TRANSNATIONAL CULTURE IN THE IRANIAN ARMENIAN DIASPORA

Edinburgh Studies on Diasporas and Transnationalism

Series Editors: Bahar Baser and Mari Toivanen

Bringing together high-quality academic works written by diaspora and transnationalism scholars, this series adopts an interdisciplinary approach and is open to empirical and theoretical submissions alike, making meaningful contributions to contemporary debates in the field. While focusing on economic, political, social and cultural factors that shape and maintain transnational identities and diasporic attachments to the country of origin and residence, the series is also open to submissions on different aspects of transnational interactions from an arts and humanities perspective.

Published and forthcoming titles

Diasporic Futures: Cypriot Diaspora, Temporality and the Politics of Hope
Evropi Chatzipanagiotidou

Second-generation 'Return' Migration: The Turkish-German Experience
Nilay Kılınc and Russell King

Transnational Repression in the Age of Globalisation
Dana Moss and Saipira Furstenberg

Kurdish Diaspora Mobilisation in Denmark: Supporting the Struggle in Syria
Anne Sofie Schott

Transnational Culture in the Iranian Armenian Diaspora
Claudia Yaghoobi

edinburghuniversitypress.com/series/esdt

TRANSNATIONAL CULTURE IN THE IRANIAN ARMENIAN DIASPORA

Claudia Yaghoobi

EDINBURGH
University Press

Edinburgh University Press is one of the leading university presses in the UK. We publish academic books and journals in our selected subject areas across the humanities and social sciences, combining cutting-edge scholarship with high editorial and production values to produce academic works of lasting importance. For more information visit our website: edinburghuniversitypress.com

Edinburgh University Press Ltd
13 Infirmary Street,
Edinburgh, EH1 1LT

Typeset in 11/15 Adobe Garamond by
IDSUK (DataConnection) Ltd

A CIP record for this book is available from the British Library

ISBN 978 1 3995 1237 4 (hardback)
ISBN 978 1 3995 1238 1 (paperback)
ISBN 978 1 3995 1239 8 (webready PDF)
ISBN 978 1 3995 1240 4 (epub)

CONTENTS

FIGURES

ACKNOWLEDGEMENTS

This book is a labour of love characterised by my own multiple consciousnesses, diasporic position and transnationalism. As an Armenian who was born and grew up in Iran and moved to the United States in her early thirties, my understanding of socio-cultural identity moves beyond the national and the nation-state. This is because my diasporic story departs from my ancestors' forced relocation to Iran and the pressures of assimilation into a new host culture. I trace my roots back to the seventeenth-century forced displacement of Armenians to New Julfa by Shah Abbas. History shows that many within this population later moved to the central province of Arak, Iran. My great-grandparent, my grandparents and my parents were all born in Kazaz, Arak, in Iran. To accomplish this project, therefore, I drew wisdom and guidance from the wellspring of my ancestors on my trajectory. I dedicate this book to my ancestors as an act that honours their experiences and thanks them for being a part of the web of intent that gave me life.

Having lived for thirty years in Iran, I moved to the United States not because of direct forces of resettlement but due to the indirect impacts of globalisation, the global economy and the problematics of living on the margins of a host nation that will never accept others as one of its own. The impact of my relocation on my identity formation and consciousness was naturally different from what my ancestors experienced. In my current location within the United States, I identify as someone who is twice a stranger with multiple homes. In this way, my transnationalism challenges earlier interpretations of assimilation to the mainstream society, a process usually intertwined with borders, territories and nation-building. My assimilation process is a transnational one that extends beyond the delimitations of one unified nation, geography, language, or territory. Today, I live in a liminal space where borders are blurred, identity is fluid, categories are malleable, and growth and transformation are possible and almost mandatory. And just as I live in this liminal space, I explore Armenian artists and authors who similarly live(d) in this transitory diasporic space of potentials and possibilities; within this fertile space they create transformative works that do not conform to any conventional frameworks.

To complete this book, I drew inspiration from (in addition to my ancestors) two women-of-colour scholars and activists whose courage in the world of academia, and in the world generally, inspired me in various ways. Throughout the writing process, the one and only cultural historian Gloria Anzaldúa became my muse via their concept 'autohistoria', giving me the courage to explore my own voice and history, as well as my cultural history, and to include them in the chapters. After finishing the first draft of this book, I came across the work of the fabulous Nadine Naber whose 'Liberate your Research' project provided me with the tools to offer a unique perspective and ultimately theorise a new concept for the Iranian Armenian diaspora. I have no words to thank these two women enough.

The idea for this book emerged out of my lived experiences; however, it received academic attention when I wrote to the Iranian Armenian author Zoya Pirzad to discuss her works in 2012. It took further scholarly shape in 2014 when I taught a course on the topic of diaspora at GCSU, in 2016 and 2018 when I presented (and consequently published) two papers on Pirzad's works at the Association of Iranian Studies conferences in Vienna, Austria, and Irvine, California. I taught my diaspora course twice at UNC, in 2017 and 2021, and in 2022 I taught a graduate seminar on 'Minorities in the Middle East'. My conversations with my students in these classes became the cornerstone of this book; I am grateful to them and their vibrant discussions. I presented various parts of this book in different venues such as at the UCLA, UC Irvine, UC Santa Barbara, the University of Toronto, the University of Virginia, the University of Chicago, the University of Maryland

and Australia's Iranica lecture series, among many others. I owe tremendous gratitude to all the colleagues in these venues who provided me with their insights and feedback.

However, the work would not have been possible without the support of the many colleagues and friends who in one way or another helped me formulate my thoughts, challenged me and aided me in editing/revising it, sending me books from Iran and Armenia, or acquiring images and their copyrights. Special thanks go to James Barry, Pamela Karimi, Rolando Longoria, Pamela Haag, Nasrin Rahimieh, Houri Berberian, Eric Hooglund, Esha Momeni, Alireza Korangy, Janet Afary and Lior Sternfeld, as well as many other colleagues, for reading the full manuscript, chapters, or excerpts. I would also like to thank Shakeh Amirian Petrossian, Sonia Balassanian, Edward Balassanian, Anoush Hovsepians, Sato A., Anne Der Hacopian, Garnik Der Hacopian, Linet Akbari, Marish Gevorgyan, Vanik Nazari, Argin Nazari, Azadeh Shams, Maryam Zehtabi, Marzia Milazzo, John Bechtold and Ronald Williams II, who have helped me in so many different ways to complete this book, including sending me books from Iran and Armenia, taking photos and acquiring copyright permissions for the images. Without their support and encouragement, this book would not have existed. For that, I am indebted to them. I would also like to thank my colleagues at UNC-Chapel Hill, especially the UNC Institute for the Arts and Humanities Faculty Fellowship programme, which provided me with a full semester of research leave in spring 2021, and the IAH Faculty of Color and Indigenous Group grant, as well as the IAH Publication Support Grant which allowed me to complete this book. Similarly, I offer my regards to the Edinburgh University Press editorial board, series editors, external reviewers and administrative staff.

As with everything in my work and life, this project was inspired by my family, my ancestors, my roots. Here I bow to them in the hope that I have fulfilled a mission delivered to me through their lineage.

NOTE ON TRANSLITERATION AND TRANSLATION

For transliteration from Persian, I have used the *International Journal of Middle East Studies* (IJMES) system, while for transliteration from Eastern Armenian I have employed the style of the Library of Congress for Armenian transliteration. In neither style have I used diacritical marks. However, common or established pronunciation has guided how certain names appear in the manuscript. Similarly, when using direct quotes, I have used the original transliteration. All translations, summaries and paraphrasing of the Persian and Armenian primary and secondary sources are by the author, unless otherwise stated.

PROLOGUE

A Turning Point – The Iran–Iraq War

I was born in Firuzgar Hospital in Tehran, on 20 November 1974. The first of four children, my birth as a girl was not too appealing to the family, a common Middle Eastern mindset at the time. For the first eight years of my life, I grew up with my extended family – grandparents, aunts and an uncle – in the same house in the Hishmatiyyih (Marvdasht) neighbourhood, in a single room with my parents. My oldest brother was born in 1978, but it was not until my sister was born in 1982, in the early years of the Iran–Iraq War, that we moved to our own rental apartment in the Karim Khan Zand neighbourhood (near Haft-i Tir). Later, in 1984, my father managed to receive loans to purchase his first ever property in the Hishmatiyyih neighbourhood where my grandparents used to live. Much of my childhood was spent in this house, until we moved to a new house in a new neighbourhood in Narmak (eastern Tehran) in 1989.

My mom tells me that she knew I was an old soul even from the very first years of my life (Figure P.1). I was so mature compared to my peers, she says, but I wonder if much of this maturity was because I did not enjoy a carefree childhood. As the oldest of four and looking after my siblings, I was always given more responsibility than my peers. My younger brother Ejmin was born in 1989, right after the war had ended and Khomeini had died.

The Iran–Iraq War (1980–88) was an enormous blow to my childhood and to everyone else's life in the country. One of my second cousins became

Figure P.1 The author's mother Parkooei, father Avak and the author at an Armenian wedding in Tehran in 1977. From the author's personal family albums.

the first Armenian martyr in the war, and another second cousin was held as prisoner of war in Iraqi prisons until 1990. I was six years old when the war began and fourteen when it ended. The trauma of the war remained with me, in recurring nightmares and somatic trauma responses, for decades after it had ended, until I began teaching a course on "wars and veterans" at UNC-Chapel Hill in the spring of 2017. I still teach this course every year, because talking about wars and telling stories help us heal our deep wounds.

On 22 September 1980, Iraqi armed forces invaded western Iran along the nations' joint border. Saddam Hussein, then the Iraqi leader, cited territorial disputes as his justification for the invasion. Chief among these disputes were sovereignty over the oil in the southwestern provinces of Khuzestan and control over the national boundary marked by the Shatt al-Arab waterway. It is believed that the war claimed half a million or more lives. While there is no consensus on the number of casualties, the Battle Deaths Dataset estimates the fatalities at more than 600,000, while the Correlates of War Project estimates casualties of 500,000 Iraqi and 750,000 Iranians.[1] Thousands of men from religious, ethnic and sexual minoritised groups – many of them conscripts – enlisted, fought and died for Iran during this time.[2] A 2019 publication estimates the total number of persons killed at 225,570; the number of veterans at 574,101; and prisoners of war at 43,173. Reports by the Armenian news media *Alikonline.ir* hold the number of Armenian martyrs at 74, veterans at 105 and prisoners of war at 35.[3] Of course, the numbers vary according to different sources. For example, *Armedia.com*, another Armenian news media outlet, notes that

---

[1] See Pedram Khosronejad (ed.), *Iranian Sacred Defence Cinema: Religion, Martyrdom and National Identity* (Canyon Pyon: Sean Kingston Publishing, 2012); Pedram Khosronejad (ed.), *Unburied Memories: The Politics of Bodies of Sacred Defense Martyrs in Iran* (London and New York: Routledge, 2012).

[2] I use the term 'minoritised' instead of 'minority' to highlight that Iranian Armenians have been forced into being minoritised and have had less social or political power or representation compared to their Muslim Iranian compatriots. Typically, minoritised populations endure mistreatment and face discrimination forced upon them because of situations outside of their control. They did not choose to be minoritised; it was shoved upon them. Women also contributed to this war in various capacities.

[3] 'The Number of Iranian Minority Martyrs Speaks to the Unity of Iranian People'. *Alikonline*, 26 December 2019, alikonline.ir/fa/news/social/item/10483

some 17,000 Iranian Armenians[4] participated in the Iran–Iraq War, with 260 Armenian casualties.[5] The war ended in 1988 by ceasefire, and a formal peace agreement was reached in 1990.

At the beginning of the war, Khomeini would appear on TV regularly with propaganda and mobilising announcements. I was a child, and my only reaction was fear after seeing a bearded old man talking on the TV about the war. My family has always been apolitical (if that is even a thing); however, they could not tolerate watching this highly Islamised TV. My grandmother cursed him every time he came on the screen. The only statements appealing to my working-class family in all of this were the promises of lower costs for basic needs, which were never realised. As the war progressed, we quickly learned that the state TV would announce the approach of Iraqi airplanes over Tehran's skies with a danger siren and their departure with a peace siren. In Persian, the siren indicating danger was called red siren (*azhir-i qirmiz*) and the one indicating peace the white siren (*azhir-i sifid*). Hearing the red siren, we were required to take shelter. I remember that we would run with my parents and brother from our second-floor rental apartment to the first floor or the basement of the building to take shelter. I was so scared of the Iraqi airplanes dropping bombs and missiles on our house in Tehran that, every time the red siren sounded, my eyes would become two big black saucers. Seeing my reaction, my parents decided to move the family temporarily to Rudehen, a suburban area an hour east of Tehran, beyond the reach of Iraqi missiles, or so everyone believed at the time. However, the war lasted for eight years, and so it was impossible for our family to stay on the outskirts of Tehran renting apartments, staying with family or friends, or putting up tents in people's backyards. This kind of lodging was debilitating during the winter months, when it was so cold, especially at night, that my cousin and I had to take turns all night placing our feet between each other's legs to keep warm.

[4] Hyphens have been historically used as a symbol of dual identity, as if the individual oscillates between their various identity facets; this is especially true in the case of immigrants. Clearly, this is divisive rather than providing the possibility of a unity. I refuse to use hyphens as I view various facets of identity as one whole rather than separate parts of an individual.

[5] 'Hassan Rouhani Visited Families of Armenian Martyrs Fallen during Iran-Iraq War', *Armedia.am*, 25 December 2017, armedia.am/eng/news/55931/hassan-rouhani-visited-families-of-armenian-martyrs-fallen-during-iran-iraq-war.html

Thus, we alternated between Tehran and Rudehen, sporadically living in each city for eight years. I have vivid memories of a few instances when Iraqi missiles hit Tehran, so close that our windows shattered. My father took my siblings and me to one of the spots where a missile had hit and demolished an entire neighbourhood (Northern Sabalan, near Tehran-Nu). I could not understand at the time why my father had taken us to that site of destruction, where lives had been lost; it left an exceptionally traumatic mark on my psyche. He only said that I would understand later that I needed to grow resilient. Although I did not know it then, he was referencing the millennia-old, entrenched resilience of Armenians who had fought, struggled, persevered and survived so many wars, conflicts and the Genocide. Today, I fully understand it, and while the sight from that day still remains in my psyche, I am grateful for that first lesson in my ancestral resiliency.

The war was especially difficult because during its first few years nobody knew that it would last for eight years, and so life went on. The economy had collapsed, and food was rationed, and this struck us sharply. I stood in lines with my grandmother and mother several times a week to buy our share of butter and margarine for the week. I vividly remember standing in lines to buy cigarettes for my grandfather; for some reason, cigarettes had become rare. This was strange because Iran is a tobacco-growing country to this day.

While we stayed in Rudehen, my dad had to go back to Tehran for work, and we constantly needed to retrieve essentials from our home in Tehran. All of these things required that my dad make trips back and forth, which was very traumatic for the entire family because we never knew when or where the next missile or bomb would hit. During the final years of the war, schools shut down all year but still conducted final exams in June. I was in middle school at that time, so for the final exams my dad would drive me back to Tehran to take the tests. My school, Kooshesh Middle School, was located near the Russian embassy. During our exams, the teachers would constantly remind us that the Iraqis would never come near that neighbourhood because they would not want to mess with the Russians. This was their way of reassuring us that we were safe. What they did not consider was that we were worried about our fathers who had driven us back to the city to take the exams but were not necessarily staying in that neighbourhood for their entirety. The guilt of putting my father in danger all those weeks as I took my exams, as a twelve-year-old child, remained with me for decades.

The war ended in 1988; my little brother was born in 1989; we moved to a new house in a new neighbourhood in Narmak (eastern Tehran) and hoped that this would be the end of our struggles, but alas, it was not. As Armenians who have survived much hostility at various historical junctures, it would prove an illusion to believe that life would become easier now that the Islamic Republic was beginning to consolidate and prove its legitimacy via various exclusive policies. An enormous wave of Armenian immigration to the west, particularly to the US, began immediately after the war broke out. My maternal aunt's family, with whom I was very close, were part of this wave; they left in 1986. My aunt and uncle insistently encouraged my parents to take that leap of faith with them, too. But, alas, my father was not ready to do so, as he had just purchased his first property in Iran. This is not an unusual predicament for a minoritised population (especially from a working-class segment of society) that has had to work so hard to secure the basic rights that their majority counterparts have had since birth. In part, this applies to work and employment opportunities available to the majority, as well.

It took us years to conclude that we wanted to leave. Human rights associations such as the HIAS (Hebrew Immigrant Aid Society) would take applications to help us get to the US, as a Christian minoritised family from a Muslim-majority country.[6] But we were not to be so lucky. We submitted our application to HIAS in early September 2001, a week or so before the World Trade Center was hit and all immigration to the US suspended until 2005. When the process resumed in 2005, my family's application was one of the first. Four months later, we left Iran on 29 April 2006, for Vienna, Austria. We stayed in Vienna for four months (they kept my parents and younger brother for five more months), were interviewed in the US embassy, received our visas and arrived at the Los Angeles airport, LAX, on 17 August 2006. I left Iran for the US after a horrific experience I had with the morality guard of the university as a tenured faculty. At the time, I was a tenured associate professor in the English Literature Department

---

[6] HIAS is a Jewish American non-profit organisation that provides humanitarian aid and assistance to refugees. It was originally established in 1881 to aid Jewish refugees. However, in recent decades, the organisation has aided many Iranian Armenians to move to the United States.

of Azad University in Rudehen. The guard stopped me in front of my colleagues and students and asked me to wipe off my lipstick; mind you, they had hired me with this same appearance. I told them that I was faculty; the next thing I heard was: 'We do not care who you are'. The disrespect was so deep that I ended up not being able to teach that day. There was a big lump in my throat all day long. The chair of my department complained to the president of the university, and I received a formal apology by the end of that day. But something had broken in me, between me and the existing Iran. Immediately after I came home, I decided that I would leave Iran (my 2001 application had been approved). My family was still in Iran only because of me; I was a university professor, had just bought my own apartment and led a successful life. My parents were happy for me and did not want to disrupt my life with migration. But the moment had come; we had to leave. Four months later, I was in Vienna, Austria, waiting for my visa to fly to Los Angeles. In the US I moved several times from city to city and state to state. Today, when asked where 'home' is, I first get confused; sometimes I even consider Los Angeles my home when in reality I want to refer to Tehran. Today, I think about home in the globalised world in which we live, where geographical borders matter little; however, even this hybridity and globalisation come with their own limits. I am a hybrid individual of a diaspora, with multiple consciousnesses, and what I have shared here about my personal life is based on fragmented memories, etched deeply by wounds and trauma that are still provoked but are in the process of healing – since healing never ends.

While this book is an attempt at highlighting the artistic and literary works of Iranian Armenians over the past forty years, I would like to briefly discuss the problem of cultural productions related to the Iran–Iraq War and their inadequate representation of Armenian contributions for the remainder of this prologue. Since the war was not only a turning point for all Iranians, but more specifically for Armenians (and for myself) regarding mass migrations and diaspora to the west, it indeed prompted me to write this book to acknowledge my Iranian and Armenian legacies.

Due to its protracted and profound influence, the so-called 'imposed war' – or, as the state defined it, 'Sacred Defence' – which took place from 1980 to 1988, after Iran's 1979 Islamic Revolution, influenced all layers of Iranian life, including my own. It also affected Iranian cultural productions, literature and scholarship, including otherwise independently-minded minoritised artists such as Samuel Khachikian, who made the 1984 film *Oqab-ha* (*The Eagles*). Post-war cultural productions followed two different trends: the militarised, state-sponsored official narrative, which dichotomised views of the conflict; and works by non-partisan authors, directors and artists, who advanced a humanistic perspective of the war. The effect of the official narrative was so pervasive that it produced a genre of propagandist literature and arts, including cinema termed 'Sacred Defence'. In response to non-partisan productions, the ruling establishment mobilised extensive resources to offer an official, totalising, propagandist narrative, which disregarded any alternatives. The state's official narrative (as well as non-partisan writings) failed to adequately recognise the wartime experiences and contributions of Iran's minoritised Armenian population (among others). It is as if Iran's religious, ethnic and sexual minoritised populations have been purposefully silenced or turned into clichés of minoritised people loyal to the Islamic Republic.

The dominant discourses of the Islamic Republic envisioned an exclusionary, Shi'i-defined, national identity. Officially, the Islamic Republic recognised Christian Armenian minoritised groups and granted them the same rights as previous rulers had done (such as the Pahlavi regime, 1925–79). However, life after the 1979 Islamic Revolution and during the Iran–Iraq War became more restricted and complicated. According to political scientist Eliz Sanasarian, the Islamic regime used religion (Shi'i Islam) as a political ideology of *velayat-i faqih*, which was derived from Twelver Shi'a Islam,[7] resulting in contradictions and the 'development of a sharp "us"-"them" distinction involving the Muslim citizens of Iran and the non-Muslims'.[8] For Armenians, this exclusionary discourse, palpable throughout Iranian life and culture, prompted mass migrations out of Iran.

The post-war mass migrations prompted Armenian authors and artists to create works in response to the Islamic Revolution and the Iran–Iraq War.

---

[7] *Velayat-i faqih* is defined as the Guardianship of the Islamic Jurist, also called the Governance of the Jurist. It is a post-Occultation theory in Twelver Shi'a Islam which holds that Islam gives a *faqih* (Islamic jurist) custodianship over people. The Twelver Shi'a refers to a group of Muslims who believe that the succession to Muhammad must remain in his family for specific members who are designated by divine appointment.

[8] Eliz Sanasarian, *Religious Minorities in Iran* (Cambridge: Cambridge University Press, 2000), p. 73.

However, within Iranian cultural productions, there are only a few scholarly books that briefly refer to Armenian contributions to the war, or even generally. Those books that do trace Armenian wartime participation more fully have been produced by Iranian Armenian scholars themselves, which suggests that the recognition of Armenian war veterans and martyrs falls exclusively to Armenians. In an effort to destabilise state narratives, Armenian scholars have recently begun documenting Armenian contributions to the war. Written and edited by Armenians, these books include Norayr Shah Nazarian's 2013 *Jang-i tahmili-i hasht salih va aramani-yi Iran* (*The Eight-Year Imposed War and Iranian-Armenians*) and Arman Budaghian's 2006 *Gul-i Maryam* (*Flower of Mary*). Shah Nazarian's book is dedicated to the Armenian soldiers, martyrs and veterans of the Iran–Iraq War and not only documents the Armenians' participation, but also emphasises their importance in national discourses. The book also names sixty-three Armenian martyrs of the Iran–Iraq conflict and features important documents such as pictures, wills and brief biographies. Sections are devoted to Zorik Moradian, my second cousin, the first Iranian Armenian killed, due to a mortar shell wound, during the first nineteen days of the conflict in a city in the West Azerbaijan province of Piranshahr. However, Budaghian's book begins by reviewing the Armenians' military background in the context of Armenian and Iranian civilisations, referring to the Armenians' minoritised status during the following empires: Achaemenid (550–330 BC), Parthian (247 BC–224 AD), Sassanid (224–651 AD), Seljuk (1037–1194), during the sixteenth century, the Constitutional Revolution (1906–11), World Wars I and II, and the Islamic Revolution. The text also recounts the life and death of Yurik Sardarian, a soldier of the 64th Urmia Division (West Azerbaijan Province) who was martyred at the age of twenty-two in the Haji Umran region (near Arbil, on the Iran–Iraq border). Sardarian is the only Armenian martyr noted in Iranian war literature. In his non-partisan novel *Namih-yi bih donya* (*A Letter to the World*), Ismai'l Fasih (1995) refers to Sardarian's obituary tacked on the door of an Armenian church in Tabriz – a passing reference to an unacknowledged Armenian whose death served the same nation.[9]

---

[9] Ismai'l Fasih, *Namih-yi bih donya* (*A Letter to the World*) (Bethesda, MD: Ibex Publishers, 1995), pp. 47–48.

Both of the above-mentioned studies have been written and edited by Armenians, suggesting that these volumes stand in the national consciousness as Armenian attempts to assert their own importance in a Muslim Shi'i majority country. More importantly, one of these books has been written in Persian, while the other one has been translated into Persian from Armenian; it is aimed at an Iranian public audience. Both belong to a body of literature produced by Iranian Armenians who 'introduce' themselves to a Muslim audience. That these authors write in Persian may also indicate that they are more confident in this language than in Armenian, a common phenomenon among Armenians raised after the Islamic Revolution, due to the changes in language instruction and curriculum that I will discuss in this book. While these books are significant insofar as they recognise Armenian contributions historically and within the Iran–Iraq War, questions about their dissemination and national status remain. Of particular concern to me is whether these foundational studies will be included in national histories, official wartime narratives, or future generations' historical consciousness.

In addition to these two books, James Barry, a scholar of minority studies, has documented in *Armenian Christians in Iran: Ethnicity, Religion, and Identity in the Islamic Republic* that Armenian community leaders have endeavoured to honour the legacy of Armenian soldiers, consecrating a memorial to them at the Catholic Church of Surb Grigor Lusavorich (St Gregory the Illuminator) near the Russian embassy in Tehran. In 2015 the Armenian Church participated fully in the 'Holy Defence Week' commemorations, holding a special liturgy to honour Armenian martyrs. In his sermon, Archbishop Sebuh Sarkissian emphasised 'the patriotic and fathomless contribution of Armenians to the war effort' and linked religious faith to the nation's victory.[10] To assert their legitimacy, the Iranian Armenian population has used the few opportunities that they have had to remind the nation writ-large of their contributions.

Beyond the inadequate acknowledgement of Armenians in the wartime effort, Armenian writings in Iran generally do not receive the recognition that they deserve. Part of the problem here is of course the issue of language

---

[10] James Barry, *Armenian Christians in Iran: Ethnicity, Religion, and Identity in the Islamic Republic* (Cambridge: Cambridge University Press, 2018), p. 127.

barrier, which raises questions about the politics of translation – who gets translated and who does not. The large gaps in knowledge about Armenian contributions to Iranian cultural and intellectual arenas, as well as my personal experiences as part of the collective experience, prompted me to write this book, to acknowledge the Armenian existence in the Iranian national landscape, to recognise Armenian artistic, cultural, literary and intellectual endeavours.

Wars generate a cultural milieu that is reflected in contemporary national modes, cultural productions and literature, establishing a foundation for important elements of cultural history. Examining the role of the Sacred Defence cinema in the formation of cultural memory, cultural historian Kamran Rastegar posits that the propagandist state narrative is 'a form of memory discourse that through narrative techniques – "shifting the emphasis" of particular memories and narratives, "recasting the protagonists of the action" that surrounds the war to promote specific communal memories – pursues the constitution of a particular discursive limit to how the war is remembered'.[11] These techniques have been redeployed by later generations to evoke a wartime ambiance, turning back towards wartime cultural productions that reflect civilian concerns against the cadences of life and death on the war front.

In recent years, there have been some efforts to visit Armenian martyrs' families during the Christmas season, including house visits to the mother of my second cousin, Zorik Moradian. Of note, the president and the supreme leader often visit these martyrs' families or send their condolences on 25 December, and not on 6 January, when Armenians celebrate Christmas. This is another indication that the Armenians in question are not important – they are useful for the regime, and therefore how and when they are presented follows the will of the regime. These visits primarily serve to legitimise government narratives that bring Iranian Armenians under a unified national banner (of Shi'ism), by using the term 'martyr' (*shahid*) for those who lost their lives in the Iran–Iraq War. While the word martyr is a religiously-based term utilised by the state's

---

[11] Kamran Rastegar, 'Treacherous Memory: Bashu the Little Stranger and the Sacred Defense', *Moments of Silence: Authenticity in the Cultural Expressions of the Iran-Iraq War, 1980–1988*, ed. Arta Khakpour, Mohammad Mehdi Khorrami and Shouleh Vatanabadi (New York: New York University Press, 2016), p. 62.

Shi'i ideology, it is also a blanket term that refers to all populations, including Armenians, Sunni Muslims and secular populations. Although the idea of martyrdom has roots in Christianity as well, the term takes on a unique meaning when used in Iranian culture: the Arabic root pertains to the act of 'bearing witness', with *shahida* meaning 'witness', 'gravestone', or 'epitaph'.

Through these visits, official discourses endeavour to appropriate minoritised populations' identities under a homogenising banner of a unified Shi'a nation, but these under-represented groups have been trying hard to preserve their unique identities that embody multiplicities within the larger cultural and social narrative. The question remains as to why the ruling establishment maintains silences (or at best inadequate representations) regarding Armenian wartime contributions, yet simultaneously celebrates Armenian martyrs, veterans and their families, filling media outlets with stories on strategic holy days and seasons.

For example, the state paid a superficial visit to veteran Norik Mahmudi's house in 2016. Mahmudi's wife, Rubina Madadi, in an interview with the Mehr News Agency recounted her family's struggles after her husband had returned from the war injured and traumatised. A twenty-year veteran, Mahmudi passed away in 2007. In 1985, he had sustained severe injuries while deployed on Operation Dawn 8 (*Valfajr* 8), one of Iran's greatest achievements during the war. During the operation, Iran captured the al-Faw Peninsula, impeding Iraq's access to the Persian Gulf. Over time, Mahmudi's wounds became infected, resulting in progressive limb amputations over the course of many years, with his family witnessing his gradual deterioration. Iranian government officials, however, denied his participation in Operation Dawn 8, asking his family for documents that the government claims do not exist.[12] This insistence on non-existent documentation illustrates how the state resists recognition of minoritised populations when it comes to their legal rights; however, simultaneously the state officials pay visits to their families.

In its propaganda, the Islamic Republic has likewise dedicated spaces to Armenian, Zoroastrian and secular war martyrs in established national institutions such as Tehran's Sacred Defence Museum and the Martyr's Museum. Similarly, the intersection of Tehran's Mirdamad and Vali Asr Streets sports a

---

[12] Zahra Shahrizai, 'Rivayat-i khandani az iyd didani dar khani-yi avalin shahid-i Armani' (An Interesting Narrative about a New Year's Visit to the House of the First Armenian Martyr), *Mehr News Agency*, 10 January 2016, mehrnews.com/xxH3V.

Figure P.2 Commemorative mural of non-Muslim martyrs. Courtesy of Dr Pamela Karimi.

commemorative mural that includes portraits of several non-Muslim martyrs: an Armenian, an Assyrian, a Chaldean, a Jew and a Zoroastrian (Figure P.2). The martyrs' names are inscribed below each portrait in Persian and in their respective language (Armenian, Assyrian/Chaldean and Hebrew). Above the images of these non-Muslim martyrs sit two larger portraits of Ayatollahs Khomeini and Khamenei, with a Persian quote from Khomeini: 'The religious minorities have respect for Islam, and they serve the country with Muslims as a single unit'.[13] The convergence of these images with the text clearly illustrates the discourse of margin versus centre, thoroughly shaped by the state propaganda of a 'unified' Iran. This insinuates that even the minorities think Islam is a good religion, if not better than their own.

Thus, responsibility has fallen on the Armenian minoritised population to assert their legitimacy as Iranian citizens, by repeatedly documenting and

[13] Barry, *Armenian Christians in Iran*, p. 127.

reminding the nation of their participation in the war and other national endeavours. The aggregation of public efforts such as museums, murals, official visits and government accounts are not inclusive, unless they can be written in a non-partisan, non-propagandist fashion. Unfortunately, even non-state narratives fail to recognise the contributions and, to an extent, even the existence of marginalised groups. As Kaveh Ehsani argues, '[t]he continued imposition by the ruling establishment of the dominant narrative of "Sacred Defence" as the universal and legitimate version of the war aims to silence alternative experiences and dissenting perspectives'.[14] It is also important to acknowledge that these narratives fail to mention that Saddam Hussein sought a ceasefire and essentially admitted that he had lost in 1982, but Khomeini refused to accept this; another six years of fighting (and hundreds of thousands of deaths) ensued until he was forced to accept a ceasefire (Khomeini knew that he was about to die at that time).

The exclusion or erasure of many Iranians' experiences has resulted in a false narrative that shores up the legitimacy of national leadership. On the few occasions when the state does mention Armenians, any recognition occurs through an overt appropriation of their identity under a unified nationalist agenda. In other words, the official, state-sponsored policies tried their best to use conscripted minoritised soldiers, yet to 'unify' them under official language and images that advance the concept of a united Shi'i-Iranian entity. Iranian cultural productions and scholarship concerning the Iran–Iraq War inadequately represent, or at times remain silent about, minoritised groups, especially in their treatment of Christian Armenians.

This erasure of Armenian experiences is significant because state-sponsored documents that detail national conflicts are eventually enshrined as a nation's material history, providing a foundation for representing and teaching an 'official history' of the disputes to future generations. According to critical race theorist Margaret Montoya, 'silence is not just the absence of voice;'[15] silence

---

[14] Kaveh Ehsani, 'War and Resentment: Critical Reflections on the Legacies of the Iran-Iraq War', *Middle East Critique* 26.1 (2016), pp. 8–9.

[15] Margaret E. Montoya, 'Silence and Silencing: Their Centripetal and Centrifugal Forces in Legal Communication, Pedagogy and Discourse', *University of Michigan Journal of Law Reform* 33 (2000), p. 275.

can make people 'complicit in [their] own marginalization'.[16] Applying this definition of silence, dominant and subordinate groups both re-craft language to their advantage, with the dominant group centralising power and privilege to maintain the status quo, while the subordinate group attempts to decentralise and destabilise that same power and its associated privileges. While silence can be liberating and accommodating, it may constitute collusion with the marginalising discourse, rather than resistance to it. To avoid this quandary of complicit silence, this book negotiates the complexity of Armenian contributions to the Iranian nation-state by bringing to the fore Iranian Armenian cultural production. Moving beyond the Iran–Iraq War within the Iranian intellectual landscape, it includes Armenian contributions, not only to Iranian art and literature, but also to American culture.

---

[16] Ibid. p. 308.

For my ancestors

INTRODUCTION

From Nationalism in Exile to Transnationalism in Diaspora

I received my Ancestry DNA kit on 19 February 2021 and the results on 5 April 2021. It took me years to muster the courage to order it – there are rumours (perhaps true) about the DNA collection and DNA banks by governments. I had been thinking about my ancestry for some time, but it was not until I became deeply immersed in writing this book that I really felt the urge and the calling to send in the kit. The results estimated my ethnicity as follows: 84 percent Anatolia and the Caucasus, 12 percent Iran/Persia and 4 percent Cyprus. I click on the results page and am taken to another page with some descriptions and maps.[1] Anatolia and the Caucasus are located in Armenia, Azerbaijan, Georgia and (the Republic of) Turkey, and it is defined as follows: 'A physical bridge between Europe and Asia, this region has seen empires – Greeks, Persians, Romans, Ottomans – come and go for thousands of years'. However, Iran/Persia is described as located in a few countries in the Middle East, including Iran. And Cyprus is marked primarily as Cyprus, but it also was a region which '[t]he Phoenician, Persian, Egyptian, Roman, and Byzantine empires have each claimed [. . .]'. All three categories are somehow

---

[1] The borders and lines on ancestry tests typically conform to the understanding of borders and nations in the contemporary world; yet, historically these borders have shifted and have been more malleable than we tend to believe, so there are doubts about the accuracy of these tests.

included in each other's definitions, including migrations to and from regions, and this is because DNA profiles nowadays use geopolitical borders familiar to us in the modern world. In short, the profile indicates that my ancestors come from the Caucasus region, probably historic Armenia. They were uprooted from Armenia to Iran. And this is how I came to be an Iranian Armenian.

As I examined my DNA results, I first noticed all the movements and the fact that my ethnicity involved three different regions/countries, rather than one – my Iranian friend tells me that she has one category. This means that my ancestors most likely moved through that area many times, even if only to a limited extent, and probably in a circular fashion. The exposure to various cultures in these regions, with different languages and dialects, may also account for certain linguistic skills, a special talent where the brain stays more malleable than the norm. The movement across regions that resulted in such mixed DNA clearly demonstrates many ancestral uprootings and displacements. As they moved through, into, or out of a space, as merchants or travelling scholars and teachers, or a displaced community, they probably picked up new people through intermarriage, immigration, religious practice, sexuality (free or forced) and other sources that consequently infused a great deal of diversity. The genetic diversity that emerged from interactions with new people was also reduced and narrowed, however, by events such as war, famine, genocide and disease. Naturally, they took what was left and continued moving, which led to new and different kinds of diversity.

The inclusion of these regions is proof inscribed within the genes (and genetics) of what I discuss in this book: historically, Armenians have experienced many conflicts, displacements and forced and voluntary dispersions; they have persevered and survived; and they have transformed themselves and their culture – moving from national to transnational identity.

Second, I notice that my ethnicity was predominantly within the Caucasus, which also corroborates this book's argument. It demonstrates that Armenians endeavoured to maintain the core of their Armenianness and heritage, even through multiple displacements and forced assimilations, within their host nations. The fact that Armenians have been displaced forcibly several times has had an immense impact on their collective consciousness as a population that has never felt a complete sense of belonging within their host nations.

My ancestors were most likely part of the group of Armenians displaced by Shah Abbas to New Julfa, part of the Iranian city of Isfahan, in the seventeenth century. They later migrated to Arak and finally to Tehran. Many of the Armenians who ended up in Arak, Iran, were displaced by Shah Abbas from Western Armenia's Van region, which is in historic Armenia. Sources have documented that they later migrated from New Julfa to other cities, including Arak. In Arak, a group of these migrants settled in the Gurihzar village of the Kazaz region, and my ancestors were part of this group. The first documented Armenian named Murad (called Armenian Murad) resided in Gurihzar in the 1800s with his grandchildren.[2] According to Hovik Minassian's oral history fieldwork, in 1894 Avedis Torosian moved from New Julfa, Isfahan, to Arak to begin working at the Hudson Company. Gradually, between 1902 and 1903, others joined him there. They moved to Arak in part because a branch of the rug-making Ziegler Company had been established in Arak. Many artistic Armenians and craftsmen moved there to work for Ziegler, were hired, participated in the rug industry and amassed wealth. In 1905, eight families (twenty-seven persons) lived in Arak, but by 1913, this number had risen to fifteen families. Armenians had a significant impact on the rug industry in Arak.[3]

In the absence of a family tree, I cannot determine when my ancestors migrated from New Julfa to Gurihzar in Arak. I only know that they were among the displaced in the seventeenth century and that my paternal and maternal great-grandparents were in Gurihzar at the time of the 1915 Genocide. As it is with most immigrants, not everyone who moved from New Julfa to Arak was fortunate enough to be hired in the rug- and carpet-weaving industry. My great-grandparents engaged in farming, gardening and ranching, and they led a traditional lifestyle. My father tells me that my great-grandfather, Jahangir Khan, was the chief (*kad-khuda*) of Gurihzar village, who for some reason at some point ceded all of his power to his brother Qasim and donated his wealth to the poor. As you notice here, my great grandfather's

---

[2] Harutun Der Hovhanian, *The History of Isfahan's Julfa* (Isfahan: Naqsh-i Khorshid Publications, 2000).

[3] Hovik Minassian and Mojtaba Qanbari, *Gurihzar: A Relic from Ancient Iran* (Tehran: Navayih Danish, 2005). See also Hovik Minassian, Mojtaba Qanbari and Leyla Mohtasham, *History and Culture of the Armenians of Arak and the Kazaz Region* (Tehran: Nayiri Publishers, 2019).

name, Jahangir, and his brother's name, Qasim, are not typical Armenian names – this is evidence of the historical influence of Iranian culture and how names were translated by name/birth registrars from Armenian into Persian or Arabic to make them sound more local.

Both of my parents were born in Gurihzar. How and when they moved to Tehran is unclear, as they do not remember exact dates. From the dates they do remember, this migration to Tehran was most likely not part of the Armenian *Nergakht* – the post-World War II Soviet policy of repatriation of the Armenian community – which means that my grandparents did not intend to return to Armenia. In Tehran, both families resided in the Hishmatiyyih (Marvdasht) neighbourhood. What I know with confidence is that, at some historical juncture, my ancestors, who were probably from the Van region of historic Armenia, were forced into displacement, relocated to New Julfa in Isfahan and ended up in the Gurihzar village of Arak. This dispersion and other migrations (including to the US) throughout history have shaped my ancestry today.

Armenians, including Iranian Armenians, have historically undergone many displacements. Iranian Armenian cultural analyst and film critic Robert Safarian delineates several forced mass relocations and migrations of Armenians in his *Sakin-i du farhang: Diaspora-yi Armani dar Iran* (*Living in Two Cultures: The Armenian Diaspora in Iran*). These displacements occurred during the 1048 Seljuk attacks on Armenia, when 150,000 Armenians were forcibly relocated to Iran. In the eleventh century, after the collapse of an independent Armenian nation, the regions of Maku, Salmas, Khoy, Urmia and Karabakh were absorbed into Iran. During the Mongol reign in 1237–38, a large number of Armenians was once again relocated to Iran as captives and slaves. These were forced displacements, but voluntary migrations began in the thirteenth century, spurred by changes in international trade routes that prompted many Armenian craftsmen and merchants to migrate. From the eleventh to the fifteenth century, Armenians migrated to and resided in cities such as Tabriz, Sultanieh, Maragheh and Rasht.[4]

---

[4] Robert Safarian, *Sakin-i du farhang: Diaspora-yi Armani dar Iran* (*Living in Two Cultures: The Armenian Diaspora in Iran*) (Tehran: Nashr-i Markaz, 2020), pp. 9–11.

In the sixteenth century, the Persian and Ottoman Empires competed over a few regions, including Armenia. Armenia was the frontier between the two empires and, therefore, the frontline of their battles and shifting borders. During the Imperial Wars of the fourteenth to the sixteenth century, Armenia was plundered.[5] In 1603, Shah Abbas I (1588–1629) re-launched his campaign against the Ottomans and relocated Armenians *en masse* to his capital city, to New Julfa in Isfahan. This forced emigration relocated the entire population of the Ararat Valley and 10,000 to 12,000 residents of Julfa to the interior of Iran. Many of these Armenians were from Yerevan, Nakhichevan, Shiravan, Van and other cities. Through a 1639 treaty the Ottoman sultans became rulers of the Armenian enclave, who bore the brunt of the Persian Safavid kings' war against the Ottomans by being forcibly relocated once more, this time from Julfa to New Julfa. Many Iranian Armenians trace their roots to this seventeenth-century deportation from the historic Armenian homeland in the South Caucasus to the Iranian Plateau.[6]

According to James Barry, Iranian Armenians are by definition part of the Armenian diaspora which is usually applied to all Armenian communities outside of the Republic of Armenia and the territory of Artsakh or Nagorno-Karabakh.[7] Iranian Armenians rarely use the term 'diaspora' to define themselves but are simultaneously aware that they fall under the jurisdiction of Armenia's Diaspora Ministry. Barry writes that 'Iranian Armenians are neither entirely a stateless diaspora (lacking a homeland that is an established nation-state) nor a state linked diaspora but are both

---

[5] Razmik Panossian, *The Armenians: From Kings and Priests to Merchants and Commissars* (New York: Columbia University Press, 2006), pp. 76–77.

[6] Vartan Gregorian, 'Minorities of Isfahan: The Armenian Community of Isfahan, 1587–1722', *Iranian Studies* 7.3–4 (1974), pp. 662–63. See also Vartan Gregorian, 'Minorities of Isfahan: The Armenian Community of Isfahan, 1587–1722', *The Armenians of Iran: The Paradoxical Role of a Minority in a Dominant Culture*, ed. Cosroe Chaqueri (Cambridge, MA: Harvard University Press, 1998), pp. 27–53.

[7] Artsakh or Nagorno-Karabakh is a disputed territory, internationally recognised today as part of Azerbaijan but governed by the Republic of Artsakh/Nagorno-Karabakh. Since 1994, mediated by the OSCE Minsk Group, peace talks between the representative of Armenia and Azerbaijan have been held about the status of this disputed territory.

at once to varying degrees'.[8] However, in Iran, they are considered foreigners, even though they hold Iranian citizenship. Most Armenians in Iran claim to be decedents of the seventeenth-century Shah Abbas deportations, hence in forced exile: 'Most see Armenia as their ancestral homeland and even maintain a myth of return, while a number also maintain a nationalistic sense of anger at being deported to Iran'.[9] This is the context in which I use the word 'diaspora' for Iranian Armenians in this book.

In this book, I focus on Armenian dispersion and displacement in Iran historically and, later, to the United States. This diaspora has been difficult and has helped to construct a malleable and fluid Iranian Armenian identity. Iranian Armenians have settled in their host nations and assimilated while also maintaining their roots and core Armenianness as a survival tactic. They have occupied a liminal space that has impacted and shifted their consciousness, and they have transformed it from nationalism to transnationalism. While conforming to the social norms of their host nations, they have found ways to negotiate and preserve their ever-changing identity.

A defining characteristic of the Iranian Armenian diaspora, consciousness and liminality is a highly developed ability to negotiate identity within a codified legal hierarchy – in Iran, within an ethno-religious hierarchy and, in the US, within a racial one. As Christians in Muslim-majority Iran, Armenians define their identity by its ethno-religious minoritised status within Iranian official narratives. When Iranian Armenians enter the US, they are defined according to their racial status. In the US, Armenians are considered a white ethnic minoritised group, yet are lumped together with Muslim Middle Easterners (inscribed as Iranian nationals in their passports), also considered white, and subjected to racism and Islamophobia.[10] Migration from Iran to the US only transforms rather than remedies this predicament, shifting it from a religious to a racial minoritisation. Hence, in both national contexts, Iranian Armenians must negotiate identity within a codified legal hierarchy that constructs them as the 'other' or as 'inauthentic' citizens. In practice, this translates into a host nation that carefully guards the coveted space of citizenship and excludes

---

[8] James Barry, *Armenian Christians in Iran*, pp. 19–20.

[9] Ibid. p. 163.

[10] The way in which 'white' is listed in the US census includes (in brackets) Middle Easterners.

minoritised members – even when these marginalised members are legally citizens, they do not hold economic, cultural, or political power.[11] In this case, they are not actually negotiating identity within a 'codified legal hierarchy'; they do indeed hold citizenship in the codified legal sense but are culturally excluded.

Diasporic Armenian Iranian authors and artists negotiate their identities as marginalised individuals who occupy a space of liminality and embody multiple consciousnesses that includes religious, ethnic, national, racial, cultural, gender and sexual factors, both in Iran and in the US. According to ethnographer and folklorist Arnold van Gennep, liminality is the transitory space as an individual moves from one group to another, through a ceremonial rite of passage or social mobility, and is comprised of pre-liminal, liminal and post-liminal phases. It is the space 'between two worlds'.[12] For cultural anthropologist Victor Turner, liminal individuals occupy the margins of society and therefore can be viewed as dangerous, with the potential to pollute society.[13] This fluid state helps them to develop resilience towards ambiguity and ambivalence, as cultural theorist Gloria Anzaldúa has argued regarding Chicanx writers.[14] Embracing multiplicity, they resist dualistic

---

[11] For a few sources that look at the inconsistency with the US claims to civic nationalism and the pervasiveness of a colour bar in countries that also promote civic nationalism (such as Australia and Canada), see the following: Kristina Bakkaer Simonsen and Bart Bonikowski, 'Is Civic Nationalism Necessarily Inclusive? Conceptions of Nationhood and Anti-Muslim Attitudes in Europe', *European Journal of Political Research* 59 (2019), pp. 114–36; Will Kymlicka, 'Misunderstanding Nationalism', *Theorizing Nationalism*, ed. Ronald Beiner (Albany, NY: State University of New York Press, 1999), pp. 131–40; Farida Fozdar and Mitchell Low, '"They Have to Abide by Our Laws . . . and Stuff": Ethnonationalism Masquerading as Civic Nationalism', *Nations and Nationalism* 21.3 (2015), pp. 524–43; Stephen J. Larin, 'Is It Really about Values? Civic Nationalism and Migrant Integration', *Journal of Ethnic and Migration Studies* 46.1 (2020), pp. 127–41; Siniša Malešević, *Grounded Nationalisms: A Sociological Analysis* (Cambridge: Cambridge University Press, 2019); Yael Tamir, 'Not So Civic: Is There a Difference Between Ethnic and Civic Nationalism?' *American Review of Political Science* 22 (2019), pp. 419–34; Bernard Yack, 'The Myth of the Civic Nation', *Theorizing Nationalism*, ed. Ronald Beiner (Albany, NY: State University of New York Press, 2019), pp. 103–18.

[12] Arnold van Gennep, *The Rites of Passage* (Chicago: University of Chicago, [1909] 1960), p. 18.

[13] Victor Turner, *The Ritual Process: Structure and Anti-Structure* (Ithaca: Cornell University Press, 1969), p. 7.

[14] See Gloria Anzaldúa, *Borderlands/La Frontera: The New Mestiza* (San Francisco: Spinsters/ Aunt Lute, 1987).

thinking within the diaspora, where they produce works that move beyond national boundaries yet simultaneously display the collective Armenian identity characterised by flexibility, adaptability and continuity.

Theorising Iranian Armenian Diaspora: *Verants'ughi*

Focusing on various Iranian Armenian cultural productions in this book, I theorise a concept specific to Iranian Armenian diaspora, which I term *verants'ughi* (վերանցուղի) – that is, a transformational passageway. This concept builds upon Gloria Anzaldúa's theories in *Borderlands/La Frontera*; however, it also departs from them extensively, as it acknowledges that the condition of Iranian Armenians in Iran and in the US differs from that of the Chicanx community. I argue that, as they carry the legacy of multiple uprootings and Genocide, Iranian Armenian authors and artists try to craft their identity in the context of a double burden: the dualling desires, often clashing, to be integrated into their mainstream host culture while maintaining ties with their homeland(s), Armenia and Iran. The term *verants'ughi* (վերանցուղի) is derived from the Armenian phrase *verap'okhakan ants'ughi* (վերափոխական անցուղի), which literally means a transformational passageway. *Verap'okhakan* – transformational – refers to a metamorphosis in the form or shape of something that moves beyond the boundaries of a solid shape. It can be defined as a process of rather sudden developmental transformations in condition, habits and/or appearance. However, this transformation and development is an ongoing, repetitive process of growth, for the better. In the context of diaspora, *Verap'okhakan* can also imply a rebirth and renewal; however, this rebirth is not a final destination, as it is often partial and includes intermediate stages of growth. The Armenian term *ants'ughi* refers to passageways, defined as long and narrow and typically with walls on either side, that afford access between buildings or between different rooms within a building. *Ants'ughi* allows passage in, out, or through – one may even pass along the same route repeatedly; however, it ultimately leads to a destination that is not necessarily the final one. The walls on either side of the passageway evoke constriction, since they narrow the path; however, because the passageway allows access between spaces, it is an in-between, transitory state characterised not only by uncertainty, constriction and pain, but also by potential and possibility, as it affords a means of communication with others.[15]

Combining these two Armenian terms, I use *verants'ughi* to refer to the liminal space, the bridge, or the threshold to shifting consciousness, border-crossing and perspective transformation for diaspora Iranian Armenians. For Iranian Armenians, liminality is a space where identity manifests itself as malleable. This identity is simultaneously quite difficult and sometimes traumatic but has some version of Armenianness at the core as a powerful survival tactic. *Verants'ughi* refers to an Iranian Armenian diasporic existence that retains a transformative power to move beyond nationalism into the realm of transnationalism, whatever this transnationalism might entail, including the limits of it. Therefore, *verants'ughi* is the threshold, or phase, during which a diasporic individual holds no social power, remains invisible and conforms to prescribed social norms within the liminal space of the passageway, or diaspora; however, this individual is open to change, growth and transformation while typically retaining parts of their core identity. They return to this same pathway repeatedly – constantly, but partially changing.

Within the context of *verants'ughi*, I highlight the despair that diasporic Iranian Armenian authors and artists endure in the diaspora, yet delineate how they simultaneously move towards transformation, growth and possibility as they confront and contend with marginality. Taking this approach, I note – especially when analysing their works – the ways in which they may find themselves misplaced between identities; in other words, they may be considered inside one identity or another (Armenian, Iranian, or American),

---

[15] Examining Muslim migrants' liminal state in Australia, James Barry and Ihsan Yilmaz have called this transitory period a 'migrant hazing' period. According to Barry and Yilmaz, migrant hazing takes place in public discourse and stops when there is a replacement for a particular group of migrants – that is, each new wave of migrant is subjected to the hazing during their first arrival and acceptance by mainstream Australian society. The hazing and racial profiling might be because of criminality, land ownership or use, or dual loyalty. See James Barry and Ihsan Yilmaz, 'Liminality and Racial Hazing of Muslim Migrants: Media Framing of Albanians in Shepparton, Australia, 1930–1955', *Ethnic and Racial Studies* 42.7 (2019), p. 1170.

but not identify with that culture, society, or language. This instability and uncertainty allow them to create works that question borders and cultural rigidities and to communicate with various cultures through their works. It also provides them with the opportunity to undergo the transformative process repeatedly through the same diasporic passageway – it is a never-ending process.

Living in a space between centre and margin, minoritised Iranian Armenian authors and artists may be viewed as a threat not only to the dominant discourse but also to their own. Viewing identity labels as limiting and refusing to be reduced to mere victims on the margins, they walk a path of consciousness that is both personal and collective. The ambiguity and uncertainty of living in multiple cultures results in multiple identities and consciousnesses – a state of constant struggle, negotiation and reconfiguration which speaks to the limits of multiplicity and transnationalism.

Methodology, Scope and Theoretical Approach

I analyse multiple consciousnesses amid the global transnational evolutionary process that involves social, cultural and diasporic influences. At the core of this analysis is the tension between maintaining Armenian heritage, culture and identity, on one hand, and constructing an Armenian identity and heritage through exchanges with Iranian Shi'i Muslims and diverse US cultures, on the other. To this end, I approach transnational Iranian Armenian authors and artists (and their characters and personas) as flexible and fluid in their understanding of identity – I view them as diasporic transnational individuals for whom the maintenance of ethnicity, language, religion, shared history and memories (the cultural markers of ritual and tradition) are no longer as significant as 'feeling' Armenian (Iranian or American). These authors and artists have symbolic and spiritual ties to the homeland of Armenia, even as they are settled in a host nation. The authors' and artists' hybrid identities and their negotiation of complex identities reveals an anxious desire to maintain an Armenian (at times Iranian) identity, yet the reality of Iranian Armenian culture necessitates multiple cultural flows and exchanges.

My approach problematises our understanding of concepts such as multiculturalism and transnationalism in Iran and in the US, comparatively.

Typically, we consider the US (and the west) more multicultural than countries in the Middle East. This is, of course, one of the consequences of the colonialism of the west, a concept associated with the mobile and transnational, while the Middle East is viewed as rooted in time and space. This study rejects this perception, specifically regarding Iran and its Armenian population.[16]

Forces that push us to see identity as monolithic and whole, and the idea of multiple identities as problematic (even though we all have multiple identities) are also crucial here. The dynamic in the Armenian world is a very Dashnak-based view of what it is to be Armenian, overlaid on a definition of Armenianness based on the Armenian church as a national church.[17] In this way, we have an Armenian nation that has a fixed territory (albeit with ambiguous borders; take for instance historic Armenia/Patmakan Hayastan) that can apply both to the Republics of Armenia and Artsakh (Nagorno-Karabakh) and to Armenians wherever they are. Today, when transnational citizenship is becoming the norm – to be a citizen, one need not live on the country's territory – this dual idea of the Armenian nation is strengthening. Hence, undoubtedly, one of the most significant contributions of Armenian diasporic literature and art has been to question a fixed idea of Armenianness established on the idea of geographic, cultural and linguistic homogeneity.[18]

Iranian Armenian diasporic artists and authors manoeuvre ethno-religiously and racially hierarchical host nations, assimilate into mainstream society and simultaneously maintain ties with the Armenian and, later, Iranian homelands.

---

[16] The Ottoman Empire and its era have been documented as one of the most multicultural empires and times in world history.

[17] Armenians are divided by political orientation (leftist, Tudeh, dashnak, hunchuk and so on). They have incredibly divergent philosophies, too. Dashnaks and the Prelacy argued for Armenians to live in Iran but as separate as possible from the majority. Tudehs wanted equal rights as Iranian citizens and a more integrated existence. It is interesting that the Tudeh segment of the Armenian community lost out and was silenced, while most institutions in Iran are either controlled by the Dashnaks or run by their sympathisers (such as the Ararat Sports Complex and the newspaper *Alik*).

[18] For transnational citizenship, see Christian Joppke, 'Citizenship between De- and Re-Ethnicization', *European Journal of Sociology* 44.3 (2003), pp. 429–58.

These confluences distinguish the Iranian Armenian diaspora, its cultural productions and the authors' and artists' multiple consciousnesses and transnationalism as a remarkable yet unexplored field of study that can enrich the larger discourse about global diaspora, because it is nuanced and multifaceted.[19]

To date, no comprehensive book on Iranian Armenian cultural productions in the context of diaspora, in both Iran and the US, has been published. While I have benefitted from and owe tremendously to the works of Eliz Sanasarian, Houri Berberian and James Barry, my focus not only on cultural studies, but also on the last forty years, as well as in Iran and the US comparatively, distinguishes my work from the previous scholarship. Similarly, Khachig Tölölyan's works on the Armenian diaspora have been extremely beneficial to my own study of diaspora; however, my work focuses specifically on Iranian Armenians, whereas his studies cover the Armenian diaspora more broadly. I have also benefited from Iranian diaspora scholarship such as Hamid Naficy's works on Iranian cinema. In addition to the field of Armenian studies, my book fills a gap, contributing to the broader topic of Iranian diaspora studies, Iranian nationalism, Iranian cultural studies and the historical exclusions of Iranian minoritised populations that has resulted in their global migration. In addition, I address questions of ethnic profiling and discrimination in the US to contribute to the study of the historical marginalisation of ethnic and racial minoritised communities in the US as well as globally.

Here, I focus on creative works of literature, painting, film, sculpture, graphic arts and music central to the Iranian Armenian diasporic experiences. Literary examples include works by Sonia Balassanian, Azad Matian, Khach'ik Khach'er, Khoren Aramouni, Zoya Pirzad, Vahe Armen, Sato A., Leonardo Alishan and

---

[19] For the concept of double diaspora, see David Wacks, *Double Diaspora in Sephardic Literature: Jewish Cultural Production Before and After 1492* (Bloomington: Indiana University Press, 2015); Maya Parmar, 'Reading the Double Diaspora: Representing Gujarati East African Cultural Identity in Britain', *Journal of the Spanish Association of Anglo-American Studies* 35.1 (2013), pp. 137–55; Shibao Guo, 'From International Migration to Transnational Diaspora: Theorizing "Double Diaspora" from the Experiences of Chinese Canadians in Beijing', *International Migration and Integration* 17.1 (2014), pp. 153–71.

Vartan Gregorian;[20] paintings include works by Marcos Grigorian, Garnik Der Hacopian and Sato A.; films by Arby Ovanessian; sculpture by Lilith Terian; and music by Vigen Derderian, Andranik Madadian and Loris Tjeknavorian.[21] More importantly, I focus on select works produced over the past forty years that respond to the two main turning points in Iran: the 1979 Islamic Revolution and the 1980s Iran–Iraq War, which resulted in the mass migration and diaspora of Armenian people from Iran to the US. While my focus is on the period after the 1979 revolution, I also investigate works from the 1960s as pioneering forms that were precursors to the socio-politically savvy artistic wave of the 1980s. Unsurprisingly, the majority of the literary works that I examine was written in Armenian and published by Armenian publishing houses, regardless of the author's country of residence. This trend marks their diasporic minoritised status. I translated the works written in Armenian and Persian, unless they already had published translations. In this book, I make references to theories of nationalism and national identity, diaspora, hybridity of identity, and transnationalism, but my main approach is to introduce the concept of *verants'ughi* – the transformational passageway.

---

[20] Written in Armenian, Almin's *Shk'egh Banasteghtsutyun* (*Rich Poetry*), Armand's *Shk'egh Merkutyamb* (*Magnificent Uncovering*), Sonia Balassanian's *Yerku Girk Banasteghtsutyun* (*Two Books of Poems*), Azad Matian's 'Mi Yerazanki Masin' (About a Dream), Nerses D. Mesrobian's *Karot Hayi* (*Armenian Longing*), Leonid Sarvarian's *Sirt Gravor* (*Written from the Heart*), Varand's *Sharach'ogh Shght'aner* (*Thundering Chains*) and *An-veradardz* (*Irreversible*), Grish Davtian's *Norjughayakan* (*Of New Julfa*), Sato A.'s *Herazheshtits' araj* (*Before Farewell*), Khach'ik Khach'er's 'Hakasutyun' (Contradiction) and 'Hayots' yerg' (The Armenian Song), and Khoren Aramouni's *Znhal* (*Thaw*). Written in Persian are the following works by Iranian Armenian authors: Vahe Armen's *Pas az ubur-i Dorna-ha* (*After the Passing of the Cranes*) and *Baran bebarad, miravim* (*If It Rains, We'll Go*), Khach'ik Khach'er's *Ashk-i Sheshum* (*The Sixth Tear*) and Zoya Pirzad's 'Yik Ruz Qabl az 'iyd-i Pak' (The Space Between Us) and *Chiragh-ha ra man khamush mikonam* (*Things Left Unsaid*). Written in English by Iranian Armenian American authors, I have discussed Leonardo Alishan's *Dancing Barefoot on Broken Glass* and *Free Fall: Collected Short Stories*, Vartan Gregorian's *The Road to Home: My Life and Times*, Henry A. Sarkissian's *Tales of 1001 Iranian Days* and Emmanuel P. Vardanyan's *The Well of Ararat*.

[21] My main rationale in choosing these works has been giving voice to those who are less acknowledged, while also including those who are well-known. However, as it is with research in all areas of Iranian studies, another criterion has been what works I have managed to access. I have received many of these works either from Iran or from Armenia.

Discussions of Armenian dispersion around the world frequently use the word 'diaspora'; however, the word itself assumes a homogenous and clearly defined entity with a cohesive network of institutions, as opposed to fragmented organisations. For Armenians, dispersed all over the world and in diverse cultural contexts, a cohesive uniformity of norms is an illusion. Hence, when discussing the Armenian diaspora, it is important to keep in mind the diversity of Armenians living in different countries and to avoid any assumptions of a homogenous cohesive community. Iranian Armenians and Iranian American Armenians, while they may seem to hold the same set of values as Lebanese Armenians or Canadian Armenians, have distinct and diverse perspectives because of the many ways in which Armenian identity is formed and sustained by schools, churches and socio-political organisations in different countries.[22] For instance, the Iranian Armenian community is diverse in its political affiliations, senses of belonging and social class, among many other factors. Along with their national affiliation, Armenians also define themselves as a Christian community with roots extending throughout the Middle East, Iran and parts of Turkey. Armenians whose families emigrated to Tehran from Iranian Azerbaijan (Urmia, Salmas and Khoy) often identify as an Iranian indigenous population, while others consider themselves part of the population moved to New Julfa by Shah Abbas. However, some Genocide survivors who fled Anatolia identify as Russian Armenian, as do others who migrated toward Russia. These differences are significant for Armenians in terms of their collective consciousness and as tools to define their identity and place within the larger Armenian community.[23]

Likewise, the Armenian diaspora's challenges are diverse. The burden of involuntary dispersion or threats to their very existence after the 1915 Genocide weighs heavily on their identities as a transnational community. A community with a rich thousand-year-old collective memory, culture, language, religion and heritage, Armenians all around the world connect to one another in a single pursuit: justice for the survivors of the Genocide, with

---

[22] Aghop Der-Karabetian, *Armenian Ethnic Identity in Context: Empirical and Psychosocial Perspective* (Beirut: Haigazian University Press, 2018), p. 229.
[23] Barry, *Armenian Christians in Iran*, p. 157.

justice for Artsakh (Nagorno-Karabakh) beginning to claim equal promi-
nence. This pursuit is the cornerstone of Armenian transnational identity
today.[24]

While creating a national identity, the use of language and the knowledge of religion and culture are important; the past and history are also crucial elements, as they provide images and cultural markers through which
people can lay claim to identities, even as the roots of heritage establish the
limits of identity. Often, community identity and consciousness are linked
to discrete elements of culture – antecedents such as language, religion,
a shared history and geography. In discussions of Armenian nationalism
and national identity, two significant historical moments have been influential – the first occurred in the early fourth century, when king Dertad
III declared Christianity as the official religion of his kingdom in 301 CE;
and the second was the introduction of the Armenian alphabet by Mesrop
Mashtots' in 405 CE.[25] According to Aghop Der-Karabetian, '[a]s a political act it helped unify the king's subjects. At the sociological and political
level it became a boundary-defining act. It helped define the collective as a
distinctive entity in comparison to other groups in the region and solidified
the collective as a more integrated whole'.[26] Hence, Christianity became
a collective Armenian identity marker for which Armenians historically
have been persecuted by neighbouring nations.[27] Mashtots' was a priest
and scholar of languages, proficient in Greek, Latin, Hebrew, Persian and
Syriac. Since a priest had invented the alphabet, the event 'was sanctified
as a divine revelation'. This clearly solidified the importance of religion,
which probably explains the swift acceptance of the alphabet among the
general population and the clergy. While it is believed that his motivation
was solely religious – he wanted to disseminate Christianity among the
population – 'the alphabet formalized the distinctiveness of the language

---

[24] Der-Karabetian, *Armenian Ethnic Identity in Context*, p. 234.
[25] He is also known as Trdat or, in the Hellenised form, Tirdates.
[26] Der-Karabetian, *Armenian Ethnic Identity in Context*, p. 14.
[27] Ibid. For instance, in 451 ACE, under the leadership of Vartan Mamigonian, the Armenians
fought the Persians to preserve their faith; they lost, but ultimately preserved their faith. This
battle is symbolic for the national preservation for the collective.

used by the people and became yet another boundary-defining mark'.[28] Nonetheless, as I will discuss in this book, even language has its own limits – specifically the Armenian language, with the two dialects of the Eastern and the Western contributing to its heterogeneity.

A nation is, however, created on the premise of ethno-cultural factors rooted in the past, as well as a sense of subjective belonging built in modernity. Paradoxically, the modernist sense of belonging tied to subjectivity counterbalances the historical and ancestral factors of belonging by inflecting specifications connected to the national (things such as minority or majority status, or religious affiliation) without necessarily specifying any nation, its social composition or political orientation.[29] For Armenians, history is a nexus where national myth and collective memory are crafted. Armenian identity is sustained through the belief that history, cultural categories and political structure are as important as historical roots. National identity is premised on a territorial foundation called the homeland, which individuals may not reside in geographically; yet the image of the homeland is imbued with national identity. However, in this system, nation and nationalism are not bound to one specific political ideology.[30]

In a world increasingly connected across borders by globalisation, where there is 'a gradual spectrum of mixed-up differences', hybridity is a crucial concept to grasp, however.[31] Unlike concepts such as diaspora and multiculturalism, notions of hybridity foreground complicated and nuanced entanglements often taken for granted in works centring identity, nation and minoritised status. Generally, communities construct identities through exclusion; they define who and what they are or are not, by drawing lines and speaking about

---

[28] Ibid. p. 15. Mashtots' is credited with creating the Georgian and Caucasian Albanian scripts as well, although Georgians do not necessarily accept this according to their tradition. There is one theory that a group of Christian scholars developed these three alphabets (which is why they share some similarities), and hierarchically no difference between the Armenian, Albanian and Georgian churches existed until after the Chalcedon controversy, which only became an issue about a century after Chalcedon anyway.

[29] Panossian, *The Armenians*, pp. 23–27.

[30] Ibid. p. 29.

[31] Clifford Geertz, *Works and Lives: The Anthropologist as Author* (Cambridge: Polity Press, 1988), p. 148.

differences. This focus must shift from exclusion to inclusion – something that Anzaldúa has theorised in terms of identity reconfiguration as flexible, hybrid, fluid. Hybridity prevents the absorption of all differences into a hegemony of sameness and homogeneity.[32] Centrally, therefore, my book elucidates how hybridity embraces togetherness-in-difference, as opposed to separateness. Hybridity is significant in a world where it is no longer possible or feasible to draw a line between 'us' and 'them'. In such a world, claiming one's difference and transforming it into symbolic capital can be a tool of reclaiming power among those who have been marginalised from hegemonic majority structures.[33] A diasporic position can provide a powerful sense of connection and belonging that both traverses national boundaries and welcomes populations with similar historical origins based in dispersion. This position can also provide space for transformation and growth.

In the case of Iranian Armenians, this hybridity manifests itself in their various forms of identification, including Iranahay, Parskahay, Iranian Armenian and Iranahayutyun (Iranian Armenian community). These terms reflect the amalgamation of Armenian and Iranian cultures and identity. In his book, Barry explains how, when asked about their identity, Iranian Armenians identify as 'Armenian' to the exclusion of all others.[34] However, the hyphen, slash, or double or triple identity opens up space for the exploration of identity and, as Rebecca Forney puts it, 'resists "fixing" the subject's identity, thereby producing different models and allowing for different negotiations than a hyphenated name'.[35] In this sense and in the service of non-fixity, I will be using a flexible

[32] Ien Ang, 'Togetherness-in-Difference: Beyond Diaspora, into Hybridity', *Asian Studies Review* 27.2 (2003), p. 141. Sources of social psychology literature on hybrid identities include Rebecca Malhi, Susan Boon and Timothy Rodgers, '"Being Canadian" and "Being Indian": Subject Positions and Discourses Used in South Asian-Canadian Women's Talk about Ethnic Identity', *Culture and Psychology* 15.22 (2009), pp. 255–83; Maykel Verkuyten and Angela de Wolf, 'Being, Feeling and Doing: Discourses and Ethnic Self-Definitions among Minority Group Members', *Culture and Psychology* 8.4 (2002), pp. 371–99.

[33] James Clifford, *Routes: Travel and Translation in the Late Twentieth Century* (Cambridge, MA: Harvard University Press, 1997), p. 255.

[34] Barry, *Armenian Christians in Iran*, p. 157.

[35] Rebecca Forney, 'Negotiation/négation of Double Names in Assia Djebar's "Le corps de Félicie"', *The Many Voices of Europe: Mobility and Migration in Contemporary Europe*, ed. Gisela Brinker-Gabler and Nicole Shea (Berlin: De Gruyter, 2020), p. 31.

format of the various facets of identity rather than solely Iranian Armenian or American Armenian; I will also avoid using hyphens which to me are indictive of separations rather than togetherness.

While Iranian Armenian identity invokes a specific geo-historical origin, it is still very much alive in the Armenian imagination, and it is constructed through a process of becoming – a conscious negotiation – rather than a fixed notion of being.[36] Armenian identity is as much a product of an anticipated future as it is a product of an ancestral past: it develops in a matrix of history, culture and power.[37] In Khachig Tölölyan's words, the Armenian diaspora has undergone 'an accelerating transition from exilic nationalism to diasporic transnationalism'.[38]

Focusing on Iranian Armenian cultural productions, I argue that diasporic Iranian Armenian authors and artists bridge the homeland and the host nation, occupying the *verants'ughi* – the transformational passageway – that requires them not only to risk being in a transitory, uncertain space and to give up the safe space of home and the power that comes with it, but also to create transformative works of literature and art. Becoming a bridge and accepting the challenge of occupying this transformational passageway means that they use their deeply painful experiences – their personal stories – to create self-reflective works that can become the foundation for understanding the collective Armenian diaspora. Living in *verants'ughi*, these authors' and artists' conception about themselves and their community is stripped away from them, because this is a transformative space where new identities are born and where old identities are reconfigured repeatedly.

My approach to Armenian Iranian artists' and authors' position in the space of *verants'ughi* manifests Armenian diasporic identity as flexible and open to growth, while retaining some 'Armenianness' at the core as a survival tactic due to the historical pain from multiple displacements and the Genocide. Through this repetitive transformative process going through the

---

[36] Stuart Hall, 'Introduction: Who Needs Identity?' *Questions of Cultural Identity*, ed. Stuart Hall and Paul du Gay (London, Thousand Oaks and New Delhi: Sage, 1996), p. 4.

[37] Stuart Hall, 'Cultural Identity and Diaspora', *Identity: Community, Culture, Difference*, ed. Jonathan Rutherford (London: Lawrence and Wishart, 1990), p. 225.

[38] Khachig Tölölyan, 'Elites and Institutions in the Armenian Transnation', *Diaspora: A Journal of Transnational Studies* 9.1 (2000), p. 107.

space of *verants'ughi*, even as a new identity is born, a sense of Armenian-ness remains at the core. This clash between the old and the new identity is sometimes empowering and at other times debilitating with its own limits. Armenian diasporic authors and artists illustrate how, when living in this liminal space of rebirth, boundaries become permeable, labels become less restrictive, and consciousnesses shift. Through the cultural productions studied in this book, we witness Iranian Armenian diasporic existence as flexible and fluid, yet also as one that is marked by Armenian perseverance, survival and resilience.

Iranian Armenians in Iran and the United States over the Past Forty Years

Armenians have historical connections with Iran that span millennia, but for the purposes of this book I will provide only a brief overview of the status of Armenians under the Islamic Republic of Iran and in the US. However, in various chapters, whenever relevant, I will discuss Armenian existence in Iran historically as well. Armenians have very deep roots as a collective historically persecuted and deprived of their homeland and nation. While many other diaspora communities leave their homelands due to natural disasters or for socio-economic reasons, Armenians have been uprooted from their homeland as a result of centuries of persecution. According to Thomas O'Connor, '[w]ith strong national pride, fervent Christianity, a native language, and a distinctive culture, Armenians managed to survive conquests by Persians and Byzantines, the onslaught of the Seljuk Turks, and the brutal invasion of the Mongols who drove hundreds of thousands from the Armenian Plateau'.[39] In addition, Armenians survived suppression under the Soviet Union and the massacres and Genocide of 1915 by the Ottoman Empire. For centuries, the area now considered Armenia existed under the rule of various nations and has almost always been the site of conflict between great powers. This has prevented the establishment of a settled government in the region, making it quite impossible to speak of a united and continuous national Armenian

---

[39] Thomas O'Connor, 'The Armenian Experience: Roots of the Past, Realities of the Present', *The Armenians of New England*, ed. Marc C. Mamigonian (Belmont, MA: Armenian Heritage Press, 2004), p. 8.

presence. Nevertheless, Armenian historian Hrand Pasdermajian conceptualises the Armenians' historical position as intermediaries between East and West, especially with regard to the Persian Empire: 'A nation is not only a state and a frontier, it is above all a mission. In the case of Armenia, this mission was to serve as intermediary and interpreter between East and West'.[40] Hence, Armenians have been negotiating the chronic instability of a diasporic existence and the precariousness of existence in an occupied or lost homeland. This experience of existing on the edge of a mainstream consciousness, of always being on the threshold of extinction, powerfully incentivises Armenian authors and artists to create so as not to disappear. While Iranian Armenians might not have been directly impacted by the 1915 Genocide, the brutality of the killings and surrounding events preoccupies the collective consciousness of all Armenians, regardless of their host nations.

Iranian Armenians who were forcefully relocated by Shah Abbas in the seventeenth century were considered a minoritised population in Iran. After the 1979 Islamic Revolution, Iranian Armenians continued to remain on the margins of society and negotiated their identity with the ruling government and Shi'ite society.[41] While Armenian culture and community were recognised in private spaces, they were not acknowledged in the public sphere in Iran. Hence, Armenians sought to establish a legitimate presence in the public sphere through political interests and organisations such as being part of the Tudeh Party during the 1979 Islamic Revolution, or participation in the Iran–Iraq War during the 1980s.[42]

Like many Iranians, Armenians welcomed Ayatollah Khomeini's rise to power. However, after he assumed power, a reign of terror was initiated, with policies and measures that dwarfed previous human rights violations. According to Amnesty International, an excess of sloppily-enacted reforms resulted in one

---

[40] Quoted in Robin E. Waterfield, *Christians in Persia: Assyrians, Armenians, Roman Catholics and Protestants* (London and New York: Routledge, 1973), p. 63.

[41] Elham Gheytanchi, 'I Will Turn off the Lights: The Allure of Marginality in Postrevolutionary Iran', *Comparative Studies of South Asia, Africa and the Middle East* 27.1 (2007), pp. 174, 180.

[42] The Tudeh Party was a communist party formed in 1941 and initially played ad an important role during Prime Minister Mohammad Mosaddeq's campaign to nationalise the Anglo-Persian Oil Company.

of the most repressive regimes of the twentieth century.[43] Once again, minori-tised Christian populations (and most others) were considered non-Muslim *najis* (unclean), capable of contaminating Muslim piety. Under Khomeini's regime, Christians were referred to as ritually unclean, occupying a category equal to urine, excrement and dead bodies. This resulted in social ostracism of all Christians in the workplace, including segregating Christians to certain spaces and areas, forbidding them from touching certain products and refusing to eat food prepared by Christians. They were also prohibited from entering Islamic holy spaces, including mosques or shrines, as well as other spaces such as barber shops and public baths.[44]

Although Christians faced discrimination under Khomeini, non-Muslims were allowed representation, as approved by the Guardian Council, who deemed the practice compatible with Islamic law. While non-Muslims were allowed to serve on most House committees, they could not serve on those that focused on foreign or judicial affairs. As long as they remained patriotic and loyal to the government, they would be protected by the Islamic Republic as *dhimmi*s – non-Muslims living under an Islamic state with legal protection. Since they did not enjoy the same rights as their Muslim counterparts, non-Muslims were considered second-class citizens. Hence, in all legal matters, authority was reserved for a *faqih* (the supreme jurisprudent), and even the process of vetting all Armenian, Assyrian and Jewish representatives fell to the ayatollahs. Thus, the 1979 Constitution of the Islamic Republic (revised in 1989) was a clear setback for the status of religious minoritised groups. While the constitution recognised Christians, Jews and Zoroastrians, no protection was offered to other minoritised groups, such as the Baha'is or Evangelical Christians.[45]

In addition to these measures, the post-1979 era involved structural mea-sures against non-Muslims. The prime example of this is the Bill of Retri-bution (*Qisas*), which mandated that Muslims and non-Muslims be treated differently in specific socio-economic and legal matters. For instance, if a

---

[43] Roxanne L. Euben, *Enemy in the Mirror: Islamic Fundamentalism and the Limits of Modern Rationalism* (Princeton, NJ: Princeton University Press, 1999), p. 6.

[44] Sanasarian, *Religious Minorities in Iran*, p. 86.

[45] Ibid. pp. 138–40.

Christian or Jew accidentally killed a Muslim, a substantial amount of blood money was to be paid to the family, yet a considerably smaller amount was paid in the reverse case. Non-Muslims were segregated, and all social activities (parties, weddings) had to be approved by Muslim state authorities; furthermore, Muslims could not attend non-Muslim services. Similar practices held true with regard to employment. In particular, alcohol sale as a trade was rendered illegal after the revolution, and many alcohol shops, a trade in the hands of Armenians, were vandalised. Armenian cemeteries were also vandalised throughout Iran; in one instance, in 1980, the Revolutionary Guards broke into an Armenian cathedral to demand that a painting of Jesus be repainted to cover his body.[46]

In 1983, the government introduced to the school curricula changes that reduced Armenian language instruction hours in Armenian schools, demanded that all schools include Islamic teachings and mandated all Armenian schools to install Muslim principals and government-approved teachers. The Ministry of Education prepared a specific textbook for non-Muslims to promote Abrahamic and monotheistic ecumenism within government-sponsored classes on Islam.[47] According to the late historian George A. Bournoutian, these sociopolitical and economic shifts after the revolution and the Iran–Iraq War resulted in an exodus of 100,000 Armenians from Iran.[48] The discriminatory policies were heightened during and after the Iran–Iraq War (1980–88), another turning point in Iranian Armenians' history of mass migration.

Since the Islamic Revolution, Armenians have negotiated state policy characterised by religion-based discrimination, the curtailment of community autonomy and lack of respect for the cultural traditions of minoritised populations.[49] Of course, religion-based discrimination was also prevalent during the earlier Pahlavi era: Armenians were never allowed to be promoted and largely occupied the lower ranks of the military, for example.[50] After the revolution, however, any privileges afforded to minoritised groups could only

---

[46] Ibid. pp. 131–32.

[47] Ibid. p. 77.

[48] George A. Bournoutian, 'People of Iran: Armenians in Iran (Ca. 1500–1994)', *Iran Chamber*, [n. d.], www.iranchamber.com/people/articles/armenians_in_iran2.php.

[49] Barry, *Armenian Christians in Iran*, pp. 110–11.

[50] Sanasarian, *Religious Minorities in Iran*, p. 39.

be approved if they did not violate Islamic law, which coerced minoritised leaders into side-stepping important issues. According to Eliz Sanasarian, '[e]very time a human rights violation report on Iran is issued, all recognized religious minorities, and particularly Armenians, hold a press conference [. . .] and publicly recant and criticize the report'.[51] Every time the state has been under scrutiny for the violation of minority rights, the Islamic Republic's strategy has been to invite non-Muslim religious figures to make statements about Iranian religious minoritised populations.[52] In addition, they have frequently denied any discrimination against religious minoritised groups and have referred to their freedoms with liberal concepts such as 'civil society' and 'dialogue among civilisations'. The fact that minoritised communities have to employ certain tactics to protect their freedoms, culture and religion illustrates the precarity of their collective social position on the margins of society.[53] As Vanessa D. Plumly writes, '[t]he power differential maintains its authority between those who are actually protected citizens and those who are not. Moreover, the security of some often comes at the insecurity of others, further reinforcing racist structures and cognition as well as reifying Otherness'.[54] However, breaching this security and blurring the boundaries of self and other also opens up spaces of possibility.

Notwithstanding this marginalisation, Iranian Armenians feel strong ties with their host nation of Iran. In his book, scholar of nationalism and minorities David N. Yaghoubian interviews several members of the Armenian community in Iran. In one June 1977 interview, he asked Sevak Saginian when Iranian nationalism first developed among Iranian Armenians; Saginian responded:

> Under the Qajars, Armenians weren't supposed to walk in the rain. We were considered *najis* [unclean] by Iranians. They [the Armenians] were not feeling

---

[51] Ibid. p. 158.

[52] I remember how, once as a teenager, at an Armenian wedding in the Ararat Sports Complex which is forbidden for Muslim Iranians, there were Europeans or maybe Americans documenting and filming the wedding as a symbol of minority human rights in Iran.

[53] Ibid. pp. 159–63.

[54] Vanessa D. Plumly, 'Linked Security and "Rhetorical Ethics": Breaking Frames and Opening Cracks of Identification through the Narrative Fissures of Olumide Popoola and Annie Holmes's *Breach* (2016)', *The Many Voices of Europe: Mobility and Migration in Contemporary Europe*, ed. Gisela Brinker-Gabler and Nicole Shea (Berlin: De Gruyter, 2020), p. 14.

very Iranian then. We were second-class citizens. Under *mashruteh* [the Con-stitutional Revolution], things began to change. Armenians were involved. Yeprem Khan was one of its heroes. He was interested in democracy for Iran and for helping Armenia. Then, under Reza Shah, there is alienation, but also secularisation and inclusion. If anyone bothered Armenian neighbourhoods or caused problems, they would be arrested, unlike before. Reza Shah gave people the freedom, by protecting them, to leave the Armenian quarters and to be equal, yet you had to lose your language to a certain extent. It's complex. But we were the best-treated religious minority and still are.[55]

Despite being considered the best-treated religious minoritised population of Iran as 'people of the book', Armenians' affiliation with Iran is more nuanced and complex than a simple affirmation or denial of it. This complexity also emerges in Lucik Moradiance's interview, when she addresses her understand-ing of her identity, and whether she considers herself Iranian, Armenian, or both, as an Iranian citizen:

Politically we Armenians considered ourselves as Iranians, but socially we were Armenians. Going to church, attending only Armenian organisations and clubs like Ararat, the Armenian Club, and the Armenian Graduates Club. So close social contact with Persians was infrequent and usually at work. But I never lived in Armenia. I grew up and lived in Iran. So I was thinking of myself as Armenian Iranian. We had all the freedoms, all the privileges, so how could you say, 'I am not an Iranian'?[56]

While Moradiance refers to Armenians as politically Iranian, many Armenian Iranians avoid politics at all costs, and many are politically affiliated with the Armenian Tudeh, Dashnak, or other party. Yaghoubian's interviews with Iranian Armenians indicate the extent of nationalism and the loyalty that Armenians feel toward Iran, but they also point towards the construction of a hybrid identity in the context of diasporic differences and their transnational affiliations with the homeland of Armenia.

---

[55] David N. Yaghoubian, *Ethnicity, Identity, and the Development of Nationalism in Iran* (Syracuse, NY: Syracuse University Press, 2014), p. 274.
[56] Ibid. pp. 277–78.

As for the US, Armenians arrived as early as in the seventeenth century, when a few were brought to America to help grow silkworms. Armenian immigration to the US can be divided into three waves: the earlier wave from as early as 1618 until World War I; the post-World War I wave that included survivors of the 1915 Genocide; and a third wave in the post-quota era in 1965, of Armenians who escaped the political turmoil in the Middle East, including the 1979 Islamic Revolution, the ensuing Iran–Iraq War and the post-1991 Soviet migrations. Significantly, Armenians in the US are a heterogenous diasporic population. There are also second- and third-generation Armenians born in the US who are the children, grandchildren and great-grandchildren of earlier immigrants. This heterogeneity has also affected self-identifications.[57]

When they arrived in the US, so the anthropologist Vered Talai describes, Armenian presence in American cities was characterised by 'relative anonymity', meaning that they decided to remain ethnically vague.[58] While their dispersal across the US meant that they were exposed to less discrimination, it did not exempt them from stereotyping. Along with Jews, Greeks, Syrians and American Japanese, they were stereotyped as 'too ambitious and with a crafty kind of self-interested intelligence'.[59] The congregation of Armenians in different states and cities in the US depended on a variety of factors. From the beginning, however, they had limited settlement choices, and while they were not exposed to explicit discrimination in many places, their settlement relied on the permission of native residents of those cities or states.[60]

In Fresno, California, things were different, however, as Armenians were subjected to overt discrimination.[61] In 1909, Armenians were placed in the category of 'Asiatic' aliens and thus prohibited from purchasing land in

---

[57] Panossian, *The Armenians*, p. 292.

[58] Vered Talai, 'Mobilization and Diffuse Ethnic Organization: The London Armenian Community', *Urban Anthropology* 13 (1984), p. 203.

[59] George Eaton Simpson and J. Milton Yinger, *Racial and Cultural Minorities-An Analysis of Prejudice and Discrimination*, 5th ed. (New York: Plenum Press, 1985), p. 101.

[60] Isabel Kaprelian-Churchill, 'Changing Patterns of Armenian Neighborhoods in New England', *The Armenians of New England*, ed. Marc C. Mamigonian (Belmont, MA: Armenian Heritage Press, 2004), p. 18.

[61] Robert Mirak, *Torn Between Two Lands: Armenians in America, 1890 to World War I* (Cambridge, MA: Harvard University Press, 1983), pp. 144–47.

California. This continued until the case of Halladjian et al., 174 F 834, was brought to the US Circuit Court of Appeals in December 1909 and the Court ruled Armenians to be 'Caucasian' based on anthropologist Franz Boas's testimony.[62] Yet, even this decision did not support property owner-ship for Fresno's Armenians, as the areas accessible to them did not include the better neighbourhoods. In addition to red-lining, Armenians were barred from other aspects of American life, including Protestant churches (recalling to mind Iran's exclusion of Armenians from mosques). They could not hold membership in social and professional associations and were ill-treated by clerks, salespersons and other townspeople; Armenian schoolchildren were openly abused by teachers and classmates. According to sociologist Richard LaPierre's 1920s research, descriptions of Armenians were similar to negative portrayals of other communities of colour – Arme-nians were labelled as dishonest, deceitful, parasitic, heavily reliant on community welfare, morally inferior and inherently criminal.[63] In Fresno, the roots of anti-Armenian discrimination can be found in economic and social factors. They were cheap labour, in the same category as Chinese and Mexican seasonal migrants in the fruit and other horticultural industries. Racial discrimination was economically important to keep wages low and profits high, a practice that continues to this day. The influx of Armenians who purchased land and attained professional positions incited fear and anxiety in Fresno's non-Armenian population. In addition to their indepen-dent attitude, and despite their legal classification as Caucasian, Armenians exhibited a diverse set of traits, including darker complexion, a unique lan-guage and ancestral costumes. While they were exposed to discrimination, Armenians avoided any direct confrontation. This is the predicament of a minoritised population living among a dominant group that exhibits anti-ethnic discrimination. Since Armenians were not as widely known in other

---

[62] Anahid Victoria Ordjanian, 'Children of Ararat: Political Economy and Ideology at an Armenian Ethnic School in the United States' (Ph.D. diss., Temple University, 1991), pp. 60–61. On this case, see https://cite.case.law/f/174/834/

[63] Richard LaPierre, 'The Armenian Colony in Fresno County, California: A Study in Social Psychology' (Ph.D. diss., Stanford University, 1930), pp. 390–415. In William Saroyan's novel *Rock Wagram*, Armenians from Fresno are in demand in Hollywood for playing 'Indians' in Westerns, because Armenians look more 'Indian' than real Native Americans.

parts of California, Fresno natives did not succeed in mobilising opposition to pass discriminatory laws, as they had done against the Chinese.[64] This invisibility soon ended with the advent of the Americanisation process.

Between 1910 and 1930, the US Americanisation League advanced integration ideologies that affected all diasporic communities, including the Armenians. The policies inspired by the league presented diasporic Armenians with alternatives to nation-building and ancestral connections. In this adverse context, Armenian political and cultural elites established a core of committed Armenians who collectively envisioned the Armenian nation. Caught between US assimilation projects and an emerging ancestral independent nation, diasporic Armenians exhibited a range of responses, including assimilation. For Armenians in the diaspora, schooling became a cornerstone that successively connected younger generations to a new image of what Armenianness would look like. New Armenians would be conscious of their culture, heritage, history, language and nation, and they would be invested in furthering the establishment of a homeland. This type of nationalistic education significantly contributed to positive identity formation for diasporic Armenians, a direct antidote to the prejudices and social challenges of host nations. For diasporic Armenians, in political scientist Razmik Panossian's words, 'Armenian identity was located within a context much wider than family history and tradition'.[65]

Due to their affiliation with Iran, Iranian Armenians faced an additional layer of discrimination in the US, particularly after the Iranian hostage crisis (1979–81) and after 11 September 2001. Iranian Armenians were subjected to further racial profiling, along with other Middle Easterners and Arab Americans, after 9/11. Much of the scholarship on American racism describes the white-black binary. Focusing on Puerto Ricans and referring to them as 'sandwiched minorities', sociologists Elizabeth M. Aranda and Guillermo Rebollo-Gil problematise this dichotomous conceptualisation and argue that, while the white-black binary exists, it subordinates other non-white Americans who attempt to unravel the effects of racial disparity in their daily lived experiences.[66] Whereas skin colour and phenotype are the

[64] Mirak, *Torn Between Two Lands*, p. 146.

[65] Panossian, *The Armenians*, pp. 296–99.

[66] Elizabeth M. Aranda and Guillermo Rebollo-Gil, 'Ethnoracism and the "Sandwiched" Minorities', *American Behavioral Scientist* 47.7 (2004), pp. 912–13.

customary tools for racial profiling, 'the inclusion of ancestry and nativism provides an axis of racialization that differentiates citizens from noncitizens and/or Americans from non-Americans'.[67]

In the West, Iranian Armenians are frequently placed in the category of Middle Eastern 'brown' bodies which, in the words of cultural studies scholar Kumarini Silva, are 'out of control because they challenge the status quo'.[68] This type of 'browning' is based on colour, ethnicity, language, nationality and those religions associated with a racial other, often viewed as a foreigner, illegal immigrant, or non-American. Like many minoritised bodies, this brown body threatens the US racial and ethnic hegemony; hence, it is deemed deviant or dangerous. The racialisation of brown bodies does not require that one belong to a specific ethno-racial group. According to Silva, '[w]hile the processes of racializing and categorizing people based on somatic identities and perceived differences are deeply historical in the United States, it is perhaps not until 9/11 that identification – of specifically targeted communities and peoples as threats to national security – has so effortlessly become incorporated into everyday life'.[69] After 9/11 and with the rise of Islamophobia, Iranian Armenians were lumped together with other Middle Easterners and subjected to American prejudice against non-white bodies. As regards Islamophobia, however, Muslim Middle Easterners are considered anti-American because of their allegiance to Islam, although this judgment and motivating factor is misplaced when Armenians who identify as Christian are racialised.[70]

These racial constructs are even more nuanced if we consider how Iranian Armenians view whiteness. Do they see themselves as white or as people of colour? Does this influence the neighbourhoods in which they wish to live? How do they view Islamophobia? Many come from Muslim societies, so how

---

[67] Bradley J. Zopf, 'A Different Kind of Brown: Arabs and Middle Easterners as Anti-American Muslims', *Sociology of Race and Ethnicity* 4.2 (2018), p. 179.

[68] Kumarini Silva, 'Brown: From Identity to Identification', *Cultural Studies* 24.2 (2010), p. 168.

[69] Kumarini Silva, 'What is Brown? Theorizing Race in Everyday Life', *Brown Threat: Identification in the Security State* (Minneapolis: University of Minnesota Press, 2016), pp. 26–27.

[70] I have discussed this type of racial profiling elsewhere; see Claudia Yaghoobi, 'Racial Profiling of Armenian Iranians in the US: Omid Fallahazad's "Citizen Vartgez"', *Iran-Namag: A Bilingual Quarterly of Iranian Studies* 6.2 (2021), pp. 154–72.

do they react when mistaken for Muslims? How do they view the US as a Christian society? How do Iranian Armenians view or interact with other Iranians? The answers to these questions vary by context and by Armenian community.

For instance, different Iranian communities tend to avoid one another outside of Iran in a way that is not possible inside Iran. Thus, Armenians stick with Armenians, Jews with Jews, Kurds with Kurds and so forth. In the post-9/11 US, however, Armenian affiliation is irrelevant. As literary theorist Trinh T. Minh-ha points out, . . .

> At a time when the rhetoric of blurred boundaries and of boundless access is at its most impressive flourish, the most regressive walls of separation and racial discrimination, [. . .] continue to be erected around the world to divide and conquer, exacerbating existing conflicts as one world, one nation, one community, [. . .] continue to be dramatically raised against another.[71]

As the visibility of non-white and non-black minoritised groups increases, people of Middle Eastern descent are racialised into what political sociologist Eduardo Bonilla-Silva calls the 'intermediate racial categories'.[72] This intermediary group occupies 'different location[s] in the racial order, and [is] racialized through ethnicity, national origin, and/or religion, rather than strictly phenotype [. . .]'.[73] Iranian Armenians (like other Middle Easterners) are located in an ambiguous space as neither white nor people of colour, a group that is simultaneously hyper-visible and what Gualtieri calls the most 'invisible of invisibles'.[74] The racialisation of Iranian Armenians is organised less by the logic of race, ethnicity and religion, but more by the logic of

---

[71] Trinh T. Minh-ha, 'Foreignness and the New Color of Fear', *Elsewhere, Within Here: Immigration, Refugeeism and the Boundary Event* (New York and London: Routledge, 2010), p. 5.

[72] Eduardo Bonilla-Silva, 'More Than Prejudice: Restatement, Reflections, and New Directions in Critical Race Theory', *Sociology of Race and Ethnicity* 1.1 (2015), pp. 79–80.

[73] Zopf, 'A Different Kind of Brown', p. 178.

[74] Sarah A. Gualtieri, 'Strange Fruit? Syrian Immigrants, Extralegal Violence, and Racial Formation in the United States', *Race and Arab Americans Before and After 9/11: From Visible Citizens to Visible Subjects*, ed. A. Jamal and N. Naber (Syracuse, NY: Syracuse University Press, 2008), p. 149.

US foreign policy, influences that have fluctuated throughout history.[75] Significantly, however, a socially constructed understanding of race has global implications that affect nationality, language, religion and history.[76] Sociologists of race and ethnicity have called this process 'brown racialisation', a confluence of skin colour with ethnic, religious, linguistic, or national factors.[77] In Minh-ha's words, . . .

> In the quasi-neurotic state of self-inducing fear, every immigrant or voyager of color is a potential terrorist. Racial and national profiling at airport security has been well documented. [. . .] Those targeted or 'randomly selected' for security checks are not only those whose political background poses a threat to the ruling authorities, but most often those in possession of a 'Muslim name', and those who simply 'look' other, queer, or shady to the 'normal' eye.[78]

This racialisation illustrates that American citizenship is legally obtainable, yet American cultural identity remains elusive. In the context of blackness, Devon Carbado labels this as testimony to the policies of 'inclusive exclusion: inclusion in American citizenship and exclusion from American identity'.[79] This holds true as well with brown bodies that are positioned both inside and outside of America's national imagination. According to sociologist Louise Cainkar, . . .

> As a result of exclusion and denigration in American society, the normative pattern among Arab immigrants arriving in the last 40 years and their American-born children was to develop a range of transnational identities [. . .] Many of the American-born children of these immigrants shunned a hyphenated identity, while they waited for a society more willing to incorporate them as full members of the American mosaic.[80]

---

[75] Louise Cainkar, 'Thinking Outside the Box: Arab Americans and U.S. Racial Formations', *Race and Arab Americans Before and After 9/11: From Visible Citizens to Visible Subjects*, ed. A. Jamal and N. Naber (Syracuse, NY: Syracuse University Press, 2008), pp. 46–80.

[76] Aranda and Rebollo-Gil, "Ethnoracism and the "Sandwiched" Minorities', p. 913.

[77] See Silva, 'Brown: From Identity to Identification'.

[78] Minh-ha, 'Foreignness and the New Color of Fear', p. 5.

[79] Devon W. Carbado, 'Racial Naturalization', *American Quarterly* 57.3 (2005), p. 638.

[80] Louise Cainkar, 'No Longer Invisible: Arab and Muslim Exclusion after September 11', *Middle East Report* 224 (2002), p. 25.

This type of transnationalism is also the essence of the Armenian Iranian diasporic experience.

Diasporic Armenians of the twenty-first century continue to exist tenuously, as the survival of the Armenian culture is threatened by the lack of an autonomous homeland and the global dispersion of the Armenian community – the very factor that defines their social position. Furthermore, some diasporic Iranian Armenian communities themselves have been uprooted and resettled both forcibly and voluntarily, which magnifies collective anxieties about global insecurities. For example, Armenian communities in Lebanon and Iran have been uprooted, and Armenians in Baku have been murdered and expelled from their homes. In the US, assimilation has been at the forefront of the Armenian existence. While some have integrated into mainstream society and view the maintenance of Armenian culture as temporary, others view the Armenian language and culture as capable of outlasting and withstanding assimilation projects. For a majority of today's diasporic Armenians, Armenian language, religion, culture and a recent legacy of genocide are unifying factors, effectively marking them as distinct from the host nation's non-Armenian communities.[81] Regarding this shared history, William Saroyan, the well-known Armenian American author, wrote the following:

> I should like to see any power of the world destroy this race, this small tribe of unimportant people, whose wars have all been fought and lost, whose structures have crumbled, literature is unread, music is unheard, and prayers are no more answered. Go ahead, destroy Armenia. See if you can do it. Send them into the desert without bread or water. Burn their homes and churches. Then see if they will not laugh, sing and pray again. For when two of them meet anywhere in the world, see if they will not create a New Armenia.[82]

Similarly, late historian Vartan Gregorian recalls experiences at Stanford University that suggested that the majority of this community was familiar with Armenian culture and ethnicity, as opposed to other campuses, states and

[81] Anny Bakalian, *Armenian-Americans: From Being to Feeling Armenian* (New Brunswick, NJ: Transaction Publishers, 1993), pp. 2–3.
[82] William Saroyan, 'The Armenian and the Armenian', *Ararat* 25.2 (1984), p. 7 [first published as *Inhale and Exhale* (New York: Random House, 1936)].

US cities. This awareness was due to a pair of well-known university football players – the Manoogian brothers – as well as Saroyan, Hollywood movie director Rouben Mamoulian and actress Arlene Francis.[83]

Diasporic Armenians' cultural resilience to assimilation forces can be seen in the social organisations that they have founded in their host nations. In an effort to transmit their cultural heritage, Armenians have built churches and schools, founded media conglomerates and formed organisations to support the achievements of future generations in their host nations.[84] George Mardikian – an Iranian Armenian and a Republican – opened a restaurant in San Francisco named after the Persian poet Umar Khayyam. According to Gregorian, . . .

> The décor consisted of scenes that depicted some poems from his classic *Rubaiyat* in the 1859 translation by Edward Fitzgerald. In one corner, you read on the wall one of the most celebrated passages of the *Rubaiyat*: *The moving finger writes; and, having writ, moves on. Nor all thy piety nor wit shall lure it back to cancel half a line, nor all thy tears wash out a word of it.*[85]

Gregorian depicts Armenian multiple consciousnesses, an identity based in innovation and creation more than victimhood. The upcoming generation has a more fluid self-image. According to sociologist Anny Bakalian, 'American-born upper-middle-class symbolic Armenians have more freedom in deciding their personal identities. They may choose to be Armenian, Armenian-American, American-Armenian, American, or whatever else they want'.[86] Today, new generations are introducing symbolic and transnational dimensions to diasporic Armenian identity. Gregorian describes how he believed that this identity fluctuation gave him a privilege that US natives did not have – a contrapuntality that also Edward Said has discussed: 'I could be in two or more places simultaneously: I could compare my experiences, see things from different perspectives, and be both observer and participant'.[87]

---

[83] Vartan Gregorian, *The Road to Home: My Life and Times* (New York: Simon and Schuster, 2003), pp. 102–3.
[84] Bakalian, *Armenian-Americans*, p. 6.
[85] Gregorian, *The Road to Home*, p. 103.
[86] Bakalian, *Armenian-Americans*, p. 7.
[87] Gregorian, *The Road to Home*, p. 118.

The boundaries between Armenians and non-Armenians in the US are porous and self-imposed, while Ottoman-influenced Armenians or Armenians from most other Middle Eastern countries contended with a socio-political structure that proscribed Armenian identity.[88] These are all the outcomes of complex historical and dialectical processes that include country of birth, childhood socialisation, generation and cohort effect. This is eloquently delineated by Gregorian:

> How does one reconcile these legacies and realities and still retain one's individuality and the integrity of one's commitments? I realised that in each of us in such circumstances, the whole is more than the parts; the multiple heritages are not liabilities, they are assets, they provide one with a critical distance from ideological straitjackets and frozen orthodoxies. I realised then and there that my multiple legacies had played a major role in my teaching philosophy; that they had given me a healthy perspective toward all orthodoxies, a belief that they were all to be tested; that I had an obligation as a teacher to help my students develop the critical thinking and discernment that would allow them to make a conscious commitment to develop a capacity for perspective. I realised that as a teacher I had to provide my students with an intellectual compass for their travels from one culture to another, yet at the same time strengthen their knowledge of their own cultural legacies to prevent deracination and alienation, to provide them a moral, cultural, and intellectual base.[89]

Since the early waves of immigration to the US, Armenians have not only established a community in America but also effectively assisted their fellows in Armenia and their compatriots in the diaspora in other countries, particularly in the Middle East. By the end of the twentieth century, the image of being an Armenian had shifted away from an emphasis on language acquisition, nationalism, politics, religion and a desire to return home. What became important was 'feeling' Armenian, or what has been called a 'symbolic identity' by Bakalian – that is, an identity that is voluntary and practical rather than ascribed and unconscious.[90] As Tölölyan also confirms,

[88] Bakalian, *Armenian-Americans*, p. 7.
[89] Gregorian, *The Road to Home*, p. 183.
[90] Bakalian, *Armenian-Americans*, p. 6.

'[a]ffiliation is coming to replace filiation, subjectively chosen identity is challenging situationally ascribed collective identity wherever possible'.[91] Gregorian also discusses this symbolic Armenianness in his book: 'I realized that my ties to America were not legal ones alone, but spiritual ones as well. After all, America was my home, my country, the home and the country of my wife and three sons, all of whom were U.S. citizens'.[92] However, this does not mean that the diaspora was actively disintegrating. Rather, it was developing into an entity with multiple loyalties, including a loyalty to its own evolution.

This new Armenian subjectivity embraced an idealised homeland rooted in the realm of spiritual affiliations. This was a community that negotiated multiple consciousnesses, a hybrid identity that traced the origin of diaspora, the norms of the host nation and the development of a homeland. Their identity occupied an interstice between an ideal homeland, the realities of the host nation, the legacy of diaspora and the Genocide, and the multiplicity of modern identity. Their connections to the Armenian homeland involved political consciousness and national mobilisation on behalf of the emerging nation. This group of Armenians might have no real desire to return to the homeland and feel more connected to the host nation.[93] Consequently, the meaning of diaspora has changed, not only because a new word, *spyurk*, was coined to replace *gaghut*, but also because after the 1960s the idea of nationalised identities changed. Whereas Armenians would see themselves in the diaspora as Aintabtsi, Kharperttsi, or Bagheshtsi, they slowly became Lebanese Armenian, Syrian Armenian, or Iranian Armenian instead.[94]

---

[91] Khachig Tölölyan, *Redefining Diaspora, Old Approaches, New Identities: The Armenian Diaspora in International Context* (London: Armenian Institute, 2002), pp. 55–56.

[92] Gregorian, *The Road to Home*, p. 234.

[93] Panossian, *The Armenians*, p. 307.

[94] In Armenian, the word *spyurk* is used to refer to the diaspora, but in the past the word *gaghut* was used to refer to Armenian communities outside of the Armenian homeland. It is borrowed from the Aramaic cognate of the Hebrew *galut*. Aintabtsi refers to the Armenian communities of Aintab in Turkey, Kharperttsi refers to communities from Harpoot in Turkey, and Bagheshtsi refers to communities from Bitlis in Turkey. This shows that diasporic identifications were previously local-based, but now shifted to national-based ones.

Chapter Outline

The chapters in this book highlight how, as transnational diasporic individuals, Iranian Armenian subjectivity tends to be more open to other cultures in Iran and in the US. Centring around how Iranian Armenian artists and authors reach beyond the national to engage in transnational thinking, all chapters engage with theories of nationalism and national identity, diaspora, borders and trans-borders, borderlands, hybridisation of identity and existence in the transformative space of *verants'ughi*. Some chapters, the prologue and the epilogue include vignettes of my personal experiences as an Iranian Armenian American diasporic transnational individual living in *verants'ughi*. While the discussions in each chapter concern characters in the creative works, they also consider the position of the authors and artists as diasporic people. All chapters also include historical and theoretical discussions where relevant.

Chapter One, 'Diaspora, *Nostos* and Longing', describes cultural productions that provide insight into Iranian Armenian diasporic life, the longing for an ideal homeland, trauma and pain, fragmented memories and Iranian Armenians' struggles to maintain ties with their heritage while they resist assimilation to the host nation's culture. To explore the Armenian presence in Iran, I provide important historical junctures where the Armenians' minoritised position within their host nations is significant. Armenian repatriation – *Nergakht* (return migration) – from Iran to Armenia is also discussed in this chapter, as a major turning point for Iranian Armenians.

Chapter Two, 'Maintaining Heritage and Assimilation', explores the Iranian Armenian community's struggles to maintain ties with their heritage, all the while they resist assimilation to the host nation's culture. Within these cultural productions, representations of Armenians who often adopted subordinate social profiles as they were pushed to the margins predominate. This positioning resulted in a cultural practice of destabilising identity categories, embodying the values and practices of multiple identities and forging multiple, overlapping national and historically influenced identities. To explore the ways in which Armenians resisted assimilation or rather assimilated in Iran and in the US, I provide the most important theories of assimilation and examine the Armenian community's responses to each one of those theoretical perspectives.

Chapter Three, 'Language as an Ethno-national Identity Marker', highlights the ways in which Iranian Armenian authors and artists praise and speak about the significance of Armenian language as their mother tongue. I also discuss linguistic flows between primarily Armenian and Persian languages and English, and I delineate the assimilatory practices of schools within Iran and the US. In response to such state policies, cultural productions foreground characters or creations that sometimes resist linguistic assimilation, while at other times they depict multilingualism.

In Chapter Four, 'History, Memory, Collective Consciousness', I examine how Iranian Armenian diasporic correspondence with the homeland is based on a fractured memory that results in the deconstruction and reconstruction of a multifaceted Armenian identity open to diversity. While the dominant concept in this chapter is the trauma of the shared history witnessed around the 1915 Genocide, other references to folk tales, literature, landmarks and so on are also explored, such as Mount Ararat and the Arax River.

Chapter Five, 'Diasporic Transnational Identity', delves into the tension between diasporic identity and the influence of the homeland for characters and personas. It considers how Iranian Armenians give birth to a new identity in a transnational space where they are socially, politically and economically anchored in their host nations, while simultaneously standing in correspondence with their homeland. Their consequent openness to multivalent identity manifests itself in the Armenian diasporic community's physical representations of their identity, sometimes through traditions and religion, at other times through language, art and literature as represented in cultural productions.

The Conclusion, 'Negotiating Identity via Creativity', explores how Armenian authors and artists tackle questions of agency and empowerment as they attempt to carve out spaces of belonging that diverge from historical origins. Of interest is an analysis of the specific modes of power and representation that these creators employ to rehabilitate their position as members of a minoritised population. In this chapter, I view creating as a healing space that allows diasporic authors and artists to process trauma through disordered and reordered memories. Through creativity and reflection, they come to terms with the fragmented nature of their thoughts, memories, global dispersion and historical origins.

The Epilogue – 'Where is Home?' – provides a snapshot of trend lines and struggles that a diasporic transnational individual, such as myself, endures as they negotiate a self, torn between multiple nations, identities and consciousnesses during times of crisis. In this chapter, I discuss my personal experience when the global COVID-19 pandemic was raging throughout the world, the US was reckoning with its racial inequities, Armenia was once again at war with Azerbaijan (and Turkey) over Artsakh (Nagorno-Karabakh), and Iran was witnessing multiple honour killings and executions of prisoners of conscience or activists.

Anzaldúa writes: 'I am a turtle, wherever I go I carry "home" on my back'.[95] The turtle – a motif that appears in Iranian Armenian author Azad Matian's works, too – connects the Iranian Armenian diaspora to global diasporic discourse. The turtle that carries its home on its back has no understanding of borders and nation-states. Living on the border, struggling with multiple consciousnesses and identities, trying to negotiate a self constantly in flux, diasporic Iranian Armenian authors and artists, like the turtle, carry 'home' in their works, and their awakened consciousness; this is never comfortable, yet it is HOME.

---

[95] Anzaldúa, *Borderlands/La Frontera*, p. 43.

1

DIASPORA, *NOSTOS* AND LONGING

As an Iranian Armenian woman who was born and raised in Tehran, I have gone through multiple processes of identity-formation, and all this is dramatised in the context of Muslim–Christian relationships in Iran. My family is one of the most open-minded and least nationalist Armenian families I have known in my life. Contrary to the norm back in the 1990s, when Iranian Armenian women, as the bearers of the culture, used to predominantly settle down and start a family right after high school, I chose to continue my education and pursue a career as an English teacher. This of course meant that I would potentially have more encounters with the Muslim world. Much gossip circulated about my decision within the Armenian community of my neighbourhood, criticising my dad for not providing me with pocket money so that I would not go to work. Right after high school I was hired as an ESL teacher at an extra-curricular English language school to teach English to elementary school children. Both of these opportunities – pursuing higher education and employment – provided me with a chance to venture outside of my Armenian bubble (Armenian neighbourhoods are largely demarcated in Iran) and later translated into further interaction with Muslim Iranians. My parents were proud of me, but, of course, this apparent success was not without criticism from the community. At the time, a story was going around about an Armenian girl who got married to a Muslim man; the girl was a college student, like myself. I was then dating a young Armenian man who made a point to comment on the incident, saying that this was the consequence of going to college with Muslims. We broke up soon after. From my early years on, I had tendencies towards thinking outside the box and questioning old beliefs. My mother keeps telling me that she knew I was different even before I was one year old; I was curious, loved the unfamiliar. I could not box and define myself as rigidly as most others did. For example, several times in my youth, I asked my parents why we never celebrated Nowruz; after all, it was a national celebration of the New Year and not a religious one. What was hindering us from participating in a national celebration? I never received a concrete response, but I kept pushing the boundaries and casting doubts by questioning time-old conventions. My parents surely had no answer for me; all they knew was that Armenians in our circle never celebrated it.[1]

The study of diaspora and dispersion entails attention to themes such as existence, loss, trauma, an imaginary homeland and multifarious identities. Forced dispersion often assumes passivity; however, diaspora itself is not a passive state. This is reflected in the Hebrew term for diaspora, *galuth*, which means forced dispersion. *Galuth* is the origin of the Armenian word for diaspora, *gaghut*; however, the Armenian word *spyurk* was adopted post-Genocide as a European-centric word. In this book, I theorise the term *verants'ughi* specifically to refer to the Iranian Armenian diaspora, regardless of whether it was forced or voluntary. In a sense, *verants'ughi* decolonises the earlier language used for the Armenian diaspora, influenced by European or Hebrew languages and referring dominantly to the post-Genocide diaspora, by combining two Armenian words and referencing specifically the Iranian Armenian diaspora.[2]

Iranian Armenian cultural productions successfully articulate the themes of loss, trauma and nostalgia, effectively manipulating the setting and background of each work to elucidate the diasporic experience, the tensions

[1] I finally set my own haftsin up for the first time in March 2022. Haftsin is an arrangement of seven symbolic items whose names start with the letter 'S', in Persian pronounced as 'seen' – displayed at Nowruz, the Iranian New Year, on 20 or 21 March.

[2] Hence, I will not go through the definitions and evolution of the concept of diaspora. However, for a concise outline of the changing meaning and use of the term 'diaspora' (originally a dispersed ethno-religious community, until Marcus Garvey reinvented it), as well as a concise description of the different, opposing definitions of diaspora in academic use (particularly the tension between William Safran's views and James Clifford's), see Stephane Dufoix, *Diasporas* (Berkeley: University of California Press, 2008).

between assimilation and maintenance of a cultural heritage, and the ways in which a legacy of multiple forced and voluntary relocations and the Genocide have fragmented identity. Iranian Armenian diasporic existence is confining and enclosing, while it is also plural and ambiguous. Uprooted and relocated, Iranian Armenians have had to reconfigure their existence, since there is no option of a return to a home for them. Living in-between, in a state of uncertainty, quickens artists' and authors' desire to hold on to history, roots and memory, longing nostalgically for a geographical place that is no longer the space that they left or imagined. In this process, finding themselves in a new homeland (or rather the hostland), they reshape their identity and re-articulate their self, negotiating it on several levels. This negotiation is a reminder of historian Eric Hobsbawm's concepts of 'Heim' and 'Heimat'. According to Hobsbawm, 'Heim, chez soi, is essentially private. Home in a wider sense, Heimat, is essentially public'.[3] Hence, this is a double-sided phenomenon that is both public and private, and neither dimension can be underestimated. The view of diaspora as permanent while the homeland is accessible is also indicative of philosopher Edward Casey's 'homesteading' – the journey to a new place in order to make it one's permanent home – and 'homecoming' – the journey to the place of origin for a temporary return.[4] The negotiation between diaspora and home occurs every day, which illustrates their flexibility, ultimately unsettling mainstream society. In this chapter, I examine the tale of protagonists and personas (and by extension their authors and artists) in Iranian Armenian cultural productions that are fated to have a *nostos* (return home) forever suspended in liminality – they anticipate a homeland that has changed and are simultaneously aware of their displaced status, and they are aware that a return to the homeland is not possible.[5] Fuelled by longing and

---

[3] Eric Hobsbawm, *Nations and Nationalism Since 1780: Programme, Myth, Reality* (Cambridge: Cambridge University Press, 1991), p. 67.

[4] Edward Casey, *Getting Back into Place* (Bloomington: Indiana University Press, 1993), p. 290.

[5] The Greek noun *nostos* ('homecoming') is derived from the root *neomai* ('to come or go'); however, it has a range of different meanings. In early Greek poetry, *nostos* referred to homecoming, return to light and life, or salvation, not death. In later Greek, the term retained much of this meaning, but it can also mean 'sweetness'. A *nostos* is a return to the home, which is symbolically a return to the past. Ultimately, it is partly a futile wish because neither home nor person, neither the past nor the individual remembering remain the same.

nostalgia, diasporic authors and artists attempt to return to the homeland imaginatively.

Definitions of Diaspora in Cultural Productions

Diaspora is often a permanent uprooting – the traumatic loss of security and the disruption of comfort in both literal and metaphorical senses. However, diaspora is not just the predicament of displacement. It simultaneously encompasses transformation and growth. The cultural productions of Iranian Armenian artists and writers often reflect this disruption and loss through a metaphorical interpretation. In their creative artistic work, loss becomes that space of *verants'ughi* where growth and transformation occur.

Iranian Armenian painter Marcos Grigorian uses dried earth to refer to the loss of homeland. Using soil (not any particular one), straw and wood bound by polyester and paint as a symbol of eternal life, Grigorian creates two-dimensional works inspired by the earth. He elevates materials harvested from the earth as the highest source of human creativity, symbolising his personal philosophies through soil. Utilising dried clay and soil as symbols of life and the sun, these works describe the creation of the earth and the sky and express the union of soul and body during human creation (Figure 1.1). His dried earth works are an interpretation of inner symbols that signify unity with the universe. The use of earthen clay evokes associations with geography, territory and nation. Grigorian attempts to establish a sense of security after the loss of homeland with a newly-shaped bit of earth. In this way, Grigorian seems to reach back imaginatively to a lost homeland by making earthen art that speaks about stability within universality. Grigorian also alludes to geometry with squares and spirals, which refer to his signature theme of mystical teachings and a combination of knowledge, hope and love. According to Iranian artist Fereshteh Daftari, Grigorian's innovative works and his use of ethnic textures were key contributions to modernism. Focusing on minimalist structured geometry, Grigorian's artistic vision would introduce concepts and styles central to pop art.[6] In 1990, Grigorian donated a collection of

---

[6] Fereshteh Daftari, *Marcos Grigorian Earthworks* (New York: Leila Heller Gallery, 2011). See also Daftari, 'Introduction' in the same publication. Pop art, an art movement that emerged during the mid- to late-1950s, presented a challenge to traditions of fine art by including imagery from popular and mass culture. I will discuss Grigorian's more ethnic works in Chapter Five.

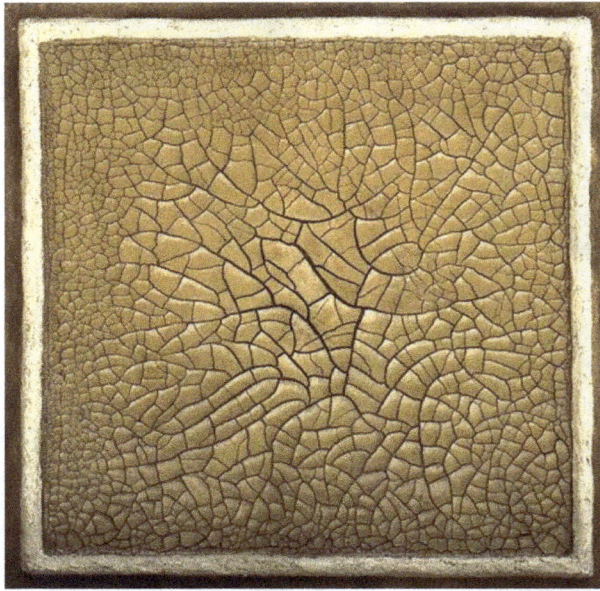

Figure 1.1 Marcos Grigorian, *Desert* (*Earthwork* series), 1972. Courtesy of Leila Heller Gallery.

5,000 artworks that he had gathered over forty years to a museum he founded in Armenia. According to Grigorian, '[a]n artist puts together a collection of valuable pieces of art over years and spends a lot of money on finding the main place for it. A time comes when he feels that he has a collection of the culture and art of a nation with himself and now it is time to return this trusteeship to the national art history so that the viewer can see the lost roots of it'.[7]

Similarly, with her minimalist style, Sato A. depicts the homeland in the image of an Armenian woman and a young girl with their traditional outfits that reflect the rich Armenian culture (Figure 1. 2). The traditional Armenian outfit is called *taraz*. Armenian women's traditional costumes are typically embroidered with gold thread. Having gone through historical developments,

---

[7] Quoted in Zhanet D. Lazarian, *Danishnamih-yi Iranihay-i Armani* (*The Encyclopedia of Armenian Iranians*) (Tehran: Hirmand Publications, 2003), p. 356.

Figure 1.2 Sato A., *Armenian Dolls in Traditional Costume*, Glendale, CA, 2021. Courtesy of the painter.

Armenian national costume is one of the symbols of self-preservation for the nation, as it not only borrows from neighbouring countries but also influences those countries. These outfits usually incorporate the colours black, white, red and yellow, which symbolise the four elements of earth, water, fire and air, respectively. It is also believed that the outfit is to portray ancestral soil/home-land with its white waters, red air and yellow fire. The outfit consists of a long dress, an apron, a sash or belt, an outer garment, a headdress, jewellery and shoes. It is a loose-fitting dress with a slit on the chest and the sides. The head-dresses were adorned with coins, jewellery and embroidery on the forehead, with a veil or kerchief that covered the head, shoulders, neck and sometimes part of the face. As in many other countries in the region, Armenian women's dress could signify their social class, region of origin, marital status and number of their children. For instance, women from the upper class would wear outfits made from silk, satin and velvet which were embroidered with gold and silver thread. Upper-class women's headdresses were embellished with gems, gold and silver. Armenian women's shoes were handmade leather shoes called *trekht*.

In addition to being a painter, Sato A. is also a poet. In the poem below, she describes home or homeland where the framework of what we call a 'house' is there, but the soul and spirit of 'home' is missing; hence, the feelings of disillusionment with the independent homeland:

The roof is there,
The walls are there,
The floor is there.

But there are no windows,
No air,
No soul.
You and I sitting here
Across one another
There is nothing to say.[8]

As for literary works, the short story 'Mi Yerazanki Masin' (About a Dream) by Iranian Armenian author Azad Matian also hints at the experience of loss and longing for a homeland. The story begins with the following statement: 'I want to live in a country whose police officers (law enforcement) are Armenian. I think this has impacted many diaspora Armenians'.[9] Matian does not address within the story why he writes specifically about the police officer. However, since law enforcement is the system through which governments and nation-states enforce laws and organise and regulate people's lives and actions in ways that engage interpersonal and structural prejudice, Matian's yearning for Armenian law enforcement may indicate his desire to be part of a nation's dominant population. This reference might also be in response to the *niruy-i intizami* (the Islamic Republic's police militia), organised after the Islamic Republic came to power. Or this statement may express the longing for an Armenian nation-state as opposed to an Iranian one.

---

[8] Sato A., 'Tun' (Home), *Herazheshtits' araj* (*Before Farewell*) (Tehran: Nayiri Publication, 2002), p. 186.
[9] Azad Matian, 'Mi Yerazanki Masin' (About a Dream), *Grakan Ashkharh* (*Literary World*), *Nayiri Newspaper* (2008), p. 160.

Matian speaks about this yearning in a documentary film produced by film and literary critic Robert Safarian, titled *Dar Fasili-yi du Kuch* (*Between Two Migrations*). Beginning with the Armenian displacement since the Safavid era (seventeenth century), Matian emphasises Iranian Armenians' architectural contributions over fifty-six years, which resulted in the construction of over twenty-four churches, including the Iranian national landmark, the famous Vank Church in New Julfa in Isfahan. Matian tells the story of the Armenians who began fleeing Iran after the community had resided there for seventy or eighty years. He considers decampment as a trend partly heightened by Armenian collective consciousness and an identity oriented around sharing stories of overcoming displacement. He discusses the many displacements and migrations in his life, including the *Nergakht*. After World War II, the Soviet Union and Iran agreed to relocate Iranian Armenians back to Armenia via an organised migration with a plan to register Iranian Armenians, move them to Tehran and then relocate them to Armenia. However, this agreement was halted. Nonetheless, throughout the Pahlavi era (1925–79), the Armenian population increased in Iran and flourished in Tehran, particularly during the 1950s homeland repatriation, or *Nergakht*. In the mid-century, many Armenian villagers who wished to return to Soviet Armenia were instead forced to settle in Tehran (and other urban cities). For example, in 1946, Arak's urban Armenian population increased from 1,000 to 6,000 in a single year. Throughout the 1960s and 1970s, this migratory rural-to-urban trend continued. By 1978, there were 110,000 Armenians living in Tehran, and after the 1979 revolution urbanisation increased, along with increased emigration to foreign countries.[10] To this day, when Armenians speak about the years after World War II, they refer to the *Nergakht*, an ancestral pilgrimage to the homeland that continued well into the 1950s and 1960s, with the number of participants declining annually.

Matian's family was among the displaced Armenians who moved to Tehran in hopes of reaching their homeland – as a result of the return diaspora or *Nergakht*. With the relocation agreement abruptly halted, Matian and his family moved to Khuzestan, where his father could work in the oil company. It was difficult for Armenians to secure employment in Tehran; however, the oil company,

---

[10] Barry, *Armenian Christians in Iran*, pp. 4–5.

predominantly managed by Westerners, was favourable towards Armenians. During the turbulent years before the 1979 revolution, the socio-political life of Armenians concerned itself with the clashes between the Armenian political parties, Dashnaks or non-Dashnaks. Dashnaks, who had left Armenia after the Soviet occupation, were opposed to the Soviets. By contrast, the Tudeh opposition believed that establishing a Soviet Armenia was a central mission – an idea that drew Matian to the Tudeh Party.

In his works, Matian ponders the Armenian diaspora and the status of Armenian diaspora poets. These subjects influenced Matian's collection of poetry, *Anapati Tsaghikner* (*The Desert Flowers*), written in Paris, in which he envisions the diaspora as a desert. For pan-Armenians like Matian, Armenia's independence was an intellectual and mental burden. The independent Armenia was not Soviet in nature, and its rulers were different from the Soviets. Thus, the dream of a homeland had come true – but that truth was fraught with wars, economic crises and cold, bleak days. These conditions, which only emphasised Armenians' sense of alienation and displacement, were difficult to reconcile. Matian moved to Armenia with his family in 1994 and lived there for six months. The short story 'About a Dream' is based on this stay in his Armenian homeland. His trilogy – 'Avarih' (The Displaced), 'Za'iran' (The Pilgrims) and 'Ba in Hamih' (Nevertheless) – were published in the Armenian literary and artistic quarterly *Handes*, for which Matian was an editorial board member during the 2000s. It focuses on diasporic themes, including the return to home, disillusionment and the lack of resolution in moving on.[11] According to Matian, 'The Displaced' is obviously the foreigner, the diaspora individual, while 'The Pilgrims' are those who want to return to a holy motherland, but experience disappointment. 'Nevertheless' is a reference to the fact that life continues, whether our crises are resolved or continue to haunt us. These poems are the outcome of Matian's relationship with the idealised Armenian homeland as well as his experiences while residing in Armenia for half a year during his return migration.[12] While Matian used to identify as a pan-Armenian, as of 2015 he feels no attachment to the homeland. Because he feels that diasporic Armenians do not exist for the benefit

---

[11] Robert Safarian, *Dar Fasili-yi du Kuch* (*Between Two Migrations*), 2010–13, https://vimeo.com/user35586486

[12] Safarian, *Sakin-i du farhang*, p. 125.

of Armenians in the homeland, he feels no yearning to return to Armenia. After Matian's son moved to Glendale, California, Matian and his wife followed. He has no expectations about a new US diasporic community and confesses that he knows that his feelings of isolation will intensify.[13]

As one of the turning points in contemporary Iranian Armenian history, *Nergakht* makes an appearance in many poems, such as 'Hayrenadardz' ('Repatriate') by Armen Ges:

> And to touch the homeland
> The man created the invisible
> Sensitive fingers and penetrating,
> Slender wings,
> Which search for the stars.
> > The huge eyes already see,
> The old homeland.
> And sometimes reaches the ears,
> The distant call of the old brothers.
> > Soon very soon,
> The man sitting on the wings of light
> Will return to the homeland . . .[14]

Ges creates imaginative and invisible wings and fingers so that the diasporic individual can reach the homeland. He makes references to the old homeland and how it no longer exists in the manner in which the diasporic individual remembers it; however, his persona still has hopes for a return.

Hrand Falian's 'Ap'ashavank' ('Apology') presents the tensions of wishing to return to the homeland in devotion yet feeling guilty because of the inability to reach Armenia. Falian asks for forgiveness:

> Homeland, homeland, forgive
> The bad behaviour of your child.
> So tender, so loving,
> > And yet,

---

[13] Safarian, *Dar Fasili-yi du Kuch*.
[14] Armen Ges, 'Hayrenadardz' (Repatriate), *Nor Ej Journal* 15 (1967), p. 74.

He did not give you that which
He had to give you. He did not give
The supreme, which he does not have, which did not exist.
And he could not give . . .
                    For he

Who has the greatest worship and devotion
What are his lavish oaths for?
When he does not give to his beloved
That which does not exist and he cannot give . . .[15]

It is important to note that, in the Armenian texts of these poems, the poets use the term *hayrenik*, which means fatherland to refer to the homeland of Armenia and not Iran (Armenians call themselves *hay*). This of course is not as clear in the English translation, which speaks to the limits of language.

The seemingly insurmountable distance between diasporic Armenians and the homeland has prompted other authors to compose encomiums to the Armenian homeland, language and music. The poem titled 'Ko yergi nman voch mi yerg che ka' (There Is No Song Like Yours) by Markar Gharabegian (also known as Dev) illustrates the interplay between tribute and longing:

How far I am, my precious homeland, from you now?
And how long have I not heard your songs; I have not heard you.
And how many, how many songs have I heard from the distance,
As far as I can remember your songs are wonderful, heartfelt.[16]

To evoke the limbo of Iranian Armenians in the diaspora, Soukias Hacob Koorkchian's (also known as Varand) poem 'Karmir Sultan' (The Red Sultan) draws on the collective memory of the 1915 Armenian Genocide:

---

[15] Hrand Falian, 'Ap'ashavank' (Apology), *Nor Ej Journal* 24 (1999), p. 11.

[16] Markar Gharabegian (Dev), 'Ko yergi nman voch mi yerg che ka' (There Is No Song Like Yours), *Nor Ej Journal* 24 (1999), p. 17.

They say that
Our rich alphabet's
First letter 'A'
Is the symbol that,
God, Himself, is
The seer from the above
Of each one of our
      Behaviours and actions
        Word-by-word.
But there are many
Words in the alphabet,
Such as the garden, the sun,
       The river,
       The Sun, the King,
       The eagle, the lion,
       The star, the moon . . .
As if only
Tears
      And blood
        Suits us.

As if something
Heavenly fortune
Or something historical
     in destiny
Has bestowed upon us
      The gloomy dark clouds
And has crushed with iron claws
      A vulnerable, tender branch. . .

Often in movement
     From a catastrophe to catastrophe,
often called
     'Poor', 'immigrant', 'hungry' . . .

Sometimes 'a friend',
      A thousand times 'an infidel' and 'unclean *najis*',
A thousand times 'a neighbour',
      A thousand times 'a looter' . . .[17]

Varand's allusions to a gloomy, dark history suspend the reader between the historical tension and trauma of the Armenian Genocide and the position of 'unclean *najis*' and 'infidels' occupied by Iranian Armenians. Referring to the 'red sultan', historian Heather Sharkey writes: 'Many who blamed Abdulhamid II for what befell the Armenians portrayed him as a blood monger and dubbed him "the red sultan". Such claims can mislead by assigning too much credit to the sultan, who did not operate solo'.[18] The lines 'First letter "A" / Is the symbol that, / God, Himself, is' are references to the Armenian alphabet, which originally began and ended with God; that is, Ayb (A) – Astvats (God) and K'eh (K) – K'ristos (Christ). This contextualises Varand's allusion. The lines 'But there are many / Words in the alphabet, / Such as the garden, the sun' refer to the Armenian word for garden, *partez*, derived from the Persian *pardis*, which is a clever and deep allusion to heaven (Paradise) as well as the earthly in both cultures. In Varand's poem, living in the diaspora deprives individuals of their cultural heritage by urging them to forget the past in exchange for inner peace. While many individuals construe cultural history as a compass that orients them in and to the present, collective history is a burden for diaspora individuals. Varand deepens this tension by the composition's structure, which situates the trauma of diasporic history between the triumph of Armenian writing and cultural productions, on the one hand, and Iranian Armenians' social position as outsider (*najis*), on the other hand. Just as the Armenian alphabet's 'A' evokes words of pride and joy, words that evoke sorrow and loss better suit the diasporic Armenian experience. Varand questions whether this calamity and darkness is due to a heavenly decree or a historical narrative, a theme underscored by the gradual constriction of lines,

[17] Soukias Hacob Koorkchian (Varand), 'Karmir Sultan' (The Red Sultan), *Sharach'ogh Shght'aner* (*Thundering Chains*) (Tehran: Alik Publishers, 2011), pp. 5–6.

[18] Heather Sharkey, 'Coming Together, Moving Apart: Ottoman Muslims, Christians, and Jews at the Turn of the Century', *A History of Muslims, Christians and Jews in the Middle East* (Cambridge: Cambridge University Press, 2017), p. 269.

choppy statements and the use of ellipses, which convey the suffocating feelings characteristic of diasporic experience. As an Armenian living and writing in Iran while homeland borders weaken, Varand's poem negotiates Armenian heritage, cultural roots, the past and collective memory.

A disconnection from ancestral consciousness – as extended families of many Iranian Armenian diasporic individuals are inaccessible due to immigration, borders and legacies of forced migration and Genocide – is an important aspect of the diasporic experience. With family histories haunted by absence, diasporic Iranian Armenians often turn to community. They strengthen their collective identity and turn repeatedly to nostalgia for the past, even if it is an unknown past, and solidify a collective identity based on collective history. This shows everyday people moving through a society constantly in transition, a group whose collective identity is woven together from diametrically opposed experiences of maintaining heritage while assimilating in the diaspora.

In his book *Dancing Barefoot on Broken Glass*, Leonardo Alishan, an Iranian Armenian author and immigrant to the US, delineates his literal and metaphorical understanding of diaspora through cultural etymology:

Pardis: Persian garden, garden of roses, roses in rows upon rows, rushing red within a rectangular crossing of rivers; perfumed Persian rug upon which no one shall walk with shoes.

Pardis: Paradise

Paradise: Forested mountains, mount of meeting, womb from which the arms of God the Giant and God the Child, the watery arms, the Euphrates and the Tigris, emerge; where the Armen rested, weary of wandering.

Paradise: Armenia

Armenia: Garden of glory, where the Armen planted the tree of life, where they fell on their knees, heavy with anticipation for the fruit; the antichrist Armilus ate the fruit, this god of miscarriage also ate many children of the Armen.

Armenia: Mother

Mother Armenia: Garden with dead gardener, begotten of woman with bleeding womb, begotten but with broken bones, tree also broken; garden begotten of woman, but also woman, begotten but forsaken; fed, but by rivers of red blood, flesh flowered with wounds of red roses, face covered with filthy footprints, forsaken but not forgetful.

Armenia: Wandering Child.

Armenia: Exiled citizen of *Pardis*, face moist with memories of perfumed red roses, faded but fair; a flower on a rectangular Persian rug, not a rushing river but a row of waves, returning to the womb, *Pardis*, Armenia, Paradise.[19]

Alishan begins his cultural etymology with *Pardis,* the Persian word for heaven or paradise (and the Armenian *partez/*garden), locating the roots of diaspora in Persian gardens. *Pardis* is also reminiscent of Persepolis, which was built as an earthly representation of Paradise. In the Qur'an, heaven is often referred to by the Arabised Persian word *firduws* ('janat ul-firduws' in 18:107), which is also the origin of the name of the famous Persian poet Abul-Qasem Ferduwsi (940–1019/1025). In addition, he references Persian roses and Persian rugs, for which Persia is well-known, and those often represent the idea of the garden, *pardis*. In moving towards Armenia, Alishan writes of features and character-istics unique to Armenian history, geography and mythology by referencing forested mountains, the Euphrates and the Tigris, and Armen, the first Arme-nians who are believed to have settled in the area. For instance, 'the tree of life' is a pre-Christian symbol still found in Armenian churches. Mother Arme-nia refers to the mother language (*mayreni lezu*) in contrast to the fatherland (*hayrenik*). He also refers to the medieval figure Armilus, an anti-messiah figure in Jewish eschatology – parallel to the Christian antichrist – who will con-quer the earth and persecute believers. Immediately after this, he writes about Armenia, the motherland, as 'begotten of woman with bleeding womb' and bloody rivers, forsaken but not forgetful. Juxtaposing these two sections, the reader understands that Armilus could be a reference to the Ottoman Empire that persecuted Christian Armenians, while the bleeding women and bloody

---

[19] Leonardo Alishan, 'Etymology of Exile', *Dancing Barefoot on Broken Glass* (New York: Ashod Press, 1991), p. 43.

rivers could refer to the Armenian women who drowned themselves in the Euphrates to avoid being raped and murdered by the Ottomans. The bloody rivers are also an allusion to the book of Revelation as well as 'Ey jan Hayrenik' (My Dear Fatherland) by Avedik Isahakian (1875–1957). Alishan's references to both mother and wandering child evoke an important psychic experience for diasporic Armenians – namely, the desire for safety and nurturing, linked to their global dispersion. His final definition integrates both Armenian and Persian features within the liminality of diaspora, pointing to a multi-layered, hybrid existence and identity.

Significantly, Alishan ultimately proclaims Armenia as a womb to which the speaker anticipates returning. For Alishan's speaker, movement away from past trauma depends on the integration of cultural hybridity, history, geography and temporal consciousness. By engaging the etymology of the Persian *Pardis* in English, he employs the new tools of the host nation to explore the Armenian and Persian ancestral legacies. To integrate into US culture, Alishan's etymologies establish a trajectory of identifying the homeland, dismantling it in his psyche and establishing new meanings for their reintegration. The speaker must first empty their soul so that the new culture can penetrate and settle. Yet, this strategy proves unsuccessful, as the past continues to haunt them, inciting a self-reinvention that melds past, present and future. These processes of disintegration and reintegration are not mutually exclusive and co-exist. Living between multiple cultures leads Alishan to multiple perspectives; seeing from multiple vantage points simultaneously makes these cultures transparent. Distancing himself from his roots and ancestry, Alishan is able to view the world around him from a new perspective and not the one to which he had been acculturated. This in-between space that he occupies – the *verants'ughi* space – debunks the myth of monoculturalism and the superiority of one culture over another. Faced with the disintegration of earlier cultural realities, Alishan needs to reconstruct his identity anew, an identity that is in constant motion and growth.

For Alishan, the impact of this diaspora and exile is so intense that he revisits these subjects in the collection *Free Fall*. In his poem 'The Exile', Alishan states: 'I'm sure you can well imagine the perplexed expression on the faces of airport officials as they look at an embarrassed man pulling at his loose tie and inhaling deeply, while they try to reconcile his faceless features with his passport photograph'.[20] In using a mundane object for many diaspora subjects – a passport – Alishan invokes the migrations of diaspora from one place to another. In diasporic literature, passports are standard motifs as identity documents that associate the individual with a specific nation; however, the passport photograph and the emotions that it embodies may contradict the individual's sense of belonging and citizenship to that particular nation. According to Lily Cho, a scholar of diaspora studies, . . .

> The 'acceptable' facial expressions reveal no emotion. They are natural only insofar as they are completely emotionally neutral. That is, they are not natural at all. They expose a citizen-subject caught and composed for identification purposes. This subject is neither angry, happy, sad, disgusted, nor even particularly present. The foreclosure of emotion in a passport photograph, the identity document that ties a person to a nation, illuminates a contradiction between feeling and citizenship. On the one hand, as these instructions for the passport photographs suggest, emotion obscures the identity of the citizen. On the other, [. . .], emotion, or the capacity for it, is very much a part of the conception of the modern citizen.[21]

Simultaneously, the passport photo provokes anxiety – Alishan's photo is different from his current appearance, which perplexes the officers. The disconnection between the passport photo and his current appearance is almost a common experience among many diasporic individuals. In this fraught moment in the airport, when Alishan is faced with the border patrol officer, it is doubtful that his anxiety-ridden facial expressions would be as neutral or natural as his passport photo. This is a moment that can also be read as the experience of being racialised. The Iranian Armenian Alishan, passing as white, presents a passport that documents his Iranian (Middle Eastern) roots, and while legally considered white in the US, he is socially deemed to be nonwhite. The scrutiny he endures is reminiscent of the racialisation that brown bodies face when assumed to be foreign-born and terrorists. Whether Alishan

---

[20] Leonardo Alishan, *Free Fall: Collected Short Stories*, ed. Gourgen Arzoumanian (Costa Mesa, CA: Mazda Publishers, 2011), pp. 59–60.

[21] Lily Cho, 'Citizenship, Diaspora and the Bonds of Affect: The Passport Photograph', *Photography and Culture* 2.3 (2009), p. 276.

is an American citizen or legally classified as white is irrelevant. He can never fully claim an American socio-cultural identity. Regardless, the same person and photograph that delineate this otherness are also symbols of his hybrid identity. They are evidence of his diasporic existence. Although it may also function as a tool of state surveillance, and although it accompanies him in his movement through the liminal space between nations, a passport implies and anticipates the borders of other nation-states. Passports, hence, hark to the limits of globalisation.

In the poem 'Sarzamin-i Man' (My Homeland), Vahe Armen uses a passport as a metaphor to portray the liminal status of a diaspora subject and their devotion to an eventual homecoming:

My feet are stuck in the dirt
My hands though
Are embracing the body of the earth

My Homeland
Is not a passport as vast as a quandary
My Homeland
Is so vast
That I suppose it's a shadow of it
When I pass by the sun
And so small
That one day
I saw it on the wings of a butterfly[22]

Beginning with an image of immobility, Armen emphasises that only his feet are 'stuck', while his hands embrace the earth and the potential of the future. Although he is suffused with possibility, it comes at the price of a monumental sense of uncertainty – a confinement to the shadow of liminality. It is as if the speaker is waiting to be given permission to exist, to have an identity based in a (perfectly imagined) homeland. These tensions are magnified by

---

[22] Vahe Armen, 'Sarzamin-i Man' (My Homeland), *Pas az ubur-i Dorna-ha* (*After the Passing of the Cranes*) (Tehran: Nashr-i Adabi, 2015), p. 62.

the image of the passport, a symbol that highlights multiple national identities within the diaspora. It also highlights the strain of resisting assimilation while maintaining cultural and political connections to an imagined homeland. Passports typically indicate a specific nation, geography, nationality and belonging, but when Armen implies that his passport is not his homeland, he revives the possibility of a belonging that transcends borders, a belonging across geography. While Vahe Armen's passport enables him to cross collapsing borders, Alishan's passport intensifies his otherness, liminality and non-whiteness within his host nation.

For Vartan Gregorian, and from his standpoint as a recent immigrant fluent in English, the meaning of diaspora shifts to the plural 'diasporas'. He realises that '[d]iasporas tend to be cosmopolitan, international. In any distant region, country, or city, one has an instant link to one's diaspora through one's extended, dispersed family, one's religion, cultural institutions, language, press and, of course, commerce. An immigrant student, a visitor finds an easy foothold, a pathway, a bridge to a foreign country'.[23] Gregorian finds solace in the knowledge that there are many different forms and types of diasporas, and that Iranian Armenians are not the only dispersed population. Given their global dispersion, the boundaries between diaspora and home are no longer meaningful, as definitions of 'home' and other locations proliferate. In this way, he finds a place for the Iranian Armenian diaspora within the larger global diaspora discourse, although this does not assuage his feelings of isolation.

Longing for a *Nostos*

Widely experienced and historically salient social crises are all but monolithic touchstones for both survivors and the collective consciousness. The trauma exists simultaneously in the past and the present. With such collective trauma, Armenians are in a constant quest for a return to the homeland – a *nostos*. However, home for them becomes what literary theorist Trinh T. Minh-ha describes as far away, yet nowhere else but here 'at the edge of this body of mine. Their land is my land, their country is my country. The source has been traveling and dwelling on hybrid ground. [. . .] It is said [. . .] that writers or

---

[23] Gregorian, *The Road to Home*, p. 98.

the diverse Diasporas around the world live in a double exile: away from their native land and away from their mother tongue. Displacement takes on many faces and is our very everyday dwelling'.[24] In this respect, while longing for a return, Iranian Armenian diasporic authors and artists endeavour to embrace the hybridity that accompanies their very existence. While they regularly desire a return home, this home can be both Armenia and Iran, depending on where in the world they are.

Iranian Armenian pop singer Andranik Madadian, known as Andy, fled the Islamic Revolution for Los Angeles, became a pop singer there and later rose to international fame after he produced music that fused western dance, Persian and Armenian heritage. His music is an amalgamation of cultures – Armenian Iranian American – that has yielded an international following, collaboration with stars such as Jon Bon Jovi and a star on the Hollywood Walk of Fame. Andy's song 'Gnank Hayastan' (Let's Go to Armenia) is a symbolic indication of this longing for and loyalty to the homeland:

> I came and saw; I loved your tasty water,
> The sweet spring of your pink cities
> I've come to satisfy my longing, you are my desire
> You're a pure fountain in my soul, in my heart
> I've come to satisfy my longing, you are my desire
> Wherever I go, wherever I live, I won't find anything like you.
> Let's go enjoy in the mountains of Armenia
> And drink sweet wine in our ancestors' gardens.
>
> Whoever hasn't seen, let them see that Armenia is beautiful
> Whoever hasn't seen, let them see that our Sevan Lake is beautiful
> Your Mount Masis and Mount Aragats are so beautiful, see
> You're the sweet longing of every Armenian's heart
> I've come to satisfy my longing, you are my desire
> Let's go enjoy in the mountains of Armenia
> And drink sweet wine in our ancestors' gardens.

---

[24] Trinh T. Minh-ha, 'Home: The Traveling Source', *Elsewhere, Within Here: Immigration, Refugeeism and the Boundary Event* (New York and London: Routledge, 2010), p. 12.

I came and saw; I loved your tasty water,
The sweet spring of your pink cities
I praise you Armenian girls with my sweet songs
Armenian beautiful girls with black eyes
You're like sweet-scented flowers, I'm going crazy
You're young beautiful women, I am losing myself
Let's go enjoy in the mountains of Armenia
And drink sweet wine in our ancestors' gardens.[25]

For Andy, the present is peppered with an unattainable yearning for a homeland that no longer exists as imagined. While this poem is about a return to Armenia, for American Andy, as an Iranian Armenian, homeland is now both Armenia and Iran, as well as the US. The poem evokes a nostalgia that straddles past and present, imbuing temporary and specific experiences of the homeland(s) with social meaning and allowing for continued engagement.

Memories of trauma are also projected into the future, as the artists and authors re-live trauma or allow it to shape their responses to their environment. With generational traumas, memory transcends temporal bounds and manifests as shared trauma from a recent crisis, or the trauma of learning about ancestral suffering. At the crux of these cultural productions and their exploration of multiple locales, ages, regions and cultural practices is the intent to convey the significance of ancestral trauma and collective memory. These themes are evoked in Varand's poem 'Nakhaedzgats'um' (Premonition) which meditates on his unresolved longing for Armenia:

I know that when I die, I will take with me a strong longing,
Longing for a scent, longing for a guest, longing for news.
I will take with me the expectation of hope on an azure morning,
Which will be replaced by the dark black kiss of death . . .

I know that when I die, I will take with me a burning longing,
Longing for stormy eyes, pomegranate lips.

---

[25] Andy Madadian, 'Let's Go to Armenia', *YouTube*, December 2014, https://www.youtube.com/watch?v=cMJ2NCVh5S0

Longing for tenderness, which is called blushing and shame
But also, suddenly changes to tremors of death . . .

I know that when I die, I will take with me a thousand longings,
Longing for the hut, the tree on the shores of the homeland,
I will take with me the bleak memories of my past,
Which swells like a sore wound and ignites a murmur . . .

I know when I die, I will take with me a passionate longing,
Longing, that no one, no one, can see in my destiny [can read on my forehead],
Longing, that all my life I will write, a strange whisper,
But never, never will the Word change.[26]

In this poem, although Varand understands that the wish to return is unfulfillable, he stresses that the 'longing' will never change. The Armenian term *karot* (longing) has a particular meaning that, although without a correlate in English, does exist in other languages, most famously in Portuguese (*saudade*), as well as in Amharic (*tezeta*), Gaelic (*cianalas*) and Welsh (*hiraeth*), all of which figure strongly in literature and music.[27]

Armenian Iranian diasporic cultural productions are replete with images of longing for a return home that is intensified by a legacy of suffering, forced migrations and the loss of the homeland. In his poem 'Ko Sevani tats' achkere minchev' (Until Your Sevan's Teary Eyes), Armand plays with themes of uncertainty and wandering from his position in the Iranian Armenian diaspora:

Who are you, what are you, unknown to me?
Dear to me more than myself . . .
See, I wander from city to city, country to country.
My loneliness with you grows in the crowds,
I am alone with you among huge crowds.

---

[26] Soukias Hacob Koorkchian (Varand), 'Nakhaedzgats'um' (Premonition), *An-veradardz* (*Irreversible*) (Tehran: Alik Publishers, 1999), p. 46.
[27] Thanks to James Barry for pointing this out to me.

Who are you, what are you, that have made me
The slave of your longing, shackled with chains?
Slave of your good, slave of your bad,
Of your radiance and glow, of your pollution,
The shimmering glow of your height
The honey-sweet sun, and the roaring snowstorms,
The greens, the greens of your lands taken away. . .
Slave of your longing, shackled in chains, I
Am wandering from city to city, country to country,
On all the roads of the diaspora inexhaustible
Open my wings seeking a bridge of love
Stranger with these shores, until your Sevan's teary eyes,
Whom in the mirror, one luminous day,
Must look, look, God justly . . .[28]

In this poem, Armand praises the characteristics of every city, region and landmark in Armenia, describing himself as enslaved by their beauty. For him, the past is integral to the national identity formation process. In the penultimate line, Armand uses the word 'mirror' as a medium to bring justice. Mirrors, as cultural theorist Gloria Anzaldúa references, speak to the act of seeing:

Seeing and being seen. Subject and object. I and she. The eye pins down the object of its gaze, scrutinizes it, judges it. A glance can freeze us in place; it can 'possess' us. It can erect a barrier against the world. But in a glance also lies awareness, knowledge. [. . .] seemingly contradictory aspects – the act of being seen, held immobilized by a glance, and 'seeing through' an experience . . .[29]

This awareness, the knowledge and knowing, is painful because there is no way back from such consciousness and visibility. Looking into the mirror seeking justice and arriving at a new awareness, a metamorphosis occurs in

---

[28] Armand, 'Ko Sevani tats' achkere minchev' (Until Your Sevan's Teary Eyes), *Shk'egh Merkutyamb* (*Magnificent Uncovering*) (Tehran: Nayiri Publishers, 1982), p. 82.
[29] Anzaldúa, *Borderlands/La Frontera*, p. 64.

the viewer. In this sense, mirrors can function as a space for *verants'ughi* – painful, yet transformative.

Themes of isolation and a deep longing to return to the homeland are central to Iranian Armenian diasporic works. This desire is expressed succinctly in Nerses D. Mesrobian's book *Karot-e Hayi* (*Armenian Longing*), but more emphatically in the collection's namesake poem:

> Among the people of the world
> And their nation's vocabulary
> You won't find so many
> Extreme longing and an overflow of yearning.
> No one feels longing
> Like an Armenian
> No one lives longing like an Armenian
> And does not yearn
> And does not suffer deep, personal longing.
> An Armenian's longing,
> Ah, how abysmal it is, infinitely deep,
> Vast and inaccessible
> Like its Mount Masis
> As vast as its Mount Masis [. . .][30]

The layered meanings built into this poem incorporate language, time, place and history. Mesrobian's position as an Iranian Armenian American writing primarily in his mother tongue of Armenian highlights the rich vocabulary and cultural depth in the Armenian diaspora's desire to maintain their cultural heritage. Yet, like Mesrobian's text, this cultural maintenance comes at the price of longing for an elusive homeland. He points out that homecoming for Armenians is 'inaccessible' – just like one of Armenia's most famous landmarks, Mount Masis, which is vast and unattainable. At times, Mesrobian's yearning is expressed through a metaphorical flight

---

[30] Nerses D. Mesrobian, 'Karot-e Hayi' (Armenian Longing), *Karot-e Hayi* (*Armenian Longing*) (Glendale, CA: Yerevan Printing, 2014), p. 7.

back home; this is demonstrated in 'Trcheyi mtkov tun' (If Only I Could
Mentally Fly Home):

> If only I could mentally fly home
> Oh if there was
> A bright and happy day
> If only I could mentally fly home
> And it's already faded
> And everything is silent
> And subtle
> Where no breaths no longer live.
> There is no one
> Alive
> A ray of sun
> A reminder of the past . . .
> If only I could mentally fly home
> Seeking my childhood,
> Craving humanity . . .
> Oh, if one day
> I could at least, fly mentally,
> If I could arrive,
> If I could see.[31]

Many Iranian Armenian diaspora authors use a textual or visual limbo that
intensifies temporality – sometimes collapsing past and future, at other times
defying the temporal logic of memory. Mesrobian's use of a bright yet fading
past opens up this kind of limbo and space within this poem. The speaker's
attempts to imagine flying into the waiting homeland are themselves woven
from memories and reminders. Although the speaker stays firmly planted
in the host nation, the motivations for returning include 'seeking my childhood' and 'craving humanity' – experiences embodied by one's own past that
suggest an inability to relate to the diaspora. One of the most significant
principles and primal drives of humanity is a biological and cultural need for

---

[31] Mesrobian, 'Trcheyi mtkov tun' (If Only I Could Mentally Fly Home), p. 14.

connection, trust within relationships, certainty and belonging. Rather than seeking these elements in the diaspora, Mesrobian turns to his memories to find them.

When circumstances make it impossible for the Iranian Armenian diasporic community to return to the homeland, nostalgia is projected onto a place that is physically non-existent yet endures in the imagination. Once the idyllic homecoming is deemed impossible, it is replaced by a return to memories – a mental flight. Memory, specifically the type of intergenerational memory that stems from the loss of the homeland, exists simultaneously in past, present and future. These temporalities cannot be separated or compartmentalised, but instead mimic the fluidity of diasporic identities themselves.

At first glance, these writings seem to propose a diametrical relationship between past and present, host and homeland. However, they actually propose a cyclic relationship that revisits movement between host and homeland and between trauma, hope, survival and struggle. The host country and homeland are held in equal regard in the transition between the two points. The journey from homeland to host nation entails the trauma and turmoil of diasporic displacement and the struggle to find safety; the journey from host nation to homeland is often a mental exercise, where the homeland may be inaccessible due to geography, genocide, or other concerns. In his *Imaginary Homeland*, novelist and essayist Salman Rushdie states that, even if the origin country still exists, return is impossible because of its transformation over time. He envisions an inevitable and natural distance between the origin of a memory and the local changes that accumulate over time. Attempting to return to the point of origin becomes impossible, since even the physical or geographic point shifts and changes, which suggests that loss of the past is inherent to human experience.[32] Because the world changes, it often is impossible to revisit important diasporic points of origins in the material world, but they are accessible in the imaginations and minds of diasporic people. The physical journey from homeland to host nation contrasts directly with the metaphorical journey from host nation to homeland, as the homeland is based in idealised memories that can never be actualised. Forced

---

[32] Salman Rushdie, *Imaginary Homelands: Essays and Criticism 1981–1991* (New York: Penguin Books, 1992), pp. 428–29.

transition for diasporic individuals starkly opposes the coveted pilgrimage to the homeland. The four points on the circle unify the homeland, the journey, the host state and the imagination as a means of return. The diasporic cycle entails leaving the origin country, encountering the traumas of migration, experiencing disillusionment with the host country and eventually arriving at a romanticised relationship with an ideal rendition of the origin country. Because this imaginary homeland does not exist, the cycle continues and creates an endless, persistent longing in the diasporic person for a homeland. The cyclical nature of this movement offers little resolution and must be disrupted to reconcile or alleviate the traumas characteristic of its subjects. Edward Said posits that, when not addressed, the diaspora further propagates new diasporas, eventually causing isolationism and nationalism.[33]

Due to this unresolved movement, there is a sense of an absent homeland origin story more often than not. In its place we hear fragmented memories – glimpses and vignettes of an inaccessible homeland. As Iranian Armenian author Henry A. Sarkissian reminds readers in *Tales of 1001 Iranian Days*, the idea of experiencing one collective memory of the homeland or a single collective Armenian identity is impossible due to Armenians' global dispersion.[34] And throughout history, that same sense of a multiplicity of identities has been extended into life in host nations. There is no prescriptive identity to be found in the host nation, as it is a perennial site of migration, language, religion, consciousness, memory and identity. Instead, diasporic Iranian Armenians move spatially and temporally between past, present and future, in ways that attempt to ameliorate fragmentation, nostalgia and uncertainty – all characteristics of diaspora.

For them, what they have been told about life through tenets of their home culture is transitional, and their lived experiences are personal. Hence, they need to break out of their monocultural way of viewing the world, not only to free themselves from their mental and emotional prison, but also to challenge the official, hegemonic narratives of the host nation. When they

---

[33] Edward Said, 'Reflections on Exile', *Reflections on Exile and Other Essays* (Cambridge, MA: Harvard University Press, 2001), pp. 173–86.

[34] Henry A. Sarkissian, *Tales of 1001 Iranian Days* (New York and Los Angeles: Vantage Press, 1981), p. 70.

travel, their perspectives on culture, home and motherland change with their mobility; 'home' travels with them, and culture remains ingrained within them, but at the same time they adopt elements of the new culture in the host nation – in fact, they co-create their cultural identity as a hybrid transnational individual. Diasporic Iranian Armenian authors and artists reinterpret the concept of home in the transformative space of art and writing within the liminal space of *verants'ughi* where they have to face their painful past yet move beyond – a never-ending journey.

Breaking away from their cyclical movement between home and host nations in hopes of disrupting nationalism, transnational diasporic Armenians embrace the host nation while maintaining ties with the homeland. Now in the new homeland, they destabilise local people's habits. While they show extreme gratitude, they are also exposed to hostility; hence, the diasporic experience 'is never simply binary. If it's hard to be a stranger, it is even more so to stop being one'.[35] Living with a sense of loss, they often feel an urge to assimilate immediately; however, '[t]he problem that prevails then is to be accepted rather than to accept'.[36]

[35] Trinh T. Minh-ha, 'Other Than Myself, My Other Self', *Elsewhere, Within Here: Immigration, Refugeeism and the Boundary Event* (New York and London: Routledge, 2010), p. 30.

[36] Ibid. pp. 29–30.

2

MAINTAINING HERITAGE AND ASSIMILATION

Since the day I have known myself as an adult, I have always had a soft spot for the underdog, for the boundary crosser, for the rebel. Anything about transgression, anything about crossing those lines of 'us' and 'them', anything about othering, and everything about inclusivity and diversity has been dominant in all my life. I am all too familiar with what it means to be marginalised. As an Armenian Iranian, I remember those tumultuous post-revolutionary and wartime days. I can vividly recall days when we had mixed-gender parties in our house and my father had to go to the local police station to receive permission, yet our house would have been raided during the party, and only after receiving some money the police would leave. As a Christian community, Armenians do not find mixed-gender parties problematic; however, after the Islamic Revolution, when everything began being defined based on Shi'i doctrines, freedom of religious and cultural practice lost its minimal meaning completely. I even remember how in the workplace, when I was teaching at the Islamic Azad University, some of my colleagues would avoid eating with me lest they would be contaminated since I was considered to be *najis* (unclean). These are only a few instances but enough to illustrate that, even though my ancestors had arrived in Iran centuries ago, the host nation of Iran has not always been welcoming of us. Naturally, this has left us wondering if we truly belong.

The diasporic experience cannot be appreciated without considering the psychological effects of the oppositional 'us' versus 'them' mentality. For the

Iranian Armenian diaspora, Vartan Gregorian encapsulates this in a few sentences: 'Muslims tolerated us. We were *their* Christians. We had been with them for some 1,400 years. We were not newcomers or foreign imports. We were good for the economy and reputation of Tabriz. We were bridges to Europe and Russia, and India'.[1] Similarly, Edward Said discusses the 'frontier between "us" and the "outsiders"', explaining how those labelled 'other' spend most of their lives 'compensat[ing] for disorienting loss by creating a new world to rule',[2] choosing to resist acculturation into the host nation. Rather than 'straddling two cultures', the complications and guilt that come with assimilation reinforce the diasporic community's cultural heritage.[3] The feeling of cultural opposition to the mainstream, however, nourishes seeds of alienation, preventing any sense that the host nation accepts and values the diasporic community's presence. The pressures to conform to the host culture often causes a sense of isolation or liminality that Iranian Armenian diasporic authors and artists grapple with throughout their lives; yet the result of this liminality is often transformative growth embodied in their creative works. For Iranian Armenians, maintaining their heritage encompasses among many other factors – tradition, language and religion.

The Armenian Church has an immense influence on Armenian identity and culture. The Apostolic Church, the Armenian Orthodox Church, is the most prominent of the Oriental Orthodox churches in Iran. To distinguish themselves from Armenian Catholics, Armenians refer to themselves as Gregorian Armenians, in recognition of St Gregory the Illuminator (c.257–c.331 AD), the Armenian spiritual founder.[4] The foundations of Armenian Christianity date back to the era of Christ's Apostles. According to Christian tradition,

---

[1] Gregorian, *The Road to Home*, p. 40.

[2] Said, 'Reflections on Exile', p. 140.

[3] Rushdie, *Imaginary Homelands*, p. 431.

[4] The largest number of non-Apostolic Armenians are Armenian Catholics or Armenian Protestants. As early as in the fourteenth century, the Roman Catholic Church was proselytising among Armenians in Armenia. However, the Jesuits had penetrated the Ottoman Empire attracting Armenians in the seventeenth century. The Crusades were also significant in the exposure of Catholicism to Armenians. Turkish Armenians were introduced to Protestantism through English and American missionaries in 1800s. For more information, see Malcolm Vartan, *The Armenians in America* (Boston: The Pilgrim Press, 1919).

St Thaddeus travelled to the southern part of Armenia, while Bartholomew travelled to the north to proclaim the message of Christ. Armenians refer to these saints as the 'First Illuminators' of the Armenian people. The first Armenian converts to Christianity were persecuted under the rule of King Ardashir I (r. 230–160 BC) in 110 BC and, later, under King Khosrow (r. 531–579 AD). Armenia became the first kingdom in the world to proclaim Christianity as the state religion, between 301 and 314 AD, shortly after King Tirdates III (250–330 AD) had been healed by prayer and converted to Christianity. A majority of Armenians promptly followed the king's edict and were baptised as Christians. Religious studies scholar Charles Kimball observes that 'the unity and strength of this [Armenian] church through the centuries has been visible to all: to be an Armenian has always been practically synonymous with being a Christian'.[5] According to Armenian art historian Sirarpie der Nersessian, the churches served as 'guardians of the language and of the traditions of the [Armenian] people'.[6] During times of unrest, the meshing of nation, church and language has been a defining element of Armenian identity and culture in general, but more particularly for Iranian Armenians who lived under a Shi'i Muslim rule. While a majority of Armenians accepted Christianity, a minority remained Zoroastrian, never converting to Christianity and taking the name *Arewordik*, or 'Children of the Sun'.[7]

The well-known Iranian Armenian filmmaker Arby Ovanessian's thirty-minute documentary in the Armenian language, *Ghara Kelisa* or *Lebbaeus Whose Surname Was Thaddaeus*, has become a vital tool to maintain Armenian heritage via its representation of religion.[8] Ovanessian's black-and-white film documents the annual pilgrimage of Armenians to the mausoleum of the Holy Thaddaeus near Maku. According to Andranik Hovian, since the eastern part of the church's structure is built from black stones, it has been assumed that the

[5] Charles A. Kimball, *Angle of Vision: Christians and the Middle East* (New York: Friendship Press, 1992), p. 28.

[6] Sirarpie Der Nersessian, *The Armenians* (New York: Praeger Publishers, 1970), p. 78.

[7] Nina G. Garsoian, *Armenia Between Byzantium and the Sasanians* (London: Variorum Reprints, 1985), p. 347.

[8] Arby Ovanessian, *Ghara Kelisa* (*Lebbaeus Whose Surname Was Thaddaeus*) (Tehran: Studio Chaplin, 1967), http://iranahaytv.com/2020/04/23/ghara-kelisa-a-documentary-film-by-arbi-ovanisian/

name of the church *Ghara Kelisa* means Black Church, as *ghara* means black in Turkish. However, Hovian notes that it is important to understand the name of the church in the historical context of the penetration of the Turkish dialect in Azerbaijan, since before this time the dominant language was Azeri and since, in Azeri, *ghara* means 'great'.[9] Hence, *Ghara Kelisa* means the 'great church' rather than the 'black church'.

As the film opens, a voice narrates the mausoleum's origin as the shrine of St Thaddaeus, disciple to Jesus Christ. The camera first focuses on a stream of light – like a single candle against a black background – then slowly pans out to display the mausoleum's location from afar – a desert hilltop. The entire documentary contrasts light and dark scenes, establishing black and white contrasts as a thematic motif. In one scene the camera pans into the church, then toward gravestones, underlining Armenian script. A background score featuring Armenian church hymns intensifies the scene. As the scene transitions, church bells toll, and the camera focuses on the church columns, ceiling and interior and exterior walls decorated with traditional Armenian architectural symbols. *Ghara Kelisa* is considered one of the best examples of the art of stone carving with its array of architectural human figures, animals, plants and geometrical shapes. The architectural ornaments are believed to be the outcome of historical fluctuations, cultural interactions and various influences from Parthian, Sassanian and Qajar art, with a touch of Christian and Hellenic art.[10] The human figures, for instance, include the Virgin Mary, Christ's Disciples and mythical and holy figures, while the geometrical shapes feature images of the cross and animal figures include lion and eagle. The film's atmosphere is solemn and sacramental, accentuating long segments with no narrative voice-over or dialogue. According to Iranian philosopher Ramin Jahanbegloo, 'the slow pace of the documentary creates questions in the viewers' minds. And this is exactly on the contrary to the fast pace of the news media or Internet to which we are used. This kind of cinema paces the images to give the viewers the chance to think about the images and the relationships between its elements'.[11]

---

[9] Andranik Hovian, 'Ghara Kelisa', *Nashri-yi barrisiha-yi tarikhi* 2.5 (1967), pp. 196–97.

[10] Aliyi Imini and Muhammad Khazai, 'Naqsh-mayiha-yi tazini dar Ghara Kelisa' (Decorative Elements in Ghara Kelisa), *Nashriyi ketab mah-i honar* 133 (2009), p. 43.

[11] Ramin Jahanbegloo, 'From the Writings, Conversations, and Photos', *Theater and Cinema of Arby Ovanessian*, ed. Majid Lashkari (Tehran: Ruzanih Publications, 2014), p. 457.

After this visual meditation on the church, the film shifts, suddenly incorporating human movement and activity within and around the structure. Cars and trucks begin arriving; two men discuss when their friends might arrive with tents for the journey. As the dialogue shifts to banter regarding the perfect camping spot, the camera pans out, capturing children playing, sheep grazing and the structure of the mausoleum beyond. Crowds slowly arrive and set up their camps with tents, tables and chairs, and a large group begins traditional Armenian folk dancing as onlookers gather. Throughout the scene we see men and women roasting kebabs over the fire, Armenian coffee pots, an Armenian woman in traditional clothing and men playing backgammon. Quickly, the church is surrounded by tents that illustrate Armenian-style everyday activities shot non-linearly, so that the boundaries of the four-day event become fluid, blending a multitude of experiences into a singular visual meditation. This moment in the film introduces the mausoleum and its surroundings as a space of in-betweenness, fluidity, liminality and transition. The crowd lives in this liminal zone for four days, without clear boundaries, to perform the rituals. Using these four days of *verants'ughi* space, Ovanessian mimics the instability, displacement and precarity that Armenians have endured historically. In this marginal space and time, the crowd forgets about the reality of their lives and resides in a space rife with transformation and possibility.

Halfway through the film, Ovanessian breaks the fourth wall by including footage of himself filming different scenes, which calls to mind the technique of acclaimed Iranian film director Abbas Kiarostami – it is unclear who influenced whom.[12] The camera then focuses on participants lighting candles within the mausoleum and then the softly glowing candlelight. As people are enjoying each other's company, we hear dialogues without the camera distinctly identifying the speakers. We can hear Armenian conversations with audible Persian code-switching and statements from the Bible. Alternating between Persian and Armenian languages, Ovanessian shows an alternative way of using language – one that has been reconfigured and

---

[12] Abbas Kiarostami, the acclaimed Iranian film director, was well-known for breaking the fourth wall in his films by suspending cinematographic conventions, such as appearing in his own films as the real director or having characters directly refer to the audience.

decolonised – changing our perception that one may think solely in one language and showing language in its natural context – how it is actually spoken. Embodying a hybrid identity, he utilises code-switches and statements from both languages that illustrate his multiple consciousnesses. In this regard, language, which can be viewed as a simple medium for communication, instead becomes a crucial means to liberate and decolonise from the idea that we live with a single consciousness.

A few of the film's scenes focus on killing sheep as a sacrifice and offering to the mausoleum. While some of the central tenets of Christianity contradict this practice on the basis of absolute forgiveness through Jesus Christ's self-sacrifice, this tradition continues as a method to distribute meat to the poor and elderly within some Greek Orthodox communities. Many world religions, including the pagan and Judaic heritage of the region, have performed these kinds of sacrifice; yet it cannot definitively be said that the Armenians' maintenance of this ritual is due to any one culture's influence – another reference to hybridity.

The religious music begins again, and the camera refocuses on the final pilgrimage ritual, with the priest and pilgrims walking to the mausoleum. As the priests walk to the altar to pay respect to the Virgin Mary and Jesus Christ, the camera hovers on a crucifix embroidered on the priest's vestments. All the while the ceremony continues. We witness a choir singing, priests burning sacred incense, reading from scripture and blessing the wine and bread to be distributed among the crowd. As they take communion, participants walk to the priest and kiss the Bible. Once the sacrament has concluded, the priests marry a couple, baptise a child and slowly move from the mausoleum to the hilltop cemetery where pilgrims and religious leaders pay their respects to the dead. This marks the end of the annual pilgrimage, and the camera briefly turns to the crowds before documenting the litter and plastic refuse that participants have discarded in the desert.

This documentation of a trashed landscape conveys Ovanessian's critical view of what happens during this pilgrimage and its rituals, illustrating how a sacred space can be demeaned by its own community. The closing shot of the documentary lasts for a full minute, consisting of a long shot of the mausoleum with a dark cloud over it, and then it slowly begins to rain. The narrator voices a sentence from the Bible: 'Build on the rocks!' – a direct contrast to the destruction left behind.

While Ovanessian's documentary is itself a piece of Armenian cultural heritage, its standing as foundational to Armenian and diasporic identity must be emphasised. According to Iranian Armenian artist Lida Berberians, . . .

> . . . the film is noteworthy in terms of its social documentary content and unique artistic look at the anthropological aspects of the event, especially as the Church of St. Thaddeus (along with the Church of St. Stephen and the Church of the Assumption), was registered on the World Heritage List of the UNESCO historical monuments in 2009, and according to the rules of this organisation, the current situation around this historical monument will soon change and the traditional form of pilgrims' gatherings will be forgotten. Such films are important to help preserve the historical memory of the future generations and to raise awareness as to how this socio-religious ceremony was performed, and the film *Labbaeus*, [. . .] with the atmosphere of neo-realist cinema of the 1960s of the twentieth century, will be a prominent example in the history of Armenian Iranian filmmaking in the future.[13]

As Berberians notes, Ovanessian's cinematic work is not just a documentary but also a tool of cultural maintenance that integrates the nostalgia of the past to create a resource for future generations.

Any discussion of cultural maintenance and the desire for Armenian heritage must consider the host nation's treatment of the subject, too. Shortly after the popular Iranian Armenian musician and conductor Loris Tjeknavorian returned to Iran from his musical studies in Vienna, he signed a contract to produce a work about the story of Rustam and Suhrab, part of Firduwsi's tenth-century epic poem, the *Shahnamah* (Book of Kings). It tells the tragic story of the heroes Rustam and his son, Suhrab. Unaware that he had a son, Rustam faces Suhrab (his son) in a battle, fighting on opposing sides. They fight in single combat; Rustam wrestles Suhrab to the ground and stabs him fatally. As he lies dying, Suhrab recalls that he is there to meet his father, Rustam. At that moment, Rustam realises that he has killed his son. Despite his success, Iranian artists criticised Tjeknavorian due

---

[13] Lida Berberians, '*Lebbaeus Whose Surname Was Thaddaeus:* A Documentary Film', *Theater and Cinema of Arby Ovanessian*, ed. Majid Lashkari (Tehran: Ruzanih Publications, 2014), p. 933.

to his Armenian descent and young age, claiming that he could not convey the emotional depth or literary roots of a story such as that of Rustam and Suhrab. However, his presence at the helm of the National Music Archives coincided with the formation of the Rastakhiz Party (Resurrection Party) by Mohammad Reza Shah Pahlavi, which mandated that all government employees participate in the party. Until then, Tjeknavorian had believed that the artist's duty was to create art that transcended politics. By disobeying the order to join the Rastakhiz Party, he paved the way for his dismissal from the Ministry of Culture.[14] The simultaneous intensification of criticism against him and his alienation from opposition artists led to the cancellation of the contract, prompting him to return to Austria.

Despite these struggles, Tjeknavorian proudly proclaims his Iranian identity and Armenian heritage, culture and ancestral roots; in a way, he prefers not to be considered a member of a minoritised community. After the Great Earthquake of 1988 in Armenia, Gyumri (Leninakan) was the second largest city affected by the disaster. In 1991, Tjeknavorian went on a pilgrimage walk from Yerevan to Gyumri to raise money for areas devastated by the earthquake. Thousands of people joined him, and many donated to his cause. Subsequently, he organised a benefit concert at Carnegie Hall to raise funds for the earthquake victims and, later, he contributed to the Armenian Independence cause by organising televised concerts and performances in various Armenian cities; some believe that he positively influenced the referendum for Armenian Independence. By melding music with humanitarian causes, Tjeknavorian became a political leader for communities in his homeland. As such, he worked to rebuild Armenia's collapsed infrastructure. According to Tjeknavorian, . . .

Armenians have always called for Armenia's independence because of their anti-communist leanings, until Gorbachev suggested that Armenia could hold an independent referendum for the next five years if there was a high turnout. But the referendum was initially welcomed by only 30 percent of Armenians because of the bitter experiences of war and bloodshed in the history of Armenians, as well as their fear of yet another bloodshed. When I

---

[14] Payam Fazlinijad, 'Musahibih ba Loris Tjeknavorian' (An interview with Loris Tjeknavorian), *Shukaran* Programme, IRIB, Channel 4, 2019.

was invited for counselling, I said that the cure for this is music, let me give concerts to people in different cities and inform them. This happened, and I gave concerts for two days and nights and talked to them and invited them to participate in the referendum. Interestingly, the turnout in the referendum increased from 30 percent to 96 percent, and this is the miracle of music.[15]

After the nation gained independence, he was influential in rewriting portions of the newly-adopted national anthem, *Mer Hayrenik* (*Our Fatherland*). During the 1992–95 energy blockade that followed a war with Azerbaijan, the city of Yerevan faced severe shortages of food, water, heat and electricity. In order to raise funds and resources and lift the residents' spirits, Tjeknavorian held weekly concerts and a series of spiritual musical concerts every Saturday, in anticipation of the 1,700th anniversary of Christianity in Armenia. Tjeknavorian's life trajectory illustrates that through his combination of music and humanitarian causes he has been involved with both Armenian and Iranian societies.

The theme of maintaining Armenian traditions in the diaspora is a staple of Armenian cultural production; it is explored by writer Khach'ik Khach'er *vis-à-vis* Iranian Armenians. In his short story 'Ashk-i Sheshum' (The Sixth Tear), Khach'er describes how Armenian men 'used to gather in the Ararat Sports Complex every two weeks on Sundays and Tuesdays to play soccer'.[16] The Ararat Sports Complex is a landmark for Tehrani Armenians; it has managed to flourish regardless of the threat of confiscation by the Iranian state governments. Khach'er narrates how Armenian men would discuss 'their kids' school situations, the Parliament elections and the Candidates of the Armenian Prelacy for the Islamic Parliamentary elections, and about the bloody war in Chechen and the tumultuous conditions of Armenia, and the unstable ceasefire in Nagorno-Karabakh'.[17] These conversations create a homosocial, culturally Armenian space where men gather to discuss not only their own Iranian conditions such as their Islamic Republic parliamentary candidates, but also global events that affect the homeland of Armenia, such as the Nagorno-Karabakh conflicts. In addition, the Armenian nationalist newspaper *Alik* is woven into

---

[15] Quoted in Fazlinijad, 'Musahibih ba Loris Tjeknavorian'.
[16] Khach'ik Khach'er, *Ashk-i Sheshum* (*The Sixth Tear*) (Tehran: Nashr-i Chishmih, 2000), p. 11.
[17] Ibid. p. 12.

the narrative by references to its articles. By incorporating all of these elements, Khach'er illustrates an intentional, Iranian Armenian cognitive and emotional investment in the homeland symbolically, and in the host nation physically. With respect to this kind of multicultural interaction, cultural theorist Gloria Anzaldúa writes: 'When two or more opposing accounts, perspectives, or belief systems appear side by side or intertwined, a kind of double or multiple "seeing" results, forcing you into continuous dialectical encounters with these different stories, situations, and people'.[18]

Khach'er's diasporic characters try to understand convergences between politics in their homeland, those in the host nation and globally. This leads them to multiple perspectives, which affords them a space to reinterpret these perspectives. As they discuss the events in Nagorno-Karabakh, they are also invested in the Iranian parliamentary elections; all the while, they are also thinking about global politics. Similar to Tjeknavorian and Ovanessian, Khach'er and other Iranian Armenian artists and authors embody the kind of transnationalism that connects them to their homeland of Armenia, while they are also invested in their host nation's politics and global causes. However, this transnationalism does not come easily to them; they experience isolation as a result of their displacement and minoritised status, even as they go through a process of transformation and identity formation.

Constructing a sense of identity and suffering from feelings of displacement are central to Zoya Pirzad's work 'Yik Ruz Qabl az 'iyd-i Pak' (A Day Before Easter), which traces the adolescent life of Edmond, who lives in a seaside town referred to as the settling place of the first Armenian immigrants to Iran. In this Armenian Iranian community, Edmond struggles with maintaining heritage, assimilating and shaping his own identity. The story begins with Edmond telling the reader about his childhood home, which is located next door to the Armenian church and school – an allusion to the important role of cultural maintenance that these two institutions play in the Armenian characters' lives. The fact that 'the church and school had been built by the first Armenian immigrants who settled in [their] seaside town' underscores

---

[18] Gloria Anzaldúa, 'now let us shift . . . the path of conocimiento . . . inner work, public acts', *This Bridge We Call Home: Radical Visions for Transformation*, ed. Gloria E. Anzaldúa and AnaLouise Keating (New York: Routledge, 2001), p. 544.

this point.[19] Edmond's recollections of students reciting morning Christian prayers before class and the annual composition about their responsibilities to their motherland – *mihan-i madari* – eloquently portray these roles.[20]

Repeatedly, in Iranian Armenian diasporic cultural productions, the significance of the church and religion and the most salient religious traditions are highlighted as signifiers of identity. Easter appears in the title of Pirzad's story and is also the season of Edmond's annual reminiscences. His description of their traditional Easter celebration is noteworthy:

> The basket of coloured eggs sat on a sideboard in the dining room. Next to it there was a big *paska* loaf topped with a chocolate cross, and *nazouk* pastries that my aunt had baked herself, and whenever someone praised them, she would say, 'No, no, they don't hold a candle to Mother's'. And there was sweet and salty *gata*, and fruit and iris candy. There were two tall silver candlesticks that were placed on the sideboard and their white candles lit every Easter night and Epiphany. On the wall there was a large picture of Grandmother in a wooden frame with a black ribbon fastened diagonally across the photo. While Grandmother was still alive, the whole family gathered at her house every Easter and Epiphany, even for those last two years when she was almost continually in bed, and the preparation of the rice and kuku and the smoked fish, as well as tending to the guests, was left to Auntie Shakeh. That final year, Grandmother had only been able to come to the table in her wheelchair for a few moments, just long enough to say the prayer before the meal and to take the holy wafer with us.[21]

Edmond goes to great lengths to explain the importance of celebrating Easter in a conventional, time-honoured manner that includes all the classic Armenian pastries: *paska*, *gata*, *nazouk* and iris candy. Generally, diasporic communities may internalise identification through emotions, food and smells associated

---

[19] Zoya Pirzad, *The Space Between Us*, trans. Amy Motlagh (London: OneWorld Publications, 2014), p. 2; Zoya Pirzad, 'Yik Ruz Qabl az 'iyd-i Pak', *Sih Kitab* (Tehran: Nashr-i Markaz, 2011), p. 226.

[20] Pirzad, *The Space Between Us*, pp. 7, 17. Also note that 'motherland' is used here as opposed to 'fatherland' (*hayrenik*) which is common in Armenian language because the story is written in Persian.

[21] Ibid. pp. 73–74.

with their homeland. In conjunction with the Easter celebrations, the reader also hears about Edmond's grandmother, the most traditional female figure in the story. Grandmother's posthumous influence – and by extension, the Armenian ancestral presence – is conveyed by a wood-framed picture from which she gazes down from the kitchen wall, still surveying and admonishing the family to conduct the celebration as she would have done. For many Iranian Armenians, gathering around the kitchen table to cook and eat clarifies what it means to be Armenian – it evokes their collective memory. Armenian food, therefore, ties living Iranian Armenians to their homeland, ancestors and roots. In addition to transmitting Armenian culture, food carries not only a personal memory but also has the potential to conjure deceased relatives. According to Arlene Voskani Avakian, 'Armenian history and culture, both personal and collective, are encapsulated and preserved in the very concrete act of preparing, eating, and sharing particular Armenian dishes or the gathering of people together to share Armenian food'.[22]

The food prepared for dinner in Edmond's household – rice, *kuku* and smoked fish – are mainstays of Persian Nowruz dishes, too. While it might be a coincidence that both nations celebrate special occasions with similar food choices, this similarity underscores the influence of a shared history between Armenia and Iran, even if Armenians do not observe Iranian national holidays such as Nowruz. According to Iranian Armenian film critic Robert Safarian, pressuring Armenians to celebrate Nowruz would have impressed upon the populace that the state supported a popular assimilationist attitude, thereby discrediting multiculturalism and denying a peaceful coexistence between minoritised and majority groups.[23]

Easter also features significantly in Vartan Gregorian's *The Road to Home*; yet, in Gregorian's work, Easter is mentioned in conjunction with Nowruz:

> The *Zadig* (Easter) that followed the Persian New Year was a major occasion of celebration, not only because it marked the Resurrection of Christ and was therefore a symbol of rebirth and hope but also because it brought family

---

[22] Arlene Voskani Avakian, 'Are We What We Eat? Armenian-American Women's Ethnic Identity and Food', *The Armenians of New England*, ed. Marc C. Mamigonian (Belmont, MA: Armenian Heritage Press, 2004), pp. 220–22.

[23] Safarian, *Sakin-i du farhang*, p. 65.

members together. It also challenged the culinary expertise and aspirations of all the families. Scores of meals had to be prepared, cakes had to be baked, cookies decorated, plates of dried and fresh fruits, chocolates, and candies had to adorn the banquet table to serve, impress, and honour relatives and friends who visited each other to celebrate Easter. New clothes were worn, along with new shoes. We got haircuts and cleaned the house. We went to church, carrying our colored eggs, we played with our friends and strangers as well, attempting to crush their eggs in a competition. We carried the broken eggs home for consumption.[24]

The influence of Iranian culture and the pressure to assimilate into mainstream society is illustrated by Emmanuel P. Vardanyan's description of why the Christian liturgy appeals to him. Located in *The Well of Ararat*, these passages also elucidate his emulation of ancient Persian and Armenian legendary heroes.[25] In a scene describing his uncle's engagement party and henna ceremony, the narrator's father explains the meaning of henna:

In Mohammedan countries the New Year, called Nove Rooz, is celebrated by decorating bazaars and mosques and streets with ribbons, flags, flowers, and wreaths, and the people put henna on their hair, hands and beards. It is a symbol of the oneness of life, of vitality; a symbol of a new life, of gaiety, because all nature dons new colors. The use of henna here indicates that your uncle and Marina are beginning a new life. Henna is the first indication, a cheerful symbol that the Second Gate begins to open for them, the garden begins to bloom.[26]

Historically, henna has been used in the Near and Middle East and North Africa, on the Arabian peninsula and the Indian sub-continent, among other places, and both Iranians and Armenians in Iran incorporate henna ceremonies into their weddings and engagement parties. Vardanyan's inclusion of the ceremony alludes to multiculturalism in traditions and rituals. While not commonly celebrated by Iranian Armenians, Nowruz captures their imagination and resurfaces

---

[24] Gregorian, *The Road to Home*, p. 37.
[25] Emmanuel P. Vardanyan, *The Well of Ararat* (Belmont, MA: The National Association for Armenian Studies and Research Inc., 2005), p. 102.
[26] Ibid. p. 110.

in many cultural productions. Gregorian notes: 'The only Persian festival that captured our attention and imagination was the Iranian New Year'.[27]

While the majority of Iranian Armenian writers refers to Nowruz in some form, Christian religion and religious traditions are even more commonly featured. Author Henry A. Sarkissian explains: 'Armenians, now dispersed all over the world, were the first nation on earth to have a Christian state; as such, they have deeply rooted religious feelings'.[28] Such a sentiment is not only found in cultural productions, but also very commonly uttered by many Iranian Armenians who take pride in being the first nation to declare Christianity as their national religion. In her book *The Survivor*, Rosemary H. Cohen spotlights the critical role of religion and tradition in the lives of Armenians in Iran. Cohen recounts history during World War II and the massacres that resulted in the 1915 Genocide of Armenians. She writes about Christianity, the Bible, Armenian priests and Easter as cornerstones of this violent period:

> The Armenian priest does not have total importance and authority in the country. He is the messenger of God, the one person who has studied the Bible more than anyone else. He is the one who will go from house to house after January sixth and after Easter to bless the families and their houses. He will listen to peoples' problems and solve their differences. He is more like a big father to all. He stays away from politics, but plays an important role in teaching the Armenian language and religion to the students, in order to perpetuate their traditions. On Easter everyone will go to church to listen to the prayers. Meanwhile, the children will play with colorful eggs decorated with dyes from onionskins and colored papers and flowers. Sometimes they return home with a lot of broken eggs. They keep the nicest one and eat the rest each day with *nazouk* and *paska*.[29]

While descriptions of Easter are deeply symbolic for diasporic Iranian Armenians, Vardanyan's *The Well of Ararat* draws attention to the importance of other Armenian religious rituals, particularly Christmas: 'CHRISTMAS

---

[27] Gregorian, *The Road to Home*, pp. 36–37.

[28] Sarkissian, *Tales of 1001 Iranian Days*, p. 42.

[29] Rosemary H. Cohen, *The Survivor* (Los Angeles: LICO Publishing, 2002), p. 13.

WAS APPROACHING. Although less spectacular than Easter, its glamour, nevertheless, had a unique effect upon the peasants. Its spiritual and mystic implications revitalized their lives; they felt expansive and exalted'.[30]

These detailed descriptions, coupled with information about the important role of religion, culture and traditions, set the scene for almost all of the cultural productions under study here. In the words of Cohen's protagonist, '[w]e [Armenians] kept our traditions, gatherings for weddings, birthdays and religious festivities. We would visit each other on New Year's Eve and other major holidays. We kept some of the traditions of Khoy and taught them to our children and grandchildren'.[31]

Even as these works explore a desire to transmit and preserve Armenian heritage, however, they also demonstrate a transnational longing to assimilate and integrate into a mainstream host culture. The tension between cultural maintenance and assimilation signals that transnational subjectivity and identity are constantly being (re)constructed. Owing to these immanent tensions, different generations of Iranian Armenians perform different cultural and religious practices in the diaspora. Gregorian expounds on the significance of the Armenian Church and how it provided him with security as a child, explaining that the church was 'the center of our religious and social life'.[32]

In addition to church, the Armenian language is the next most crucial identity marker for diasporic Iranian Armenians. In his autobiography Sarkissian recalls how maintaining both Armenian and Persian language fluency was crucial for his family, however difficult it may have been, especially when he was a small child transplanted to Paris: 'That sort of switching countries back and forth is somewhat difficult for a school-going child. When I started going to a kindergarten in Paris, it was tough for me, as I didn't know French, and when we got back to Tehran, I didn't know a single word of Persian, which was an additional burden when struggling with my written homework'.[33] Later, he comments on the difficulties of maintaining religious traditions in Paris, especially prayers, and how those traditions dove-tailed with language. He recalls

---

[30] Vardanyan, *The Well of Ararat*, p. 37.
[31] Cohen, *The Survivor*, p. 142.
[32] Gregorian, *The Road to Home*, p. 29. Gregorian, however, does not mean that Armenian social life was limited to the church.
[33] Sarkissian, *Tales of 1001 Iranian Days*, p. 27.

how he had to repeatedly say 'the Lord's Prayer in Persian while visiting the missionary, in addition to having to say it in Armenian at home when going to bed at bedtime, during which I had to sing also as a duet with my younger sister a night time hymn in French'.[34] The family's emphasis on bilingualism in the diaspora, while they also learned a third language in order to prosper in the host nation, illustrates the multiple struggles that diasporic communities face. The experience of being transplanted involves delicately balancing accultura- tion and assimilation with a cultural maintenance of language, tradition and religion. At the same time, the bilingual and trilingual experiences of diasporic immigrants point to multiplicities as a core value. Sarkissian's parents empha- sised trilingualism by using prayer as a foundation practice; yet, for Sarkissian constantly switching languages was an endeavour that left him feeling non- fluent. While in Iran Sarkissian would consider Armenia his homeland, in France he felt twice the stranger, twice in diaspora, with two homelands – Armenia and Iran. For Sarkissian's family, as is true for many Armenian families, language is the most crucial element after religion when it comes to national identity formation.

Socio-cultural anthropologist Martin Sökefeld explores the question of whether those in the diaspora hold on to religion due to religious conviction or as a cultural identity based in the homeland. He demonstrates that people in the diaspora hold on to religion as a foundation of their culture, perhaps in part because, in social contexts, 'religious communities are more easily recognised than "cultural" or "ethnic" ones'.[35] Iranian Armenian diasporic literature and art point out that many Armenians experience Christianity, Armenian language, culture and a relationship to the homeland as a strong foundation for diasporic identity formation during periods of confusion and isolation. This is even more significant for generations less exposed to trans- national discourses, who often choose to surround themselves with a like- minded community where identity is rooted in a common homeland with a shared heritage. For those who have indeed been evolving with global trans- national discourses and who question strict religious beliefs and practices,

---

[34] Ibid. p. 37.
[35] Martin Sökefeld, 'Religion or Culture? Concepts of Identity in the Alevi Diaspora', *Dias- pora, Identity and Religion: New Directions in Theory and Research*, ed. Caroline Alfonso, Waltraud Kokot and Khachig Tölölyan (London: Routledge, 2004), p. 148.

religious identity is diluted and not maintained as diligently. These variations illustrate how different groups in the diaspora establish and maintain their cultural identity and heritage differently, based on their exposure to and opinions about global transnationalism. Some hold on to their religious identity for a communal, national, cultural and religious practice, while others find a way to negotiate a more plural identity. Both cohorts cope with their diasporic experience in different ways, depending on the severity of their loss and their level of nostalgia.

The trauma of separation from the homeland instils a deep commitment to cultural preservation, often in a strict, imported style. Those who leave the space, connections and relationships that have shaped their being leave an integral part of their identity behind. This is encompassed in a feeling of unbearable loss that is magnified for diasporic individuals, exiles, immigrants and refugees. The struggle to hold on to some element of the homeland within the host nation, as well as the preservation of their culture and values, is an important practice for families in the diaspora. By passing on their culture and values to the next generation, they are able, in a way, to recreate their homeland and their previous life, even as they grapple with assimilation to a host nation.

The Dilemma of Assimilation

Immigrant assimilation is typically assessed according to four benchmarks: socio-economic status based on educational attainment, occupation and income; spatial concentration such as residential patterns; language attainment and the ability to speak the host nation's language, accompanied by a loss of the mother tongue; and intermarriage across racial, ethnic, or (occasionally) generational lines.[36] There are three major theories of assimilation in the US: the classic and new assimilation models, the racial/ethnic disadvantage model and the segmented assimilation model.[37] The classic and new assimilation model is the most prominent. It contends that immigrant

---

[36] Frank D. Bean and Gillian Stevens, *America's Newcomers: Immigrant Incorporation and the Dynamics of Diversity* (New York: Russell Sage Foundation, 2003).

[37] Since I focus on Armenian diaspora in Iran and in the US, here I will provide some information on the assimilation theories developed in the context of US immigration, before I will briefly discuss its difference with its counterpart in Iran.

groups gradually adopt the host nation's norms, values, behaviours and cultures (characteristics also known as 'straight-line convergence'). According to Richard Alba and Victor Nee, however, the incorporation of ethnic and immigrant groups also involves acceptance by the mainstream population.[38] The racial/ethnic disadvantage model argues that the assimilation of certain groups is blocked by mainstream society, based on race or ethnicity. According to this model, language and cultural familiarity may not lead to increased assimilation due to lingering discrimination and institutional barriers to employment and other opportunities that ultimately block complete assimilation.[39] Sociologists Alejandro Portes and Min Zhou combine elements of both the 'straight-line assimilation' and the 'ethnic disadvantage' perspectives into a single framework, which they call 'segmented assimilation'. Based on this theory, structural barriers hinder access to employment and other opportunities for disadvantaged members of immigrant/diaspora groups, which results in downward mobility. Here, assimilation plays into the idea of class mobility. This model endeavours to identify the contextual, structural and cultural factors that separate successful and unsuccessful assimilation.[40]

While these three models are useful, they are not adequate for all diasporic and immigrant groups around the world. Of US origin, these models were constructed in a specific socio-historical context of black-white racial relations, or non-white minoritised individuals whose discrimination is contoured by anti-African American thought.[41] To assess Iranian Armenian assimilation in Iran and in the US, the segmented model may be most useful. Today, although they are legally classified as white, the bulk of Armenian immigrants define

---

[38] See Richard D. Alba and Victor Nee, *Remaking the American Mainstream: Assimilation and the New Immigration* (Cambridge, MA: Harvard University Press, 2003); Richard D. Alba, *Ethnic Identity: The Transformation of White America* (New Haven, CT: Yale University Press, 1990).

[39] See Nathan Glazer and Daniel P. Moynihan, *Beyond the Melting Pot: The Negroes, Puerto Ricans, Jews, Italians, and Irish of New York City* (Cambridge, MA: MIT Press, 1963); Nathan Glazer, 'Is Assimilation Dead?' *Annals of the American Academy of Political and Social Science* 530 (1993), pp. 122–36.

[40] See Alejandro Portes and Min Zhou, 'The New Second Generation: Segmented Assimilation and Its Variants', *The Annals of the American Academy of Political and Social Science* 530 (1993), pp. 74–96.

[41] Jennifer Lee and Frank D. Bean, 'America's Changing Color Lines: Race/Ethnicity, Immigration, and Multiracial Identification', *Annual Review of Sociology* 30 (2004), pp. 221–42.

themselves as neither black nor white, and younger Armenians are more likely to identify themselves as multiracial or multicultural. Therefore, models developed in a binary racial context are less relevant to the historical and contemporary experiences of Armenian diaspora communities. For the transnational generations of the Iranian Armenian diaspora, while processes of racial/ ethnic identification interact with socio-economic status, they do not do so in a straightforward manner. Rather, ethnic identification appears strongest among the highest social classes. According to this theory, the working and middle classes generally stand to gain the most from assimilation and might therefore shed much of their ethnic identity. As sociologist Mary Waters notes, racial/ethnic identification – more so than other aspects of assimilation – may become both more subjective and autonomous as racial/ethnic and other ascriptive criteria become more volitional.[42] Thus, some Iranian Armenians in diaspora may maintain ethnic identifications despite considerable economic assimilation. They may also maintain social networks and even marry across racial or ethnic boundaries, providing examples of identifications that do not correspond linearly to economic mobility. This proceeds most rapidly in the absence of strong discrimination or value conflict; otherwise, external barriers might block assimilation and foster ethnic identification.

Generational gaps have also always provoked social tension in societies, but how do these gaps affect different aspects of diasporic cultural identity? Divergences in generational perspectives illustrate how different cohorts maintain their ancestral identity and heritage. Diasporic parents establish later generations in a liminal space between immigrant, diaspora and citizen. This happens all the while global discourses of transnationalism are evolving. The generations of diasporic parents who have limited exposure to or understanding of transnationalism often cling to their religious beliefs, nationalities and cultural and religious practices. As diasporic immigrants tied to a parent culture, they represent and embody the fear of losing national and cultural identity, and they demonstrate how the less transnational generations within the diaspora will hold tightly to their heritage as a stable anchor to maintain their cultural roots and identity. Meanwhile, transnational generations interrogate this singular

---

[42] Mary Waters, *Ethnic Options: Choosing Identities in America* (Berkeley: University of California Press, 1990).

definition by shaping their identity, suggesting that later generations gradually move toward a more transnational identity that fosters multiplicity.

Generally, the less transnational cohorts seem to try to adjust to their new circumstances and struggle to reconcile their ethnic identity with that of the majority. In the case of Armenians, psychologist Aghop Der-Karabetian calls this 'a state of culture shock'. For this group, feelings of anxiety and a desire to associate with one's own community are inevitable, which might prevent them from associating with the host nation's culture. Der-Karabetian explains that, while this is a result of culture shock, an excessive desire to identify with the host nation can also be considered as a form of culture shock. As opposed to older generations, the younger ones – especially those born in the host country – do not experience such struggles and acculturate to the norms of the majority population more easily; however, they simultaneously maintain their ethnic distinctiveness. Nonetheless, assimilation into the host culture is not simply a generational matter. There are other factors such as the amount of ethnic involvement that must be taken into consideration. For instance, those who are extremely involved in matters of Armenian culture and have less contact with the culture(s) of their host nation might be more resistant to assimilation.[43]

There is yet one more factor to keep in mind, which is the basic tenet of the dynamic between assimilation and acculturation. Der-Karabetian's research shows that Armenians who live(d) in majority Muslim cultures, such as Armenians in Iran, tend to assimilate less than those who live(d) in Christian cultures, such as Iranian Armenians who move to the US. He explains that, if a minoritised population looks up to the majority culture – Armenians look up to the US due to Christianity – they will feel a stronger pull to assimilate. Ultimately, when discussing assimilation, we should differentiate between 'functional integration and primary acculturation'. Individuals who adopt the majority culture's formal institutions and organisations are doing so for instrumental purposes, too, taking advantage of economic and cultural resources. However, to adopt the values and ideals of the majority culture would mean primary acculturation, which potentially leads to assimilation.[44] For diasporic Iranian Armenians, this integration, acculturation and assimilation trajectory

---

[43] Der-Karabetian, *Armenian Ethnic Identity in Context*, pp. 46–47.
[44] Ibid. pp. 231–32.

relies heavily on the majority culture; that is, if the majority culture is a Muslim one – Armenians in Iran, for example – we see signs of functional integration, while in majority Christian culture – Armenians in the US, for instance – there are signs of both functional integration and assimilation.

These themes – including anxiety over cultural loss within the diasporic immigrant experience – are eloquently explored in the mixed-media works of the Iranian Armenian painter, graphic designer and sculptor Garnik Der Hacopian. His 1985 mixed-media composition titled *Immigration* (Figure 2.1) reconfigures Edvard Munch's *The Scream*. While Munch's opus is recognised as an expression of the anxiety of the human condition, Der Hacopian chronicles the many adversities faced by diasporic immigrants. In his own words, in depicting figures such as the one in this painting, 'I have left realism behind, turning to eerie illustrations, especially where I portray faces and bodies in a distorted and exaggerated fashion. So, the aggressive and rebellious element is especially strong in these works. I have hidden what I intended to say behind a veil of vagueness, trying to be implicit'.[45] To him, these bizarre figures tell a bitter story about the turbulent world inside them.

Carved across the face of a figure in the painting is the word 'immigrants'. The left eye is being pulled at the corner by a hand, and the right eye is upside down – a commentary on the perspectives disrupted by the many push-pull factors that diasporic people face and the resulting limbo of glancing back while struggling to move forward. There are several nails in the face of the figure, reminiscent of crucified limbs nailed to a structure. A larger nail pierces the open mouth of the figure, signifying that, although it is capable of speech, it has been rendered voiceless. The left edge of the painting features many skull-like shapes with shadows, reminding of the deceased 1915 Genocide victims. An allusion to a khachkar, often found in Armenian churches and cemeteries, fills the upper left corner, tying the skeletal figures to their ancestors. A khachkar is a feature of medieval Armenian art, a small architectural monument or stele elaborately carved with a cross atop a rosette, standing on a pedestal (anchor), facing west. Throughout the image, rubble reminds viewers of loss. Fragments of newsprint or printed books on the nose of the figure may refer to a fragmented history, problematising the question of who writes history and who writes diaspora.

[45] Garnik Der Hacopian, and Ruyin Pakbaz, *The Presence of the Absent Artist* (Tehran: Nazar Art Publication, 2016), p. 158.

Figure 2.1 Garnik Der Hacopian, *Immigration*, mixed media on paper, 1985. Courtesy of the artist.

While many of Der Hacopian's other compositions feature bright colours and scenes of daily life, this particular work is rendered in black and white, possibly connoting an otherworldly or spiritual realm, or a play on life and death rituals. The painting can be understood both in the Armenian historical context with its subtle symbolism and in a broader global context of immigration. The black and white of Der Hacopian's painting hearkens back to Arby Ovanessian's black-and-white documentary *Ghara Kelisa*. Works of art such as Der Hacopian's painting are not merely dead objects; rather, they encapsulate stories; they have identity, presence and ancestral power. Images, paintings and art evoke consciousness, knowledge and emotions; hence, they are bridges between what they represent and the viewer.

According to art historian William John Thomas Mitchell, '[p]ictures are things that have been marked with all the stigmata of personhood: they exhibit both physical and virtual bodies; they speak to us, sometimes literally, sometimes figuratively. They present, not just a surface, but a face that faces the beholder'.[46] While paintings, pictures and art may be viewed as simply objects, art historians frequently consider them as works with 'consciousness, agency, and desire'.[47] Often, however, that 'desire' may speak to a lack. A painting such as Der Hacopian's work may desire to turn the gaze on the beholder. The man in Der Hacopian's *Immigration* is directly gazing at the viewer, as if in an attempt 'to move and mobilize the viewer' to comprehend the duality of desire and lack – a constant diasporic state.[48] The painting elucidates the diasporic communities' attempts to negotiate more than one culture, as assimilation within the host nation becomes difficult. Living in a transitory space where various belief systems and perceptions overlap, Der Hacopian's work illustrates the possibility of change and the fluidity of conventional categories and labels.

Iranian Armenian diasporic cultural productions reflect various methods of maintaining social networks and friendships across ethnic and religious

---

[46] William John Thomas Mitchell, 'What Do Pictures Really Want?' *October* 77 (1996), pp. 71–82, 72. See also William John Thomas Mitchell, *Picture Theory: Essays on Verbal and Visual Representation* (Chicago: University of Chicago Press, 1994); William John Thomas Mitchell, *What Do Pictures Want? The Lives and Loves of Images* (Chicago: University of Chicago Press, 2005).

[47] Ibid. pp. 72–73.

[48] Ibid. pp. 76–77.

boundaries, which vary in the Iranian and US contexts. In 'A Day Before Easter', Pirzad explores the limits of cultural and social identification with the characters Edmond and Tahereh in Iran. Throughout the story, the majority of the Armenian community refers to Tahereh as 'the daughter of the Muslim Janitor'. This phrasing imposes two layers of othering: the initial act of othering Tahereh as non-Armenian, and the second act of othering her as an individual minoritised by social class (as the janitor's daughter). The story's dynamics also speak to generational differences and divergences in how less transnational and more transnational generations think about the other.[49]

Edmond's relationship with Tahereh creates tension within the Armenian community and reverberates through Edmond's own family: Edmond's father does not approve of his interactions with Tahereh. Every time Edmond trespasses these rules, his father lectures him about social class, religious and ethnic differences among people.[50] Edmond's mother conceals Tahereh's visits from Edmond's father.[51] Ironically, the only two places where Tahereh and Edmond can freely interact and play are the two dominant cultural institutions of the Iranian Armenian community – the school's courtyard and the church.[52] The community's anxiety over this friendship is mimicked in a commentary by Anush, Edmond's classmate – 'you're in love with the Muslim janitor's daughter' – and Edmond's grandmother's constant concern 'that the children would choose someone unsuitable'.[53] The diasporic Armenian community's unwillingness to assimilate within their host nation of Iran and its active distancing from the Muslim Iranian population fosters feelings of difference, superiority and supremacy that result in the exclusion of non-Armenians.

However, these exclusions are also the consequence of a defence mechanism against an unwelcoming host nation that perceives them as the other. In Pirzad's short story Edmond's relationship with Tahereh ends when the 'scandalous' love affair between Tahereh's mother and the Armenian school principal comes to light.[54] While Tahereh's actions, such as learning the

---

[49] Pirzad, *The Space Between Us*, p. 12.
[50] Ibid. pp. 3–4.
[51] Ibid. p. 45.
[52] Ibid. pp. 3–4.
[53] Ibid. pp. 12, 76.
[54] Ibid. p. 56.

Armenian language, afford her a space within the Armenian community (the grandmother praises her fluency), she has to say farewell, ultimately, to her best childhood friend because of her mother's relationship with an Armenian man. However, her audacity becomes a source of hope and agency as Edmond crafts his future identity later. Drawing attention to the anxieties inherent in Iranian Armenians' encounters with Muslim Iranians – as well as the ways in which national, ethnic and religious demarcations are maintained (particularly within interreligious friendships, romance and marriages) – the second part of the story opens with Alenush's casual announcement of her engagement to Behzad (a non-Armenian, Iranian Turk from Tabriz) over lunch: 'Behzad and I have decided to get married'.[55] If the affair between Tahereh's mother and the school principal was a secret one, the transnational generation's mindset depicts a positive progression toward an open acceptance of non-Armenians.

Immediately after Alenush's announcement, Edmond thinks: 'What a relief it was that grandmother was no longer with us. Who would have had the heart to tell her that the light of her life wanted to marry a non-Armenian? Possibly only Alenush herself'.[56] Alenush, who ultimately becomes one of the most daring characters in this story through her marriage to a non-Armenian and her consequent flight overseas, is depicted as insubordinate. Edmond recalls an incident when Grandmother had asked the child Alenush to pray and thank God for 'creating us', to which Alenush responded: 'I didn't ask Him to create me, so why should I thank Him?'[57] To Grandmother, this would have been blasphemous; yet Alenush was Grandmother's favourite grandchild, and so it was overlooked. After Alenush's announcement of her marriage to a non-Armenian, Edmond's preoccupation with Grandmother reflects his concern with social pressure, constantly wondering, what will others think or say? In contrast, Edmond's wife, Martha, declares that *she* cannot bear the shame and social rejection that Alenush's relationship would bring to the family, telling Edmond: 'I'm begging you. You have to do something about this'.[58] While

[55] Ibid. p. 59.
[56] Ibid. pp. 61–62.
[57] Ibid. p. 62.
[58] Ibid. p. 83.

Martha holds a more singular notion of Armenianness, Edmond has a subversive attitude when he asks Alenush to invite her fiancé Behzad to the house. Immediately, Martha makes a sign of the cross and kneels to pray.[59] Behzad assumes that being a Turkish ethnic minoritised individual from Tabriz will alleviate the tension with Martha, unaware that Armenians' exclusion of other(s) extends to all non-Armenians, regardless of their religious and ethnic affiliations. In this scenario, as in many others, language plays a significant role in the otherising process: whoever does not speak Armenian is excluded.

Regarding interactions between Armenians and Muslim Iranians, Robert Safarian writes that among Muslims it is believed that Christians, including Armenians, are *najis* (unclean). This has impacted the Armenians' perception of their Iranian Muslim relations, especially in terms of bodily and physical interactions, which are often the basis for marital relationships. To maintain their traditional values, Iranian Armenians have propagated certain values within the diaspora; for example, intermarriages with Muslims are called *turkanal* or, literally, becoming a Turk. This is, of course, a pejorative term, to the extent that it refers to becoming *najis* (impure, unclean), which leans etymologically toward self-prostitution. These cultural exclusions may have something to do with living under oppressive Persian and Ottoman Muslim regimes for centuries.[60] The reference to becoming Turk also underlines the significance of the post-Genocide Armenian community's predicament in Turkey, when they were forced to abandon their Armenian identity and/or live in disguise as Muslim Turks. With interreligious marriages, Iranian Armenian parents who resist do so because they also lose their child, since, according to the law of the land, that child has to become Muslim in order to marry a Muslim man.

In Pirzad's story, Edmond, who struggles between identities, never exhibits prejudice toward Muslim Iranians. This is evident from his childhood friendship with Tahereh, and also in his disclosure to Alenush: 'Of course you know that your mother and I have no problem with Behzad as a person' To this Alenush responds: 'You don't have a problem with him as a person! You just have a problem because of some medieval notions and traditions'.[61]

---

[59] Ibid. pp. 80–81.
[60] Safarian, *Sakin-i du farhang*, pp. 44–45.
[61] Pirzad, *The Space Between Us*, pp. 85–86.

Alenush's response to Edmond positions her within the transnational generation of diasporic Armenians who do not believe that they belong to a country which they have never seen. Alenush's tendencies to transgress result in
loneliness and isolation, as her mother passes away and her father rejects her
after she moves to a foreign country with Behzad. Alenush inhabits the space
of *verants'ughi*, where her personal life and the realities of the outside world
meet; where everything is porous, and anything is possible; where reality
becomes fluid and expands. This is a transformative space in which Alenush is
granted the opportunity to see through not only her own individual lens but
also the collective, so that she can reconstruct her reality, her ways of knowing
and her identity. However, this is also a space filled with isolation and pain.

Pirzad's transnational generation defies categorisation at the same time as it
confronts isolation, loss and marginalisation. They challenge traditional perceptions of self and other, incorporating and transgressing boundaries. Like Alenush, Edmond's colleague Danique chooses self-exile as rumours circulate; she
faces much suffering because '[s]he was in love with [her] Muslim neighbour.
[. . .] Without a thought for her family's feelings on the matter, she insisted she
wanted to marry this boy! [. . .] Shamed by the public humiliation, her poor
mother became sick, and this madam, after all the trouble she'd caused, left for
Tehran'.[62] Danique's desire to move outside the norms of her Iranian Armenian community also results in loss and loneliness. Rejected by her family and
community in Tabriz, she lives a secluded life in Tehran. Edmond and Alenush
find many connections with Danique, and every time Danique is targeted with
accusations, Edmond finds himself defending her and subsequently questioning his fervour to do so: 'Why am I defending Danique? For my sake? For her
sake? For Martha's sake? Wasn't the way Martha behaved last night strange? Did
that mean she loved Danique so much that she was willing to forgive her that
mistake? It wasn't a mistake: for Martha, what Danique did was a sin! But was it
just a mistake? Was it a sin? Wasn't it?'[63] Edmond's impulse to side with Danique
resonates with desires suppressed in a distant past, in a lost childhood. It is only
after celebrating a non-traditional Easter at Danique's house, free from his own
traditional family, that Edmond decides to reconcile with Alenush and his own
multiplicities.

[62] Ibid. p. 117.
[63] Ibid. p. 119.

The story ends with the present and the past interleaved through Edmond's recollections of the past, where he achieves an inner peace in the present, with the potential for a reconciliation with Alenush in the future. His incapacity to bridge the divides of language, religion and ethnicity comes to an end in the story's final moments. Here, Edmond's newly acquired flexibility is conveyed in his willingness to fly – 'A ladybug [. . .] basking in the sun on the white petal of violet' while he regrets not having done so in his childhood.[64] More importantly, Edmond writes a letter to Alenush the day *after* Easter: 'On a piece of white paper, in green ink, I begin a letter: *Dearest Nunush*'.[65] Edmond's letter, using the endearing short form of Alenush's name, Nunush, signals his desire for reconciliation with her. Edmond's use of green ink calls to mind his earlier desire for uniqueness, yet now indicates Edmond's acceptance of Alenush's differences. These symbols acquire deeper meaning when contextualised against Edmond's mother and her desire to be transgressive and different. These tendencies are illustrated when his mother buys Edmond a fountain pen with green ink for his graduation from high school. When asked why she chose green ink, she responds: 'I don't know, maybe because it's different from black and blue'. Having similar proclivities, Edmond writes on a corner of an issue of *Alik*, the most axiomatic Armenian newspaper in Iran: 'Green ink is different from all other inks. I like people and things that are different'.[66] Edmond's mother never fully assimilates into the Iranian community or, more importantly, into her own Armenian community. She is an outsider, even to her own community. Edmond's use of green ink in writing a letter of reconciliation and acceptance to Alenush indicates his acceptance of those who are different and choose not to conform to a prescribed definition of identity.

After Alenush's marriage to Behzad and their emigration to the US, Edmond 'had become used to telephone calls and chilly reactions and being whispered about. The truth was that [he] had gotten used to it. [He] had learned how to answer curtly and not to allow friends and acquaintances and strangers to talk about Alenush'. But he could not forgive Alenush for Martha's death – something that was not overtly expressed but still present. As opposed to Edmond,

---

[64] Ibid. p. 136.
[65] Ibid.
[66] Ibid. p. 106.

Martha 'had cut back on socialising and had even gradually stopped going to church on Sundays. The only person she saw almost every day was Danique'.[67] After writing the letter, Edmond finally resolves his own bewildering sense of not belonging. Edmond's duality of consciousness and simultaneous attachments to 'here and there' or 'home away from home' defers to a kind of pacification deep within himself.[68] Pirzad's narrative ends with Edmond reconciling with the multiplicity of his identity. Throughout his journey, Edmond suffers from an inner conflict, family loss, social rejection and an isolated life. Ultimately, he accepts the reality of his life and the multiplicity of his Iranian Armenian identity within a predominantly Muslim society. Pirzad's Edmond illustrates that the diasporic individual has access to a unique consciousness that transforms singularities to pluralities. He has lived in a transitory space full of potential for transformation all his life, as he has craved different perspectives and growth; he has questioned the status quo and the fixed identities inherited from his family and culture. Indeed, Edmond had been occupying the *verants'ughi* space – different phases of inner metamorphosis that eventually can bring him peace with his outer world.[69]

Interreligious marriages between Armenians and Iranian Muslims are a thorny subject. My own appearance in the Muslim-majority society and workplace at the college doubtlessly brought with itself many marriage proposals from Muslim colleagues, classmates, or family members of my students. One instance, however, was different from all others. It happened during one of my trips to Turkey with my family. During this leisurely time, I met a Muslim man from the US whose mother was still living in Iran. His family in the US had mostly converted to Christianity, and he was willing

---

[67] Ibid. pp. 133–34.

[68] Paul Gilroy, *The Black Atlantic: Modernity and Double Consciousness* (Cambridge, MA: Harvard University Press, 1993).

[69] In the context of diaspora theories, Pirzad's work demonstrates the tension within Iranian Armenian identity between hardline, exclusionist anti-cosmopolitanism and its opposite, which mirrors the argument between William Safran and James Clifford on diaspora. According to Safran, for the term 'diaspora' to have meaning, it has to have limits, while Clifford, who is more postmodern, believes that one cannot delimit 'diaspora' with set boundaries because there will always be exceptions, and thus 'diaspora' should be defined by what it is not. Pirzad's work poignantly portrays the debate between cosmopolitan and non-cosmopolitan approaches to diaspora and also recalls the debate over transnationalism and non-transnationality, as well as the differences between the two.

to do so, too. He intrigued me – after all, the forbidden other is intriguing – and we began spending some time with each other during this trip. My father even invited him a few times to have dinner with us. When we returned to Tehran – he was visiting his mother – we kept talking on the phone. I have to say that these phone conversations were just that – phone conversations. As someone who had an English degree, talking with someone from the US was rewarding (and a language practice) for me. My long phone conversations alarmed my father. Gradually, my father became more and more curious and asked my mother about these phone calls. My mother could not help but tell him the truth. His immediate response was anger. When I heard this, I felt offended. I did not like the fact that my father had no trust in me. I wanted him to see me as an adult who could make independent and wise decisions. I have to say that this reaction was only because of the threat of potential blooming romance. For years, I had had great Muslim male and female friends who would frequent our home, and my father would be very hospitable towards them. But this was only because they were my friends. As a result, for the first time in my life, I stopped interacting with my family; when at home, I stayed in my room most of the time. This might seem a little childish, but I had to go to extremes to make my point. And, well, it worked; my father never questioned my decisions thereafter.

Nonetheless, what I would like to highlight here is the inner struggle that many Armenians have to endure when living in Iran, particularly regarding romantic relationships with Iranian Muslims. Although I was fascinated with this Muslim man, in the back of my head, in my consciousness, a voice was constantly whispering that this was wrong. After that instance, subconsciously, I would block any thought of more than a friendship with a Muslim man. I would not even allow the thought of marriage cross my mind, and if it did, feelings of shame and guilt would follow. In addition to the questions of heritage and roots, there was also the thought of entering a socially taboo zone; this was stopping me right there and then, before I would even fathom to venture outside. I knew about the shame and dishonour that such a relationship would bring to a family. At the core of my heart, I also knew that, although my parents wanted my happiness, they were concerned about the so-called 'what would others think'?

Interreligious marriages are very real in Iran and in the US among Iranian Armenians, and they feature in cultural productions. Gregorian's autobiography recounts similar, pejorative responses to his marriage with a non-Armenian, even though she is an American Christian woman:

> The news of my marriage surprised everyone, friends and relatives alike. The fact that I married a non-Armenian, an *odar* (foreigner), raised the ire of some Armenians in San Francisco, Beirut, and Tehran. They were dismayed, disappointed, and angry. I was asked time and time again – why did I not fall in love with and marry a nice Armenian girl? Rumors began to circulate that Mrs. Russell, my mother-in-law, had Armenian blood, and therefore Clare must have some Armenian blood too.[70]

Gregorian's narrative emphasises two trends in diasporic Iranian Armenian communities: first, the emphasis on religion as the basis of identity automatically excludes non-Armenians, yet Christian Americans in the context of marriage are still viewed as the other, partly due to language differences. Second, mainstream Iranian Armenian society characterises Iranian Armenians as technically white Christians, but effectively non-white individuals who become targets of discrimination. Rather than being unidirectional, Iranian Armenian diasporic experiences raise the possibility of othering as a reciprocal practice.

In the US, while the initial waves of Armenian immigrants assimilated to American life through gradual acculturation into multiple American cultures, they still maintained rigid boundaries under certain circumstances. For instance, they interacted freely with their workplace colleagues and neighbours, but they retained boundaries on more intimate matters such as marriage and religion. This indicates that total structural assimilation was not achieved due, in part, to the host nation's discriminatory practices. While Iranian Armenian Americans have documented multiple instances of discrimination, Gregorian writes about his treatment as the provost of the University of Pennsylvania:

> I had heard about Miller's alleged 'unhappiness' with my 'management ability' and 'flamboyance'. If he was unhappy, he never said so to me. I had also heard that some trustees were worried that I was 'too ethnic', that I had a

---

[70] Gregorian, *The Road to Home*, p. 140.

'thick accent' and 'unruly hair', and that there were serious questions about whether I would be able to raise substantial funds for Penn.[71]

The fact that Gregorian's ethnicity, accent and appearance work to otherise him illustrates that – despite his legally white status, his religion as a Christian and his expertise and education – he was lumped together with other, non-white minoritised ethnic populations, according to the US's scheme of race, ethnicity and non-whiteness.

Compared to other diaspora communities, Iranian Armenians have been slow in their assimilatory practices. As a nation that has persevered through wars, conflicts, dispersions, famines, occupations, persecutions, deportations and the Genocide, Armenians feel an obligation to maintain their culture and to do justice to their ancestors' memory. Iranian Armenian cultural productions certainly do justice to this past heritage while simultaneously capturing the reality of diasporic life in a globalised world. These works portray various modes of diasporic transnationalism that emphasise the multiplicity of diasporic identity. They show that the majority of Iranian Armenians have moved away from what Rushdie calls a 'ghetto mentality' that requires the community to forget that there is a world beyond their immediate Armenian community.[72] While citizens of their host nations, Iranian Armenians engage with their homeland of Armenia (and Iran) in various symbolic ways that do not translate into a loss of individual subjectivity. As they maintain their diasporic subjectivity within their transnational space, they have also come to terms with the reality of their existence. These cultural productions imply that a singular definition of Armenianness and the fixity of Iranian Armenian identity is not sustainable; they rather offer a beautifully nuanced one, as generations of diasporic Iranian Armenians cultivate new identities.

---

[71] Ibid. pp. 257–58.

[72] Rushdie, *Imaginary Homelands*, p. 19. It is important to remember that Armenians have undergone forced geographies; hence, there is a communal memory of times when they were forbidden from living in certain areas. Today, the majority of Armenians in California, for instance, live in Los Angeles, Glendale, or its vicinity.

3

LANGUAGE AS AN ETHNO-NATIONAL IDENTITY MARKER

I was raised Christian Armenian with Armenian as my mother tongue. When I was six, instead of going to kindergarten, my mother decided I was too smart for that, and so she took me to the Department of Education in Tehran to take an IQ test. At the time, this was not out of the ordinary. I passed the test, and so they placed me in first grade. Now, the problem with this was that for the first six years of my life, Armenian was the only language to which I had had exposure; and school instruction in Iran was predominantly in the Persian language. I failed my first test – out of thirty-eight questions, I answered only thirteen correctly. The teacher advised my mom to take me back to kindergarten, but my mom was adamant to keep me in the first grade. Thus, the entire following week, she spent teaching me the Persian alphabet. The doors of our cabinets at home became chalkboards. When I took my next test in the following week, I scored twenty-five out of thirty-eight; this was progress. I stayed in the first grade, and I still remember how I loved my teacher, Ms Odet.

Throughout the world, language and religion are typically considered markers of ethnic and national identity, and this holds true for Armenians as well. Religion and language became national identity markers for Armenians in the fourth and fifth century, respectively. I have already discussed Iranian Armenians' endeavours to maintain their heritage by practising traditional Armenian rituals and religion as reflected in cultural productions.

Since language is a crucial identity marker for Iranian Armenians, in this chapter I delve into the significance of the Armenian language within an Iranian and American diasporic context. While language and religion are considered integral to ethnicity, William Safran, a scholar of ethnic politics, argues that they do not correlate exactly with an ethno-nation. Because they may extend over more than one ethnic nation, and because members of one ethnic group may follow more than one religion or use multiple languages, Safran cautions that language and religion alone are insufficient to establish ethno-national identity. At the same time, they are not always the definitive factors in ethnic behaviour or political demands, as not all communities that adhere to a certain language and/or religion desire a unified nation. But all the same, language and religion are integral parts of the primordial elements into which individuals are born.[1] Depending on time and place, the relationship between the two varies, yet they are associated with each other and to some extent mutually defined.[2]

Regarding the link between language, ethnicity and identity, cultural theorist Gloria Anzaldúa expresses:

> So, if you want to really hurt me, talk badly about my language. Ethnic identity is twin skin to linguistic identity – I am my language. Until I can take pride in my language, I cannot take pride in myself. Until I can accept as legitimate Chicano Texas Spanish, Tex-Mex and all the other languages I speak, I cannot accept the legitimacy of myself. Until I am free to write bilingually and to switch codes without having always to translate, while I still have to speak English or Spanish when I would rather speak Spanglish, and as long as I have to accommodate the English speakers rather than having them accommodate me, my tongue will be illegitimate.[3]

---

[1] William Safran, 'Language, Ethnicity and Religion: A Complex and Persistent Linkage', *Nations and Nationalism* 14.1 (2008), pp. 171–90. See also Steven Gryosby, 'The Verdict of History: The Inexpungeable Tie of Primordiality – A Response to Eller and Coughlan', *Ethnic and Racial Studies* 17.1 (1994), pp. 164–71. It is important to note that, while Safran believes that religion and language are interlinked, James Clifford's arguments are quite a contrast to Safran's.

[2] Ibid. pp. 171–74. See also Jean-William Lapierre, *Le pouvoir politique et les langues* (Paris: Presses Universitaires de France, 1988), p. 99.

[3] Anzaldúa, *Borderlands/La Frontera*, p. 81.

However, sociologist Roger Brubaker believes that nationhood and nationalism must be understood within the context of the hopes, interests and longings of everyday life and ordinary people rather than just language and religion. To Brubaker, . . .

> Social life is pervasively, though unevenly, structured along ethnic lines, and ethnicity 'happens' in a variety of everyday setting. Ethnicity is embodied and expressed not only in political projects and nationalist rhetoric but in everyday encounters, practical categories, commonsense knowledge, cultural idioms, cognitive schemas, interactional cues, discursive frames, organizational routines, social networks, and institutional forms.[4]

Literary theorist Trinh T. Minh-ha, in 'Other Than Myself, My Other Self', offers a different perspective: 'Home and language tend to be taken for granted; like Mother or Woman, they are often naturalized and homogenized. [. . .] Yet, language can only live on and renew itself by hybridizing shamelessly and changing its own rules as it migrates in time and space'.[5]

Historically, before the emergence of nation-states, religion functioned as the basis for a nation's collective consciousness. The idea that one's nation was divinely decreed was a foundation for an individual's loyalty to the group and the development of a national identity. The Peace of Westphalia (1648) reinforced the close interdependency between religion and state. However, religion coincided with political frontiers rather than being subordinated to them, or to national power. During the Renaissance, cultural and humanist concerns were articulated and underscored in a language independent of religion because a secular collective consciousness was emerging.[6] In the Armenian case, religion and language are interlinked – separate in most respects but not exactly mutually exclusive. Armenian is the liturgical language of the Armenian Church, and although it is Classical *grabar* Armenian, which no

---

[4] Roger Brubaker, *Ethnicity Without Groups* (Cambridge, MA: Harvard University Press, 2004), p. 2.
[5] Minh-ha, 'Other Than Myself, My Other Self', p. 34.
[6] Safran, 'Language, Ethnicity and Religion', pp. 171–74.

one speaks, it is recognisable to speakers of Western and Eastern vernaculars as 'Armenian speech'.[7]

With the emergence of modernity and secularism, ethnic nations gradually metamorphosed into civic nations, large populations began moving from one country to another, and criteria other than language and religion became defining factors of political communities. Another important factor was the emergence of vernacular standards that replaced classical languages concurrent with the rise of the nation-states' political order and the capitalist economic system.[8] For many, the use of language was less important in crafting ethnic identity than other factors, such as economics. English, which in Safran's words became the 'supra-ethnic' medium for global communication, lost its cultural significance as a language linked to a specific nation. Non-linguistic identity factors – such as territory, sovereignty and political values – became more objective. With globalisation, sovereignty declined, territories became permeable, and political values ascended to become transnational. The importance of language as an ethnic marker was diminished by the existence of trans-ethnic languages, multilingualism within nations, the inadequacy of monolingualism for ethno-national identity and the increasing use of colonial languages by newly independent states in their nation-building endeavours.[9] In *Grounded Nationalisms: A Sociological Analysis*, sociologist Siniša Malešević has argued the contrary, by introducing the concept of 'new nationalism', which concerns the rise of a new nationalist ideology that is anti-global, anti-immigrant and anti-multicultural and aspires to 'economic protectionism, identity politics, and support for populist leaders and nativist policies' hostile to cultural and religious diversity.[10] These various debates not

---

[7] For a brief discussion of the significance of language, see Claudia Yaghoobi, 'The Significance of Armenian Language in Iranian Armenian Diasporic Literature', *The Doha Institute Arab Center for Research and Policy Studies*, September 2021, https://www.dohainstitute. org/en/PoliticalStudies/Pages/The-Significance-of-the-Armenian-Language-in-Iranian-Armenian-Diasporic-Literature.aspx?fbclid=IwAR0O8HbZWoDN3bv2k6AEo8qCtTW_SThcCpukCw8lkwy8xVImb0fMhnN8hSA

[8] Benedict Anderson, *Imagined Communities: Reflections on the Origin and Spread of Nationalism* (London and New York: Verso, 1991), p. 37.

[9] Safran, 'Language, Ethnicity and Religion', pp. 177–78.

[10] Malešević, *Grounded Nationalisms*, p. 5.

only highlight the resistance to multilingualism and multiculturalism globally, but also hint at the limits of language as medium for either ethnic identity or transnationalism.

The primacy of religion and language have changed due, in part, to shifting dynamics between the two; yet these changes do not indicate that they are no longer the building blocks of ethno-national identity. The relationship between language and religion is believed to be the weakest in trans-ethnic languages, such as English and French, and strongest in languages tied to an ethnic community. Conversely, the religious element may sometimes be so dominant in a given language that it cannot easily 'desacralize' itself.[11]

However, questions arise in some instances regarding classical or vernacular language and which of these should assume the place of the official language. This question was relevant for Jews, Greeks and Armenians in their efforts at ethno-national mobilisation. The classical languages of these ethnonations were historical and respectable. However, classical languages have been mobilised by a narrow field of elites, whereas their respective vernaculars were secular and popular.[12]

According to linguist Antoine Meillet, Classical Armenian is known quite definitely to have developed in the region of Lake Van. Ordained Catholic priest and scholar Father Ghevont Alishan of the Mekhitarist order (1820–1901) advanced the idea that Armenian literature was first written in Parthian, in the Zend language. Later, Assyrian replaced this language, which was itself eventually supplanted by Greek language and culture.[13] It is generally accepted that words entered Armenian from Finno-Hungarian and Turkish, but according to Assyriologist and archaeologist François Lenormant, Avestan and Persian were the linguistic roots of Armenian, which arose as a dialect of the Iranian group.[14] Many scholars, however, believe that Armenian is an Indo-European language that borrowed heavily from the

---

[11] See Nasim Ahmad Jawed, *Islam's Political Culture: Religion and Politics in Predivided Pakistan* (Austin: University of Texas Press, 1999).

[12] Safran, 'Language, Ethnicity and Religion', p. 179.

[13] Antoine Meillet, *Esquisse d'une grammaire comparee de L'Armenienne Classique* (Vienna: [n. p.], 1936).

[14] François Lenormant, *Histoire ancienne de l'Orient jusqu'aux Guerres Mediques, vol. 1* (Paris: A. Lévy, Libraire-Editeur, 1881).

Parthian and Iranian languages, in particular historical and family names. Yet another view holds that Armenian arose out of a hybridisation of the language spoken by indigenous ancestral Armenians and migrant peoples from the Balkans, who settled alongside Armenian progenitors.[15]

For diaspora Armenians, the clergy have been positioned as the guardians of Classical Armenian. However, most Armenians did not master Classical Armenian because emphasis was placed on fluency within the host nation, which encouraged a form of Armenian vernacular. Then came the standardisation of vernacular languages in the eighteenth and nineteenth centuries. While the language of the Church and the clergy was not completely abandoned, the vernacular began to be used more widely. The first Armenian periodical to use an amalgam of classical and vernacular Indo-Armenian dialect and printed in the Armenian alphabet was published in India.[16]

Hence, the idea that nationalism is a strictly secular ideology does not apply to Armenians, for whom religion plays an important role and for whom many Armenian ethno-symbols are religious in nature.[17] Secular conceptualisations of ethno-identities have incorporated socio-economic and political-territorial elements. However, for ethno-national communities outside the homeland, a common language and/or religion are still major markers of collective identity, and this holds true for diasporic Armenians, Chinese, Greeks, Indians, Jews, Sikhs and Tibetans.[18]

In terms of the use of a unified vernacular Armenian language, Armenian intellectuals of the early eighteenth century had become keenly aware of the need for a common Armenian language that could unite a widespread diaspora. By the second half of the nineteenth century, 'the vernacular was victorious as the hegemonic language', in political scientist Eliz Sanasarian's words, due to the widespread and fragmented nature of the diaspora, which ultimately resulted in two vernaculars: Western Armenian with a Constantinople

---

[15] Esat Uras, *The Armenians in History and the Armenian Question* (Ankara: Documentary Publications, 1988), pp. 330–31.

[16] Panossian, *The Armenians*, 133n.

[17] Safran, 'Language, Ethnicity and Religion', p. 181. See also Anthony D. Smith, 'Nations and History', *Understanding Nationalism*, ed. Montserrat Guibernau and John Hutchinson (Oxford: Polity Press, 2005), p. 21.

[18] Ibid. p. 184.

dialect, and Eastern Armenian with an Araratian Plain, Yerevan dialect. Classical Armenian – used only by intellectuals – was unsuitable for the unification project and perceived as inadequate for contemporary communication.[19] Since Armenian intellectuals believed that language was a tool to demarcate one ethnic group from others, a unified language was used to facilitate in-group communication. It was also meant to remove foreign, mostly Turkish, influences. In turn, the relationship between ethnicity and language would also influence national and diasporic identity.

Regarding the difference between Western Armenian and Eastern Armenian dialects, in *Chiragh-ha ra man khamush mikunam* (*Things Left Unsaid*), Zoya Pirzad introduces characters who recognise the differences between the two dialects, acknowledging the non-monolithic and non-homogeneous nature of Armenian identity by way of Armenian languages.[20] In Pirzad's novel, Khatun Yeremian from the city of Van, who speaks in a Western Armenian dialect, is an eyewitness to the 1915 Armenian Genocide and shares her experiences with the Armenian community of Abadan, Iran, during an annual commemoration:

> We all watched her in silence. For a few seconds she looked back at us, then began to speak in a weary voice. She spoke in a different dialect from ours, in the western Armenian of the city of Van, saying things like 'a wee bit' instead of 'a little bit'; and 'gusto', in place of 'joy'. She said that before talking about those days of hardship, she wished to speak 'a wee bit' about the days of 'gusto'. She wished, she said, to journey with us to the past.[21]

---

[19] Sanasarian, *Religious Minorities in Iran*, pp. 133–34. Western Armenian shares more features with Classical Armenian than Eastern does, especially in some of the grammar, such as plurals and some declensions. Therefore, even though the vernaculars were used to replace the classical, they still modelled themselves on Classical Armenian to build a connection with it. A correlation would be how Sanskrit is used to form new words in modern Hindi.

[20] The differences between Eastern and Western Armenian dialects are important in so far as the construction of an Armenian (national) identity within the homeland and in the diaspora is considered. Armenians in the homeland speak Eastern Armenian, while those in the diaspora (with the exception of Iran) speak Western Armenian.

[21] Zoya Pirzad, *Things We Left Unsaid: A Novel*, transl. Franklin Lewis (London: OneWorld Publications, 2013), p. 144; Zoya Pirzad, *Chiragh-ha ra man khamush mikunam* (Tehran: Nashr-i Markaz, 2002), p. 133.

This heterogeneity in the Armenian language and the ways in which dia-sporic Armenians negotiate language appear in several other works. On his way to the US, Vartan Gregorian lived in Lebanon for a short time. In his memoir, he highlights how Armenians in Beirut spoke the West-ern Armenian dialect; yet, being from Iran, he spoke the Eastern dialect. Nonetheless, this did not create misunderstandings. However, not creating misunderstandings does not necessarily mean that there was full communi-cation. Right after his discussion of language, he reflects on his loneliness in Beirut: 'My first night in Beirut was depressing. All of a sudden, I felt alone in the world. I was in a faraway place, in a strange city and strange hotel and bed, uprooted and transplanted to follow the unknown. I had neither friends nor acquaintances'.[22] Without the shared language identification, Gregorian experienced a sense of non-belonging, even while he was among other Armenians, which speaks to the importance of language to collective identity, down to the level of dialect.

The Significance of the Armenian Language

History, language, culture, literature, art and religion have always been critical tools in the construction of Iranian Armenian identity; however, religion and language have been the cornerstones of Armenian identity. Iranian Armenian poet Soukias Hacob Koorkchian (Varand) captures the significance of the Armenian language to Armenian identity in the follow-ing poem titled 'Hayeren' (Armenian Language):

> All over the world
> Monasteries
> Chapel-tabernacles,
> If need be
> (in front of the Christ,
> Or the Virgin)
> I'll say in your language
> The words of my prayer.

---

[22] Gregorian, *The Road to Home*, p. 66.

All over the world
Rich in languages
Covered in a book's
page
If need be
I'll only write
Letters in your language.

All over the world
In missiles
If one missile
Flies toward the sun,
And if it happens for me
In that sharp moment
To release a new wing
My song of faith
My breath and existence
It'll be in your language
Infinite-eternal
Whispering *barev* [hello]

My luminous Armenian.[23]

It is interesting that Varand links the Armenian language to the practice of Christianity, the worship of Christ and the Virgin Mary, which alludes to Armenians' nationalisation of Christianity in the fourth century and the invention of the Armenian alphabet by Mesrop Mashtots' shortly thereafter. He refers to the chaos surrounding the Armenians, metaphorically alluding to the historical position of Armenia as the crossroads for many wars and conflicts. Notwithstanding all of this chaos, the Armenian language will acquire a 'new wing' and survive. This conveys the precarious existence of a diasporic community whose language is on the verge of disappearance (Western Armenian is at risk) and who strives to maintain heritage and roots.

---

[23] Soukias Hacob Koorkchian (Varand), 'Hayeren' (Armenian), *An-veradardz (Irreversible)* (Tehran: Alik Publishers, 1999), pp. 79–80.

The significance of the Armenian language and its praise also appears in Almin's poem 'Herashalik Hayots' Lezu' (Marvellous Armenian Language):

> *Whoever says that*
> *There are seven wonders in the world*
> *And I say*
> *An Armenian teacher and poet*
> *That of the eight wonders of the world*
> *You are one of them, our Armenian language*

Our and the world's love for the Armenian language,
You are beautiful, gentle and rich,
And a miracle,
The one who speaks you becomes beautiful,
Nobler and . . . more magnificent . . .

My friend, my good one,
Keep this miracle pure,
Keep it pure,
Get rid of foreign words
And the unfamiliar ones.

Why distort,
Why distort?
This miracle
God-given.
Our mother tongue and the jewel,
Magnificent and wonderful,
The most Armenian . . .

So come on
And become beautiful,
And gentle,
And rich
by the Armenian language's
great miracle . . .[24]

[24] Almin, 'Herashalik Hayots' Lezu' (Marvellous Armenian Language), *Shk'egh Banasteght-sutyun* (*Rich Poetry*) (Tehran: Alik Publishers, 2018), p. 28.

In praising the Armenian language, Almin emphasises a lingual purity impervious to the host nation's language and culture. The preservation of the Armenian language is a significant motif in many diasporic Iranian Armenian authors' works, which suggests a preoccupation with resisting assimilation and cultural motivations to maintain ancestral heritage. However, the aim is not just the preservation of the Armenian language, but its pure form, which alludes to the anti-hybridisation of language.

Gender plays a significant role in how Armenians talk about language. In a deliberate contrast, language is female (mayreni lezu/mother tongue) and land is male (hayrenik/fatherland). The language is the mother, nurturing and emerging through home life, whereas the land is masculine, in need of strong men to defend it and be willing to die for it. Otherwise, the Armenian language is not as gendered as the languages in the neighbouring communities or countries, such as Kurdish, Arabic, Russian, Georgian and so on. Turkish and Persian, like Armenian, are not heavily gendered in their nouns, pronouns, or verbs, either. Almin's poem also reminds the reader of the well-known Armenian poet Silva Kaputikian and her poem 'Khosk im vordun' (A Word with My Child). Here, Kaputikian also includes an allusion to migration and Armenian mobility, as well as the importance of language maintenance.[25]

In occupying multiple diasporic consciousnesses, the less transnational Iranian Armenians work to instil correct and 'pure' knowledge and use of the Armenian language, confronting cultural anxieties around loss of the ancestral language. The conflict between the uses of two or more languages distorts the speaker's articulation, producing incorrect grammar and jeopardising analytical clarity and integrity. This is because the hybrid speaker's mind is divided into conflicting parts, complicating the average person's ability to automatically organise two or more languages.[26] By its nature bi- and multilingualism transforms language from many discrete entities into hybrid possibilities, including the creation of a hybrid identity.

From a very young age, Iranian Armenian children learn about these tools through a social progression – namely, from family, school and church.

---

[25] Thanks to James Barry for reminding me of this.
[26] Murat H. Roberts, 'The Problem of the Hybrid Language', *The Journal of English and Germanic Philology* 38.1 (1939), p. 23.

Later these are reinforced in adolescent and adult social interactions. It is important to note that Iranian Armenian children become fluent in their ancestral language while simultaneously listening to the host country's language through mass media. This naturally affects their language skills, and the Iranian Armenian authors and artists discussed in this book, the majority of whom produce works in their first language, Armenian, are no exception. In the diaspora, however, manifestations of Armenianness *vis-à-vis* lingual fluency exist alongside the dominant language and culture of the host nation.

For some diasporic communities, memory and folkways can replace religion and language as the integral foci of ethnic identification. For instance, the memory of the 1915 Genocide has played a major role for diasporic Armenians. However, as successive generations remain in a host nation, memory fades, as does the value of long-term diasporic traditions. Accordingly, the language of the homeland becomes the most effective way to carry vestiges of the ethnic narrative if maintained. But when this homeland language is no longer current, diasporic consciousness moves between an ancestral language and the language of the host nation. As transnational generations move towards utilising the host nation's language, previous narratives and religious rites and rituals may come to seem inauthentic. For example, English Armenian Apostolic church services become increasingly less distinct from standard American Catholicism in the west. The shift away from the ancestral language may also facilitate conversion to the dominant religion, although this is not a guarantee. Therefore, according to Safran, 'without the maintenance of language and/or religion, the dissolution of the ethnic culture is only a matter of time'.[27] However, religion and language are not themselves adequate foci for diasporic Iranian Armenian ethnic identification, either. This is especially true in North America and Western Europe, where the dominant religion (usually Christianity) is not very different from the Armenian Apostolic faith, making conversion seem more familiar rather than different. Movement away from the Armenian Apostolic Church is facilitated by a common language, and language alone is not adequate to

---

[27] Safran, 'Language, Ethnicity and Religion', p. 185; Shompa Lahiri, *Indians in Britain: Anglo-Indian Encounters 1880–1930* (London: Frank Cass, 2000), pp. 162–63.

maintain diasporic ethnic identity.[28] Hence, Armenian instruction at schools incorporates wider cultural and historical narratives, such as poems, songs and religion itself as an important tool for preserving heritage.

Language influences identity in two ways: it is a behavioural attribute, and it establishes the context and lexicon through which identities are expressed.[29] From a social constructionist standpoint, 'identity is not one thing for any individual [. . .] Rather, it may be a place from which an individual can express multiple and often contradictory aspects of [themselves]'.[30] As linguist Andrée Tabouret-Keller indicates, identity is both an objective social construct and a personal subjective construct established by individual mental processes and choices. Language, which connects both of these elements of identity, is a powerful symbol that represents many affiliations.[31] Individuals access a range of self-identificatory measures when they construct their ethnic identity, and bilingual individuals, in particular, possess rich linguistic and cultural repertoires to draw upon.[32] Language is also an agent of hegemony through which cultural beliefs and values are adopted.[33] According to cultural theorist Stuart Hall, '[i]dentities are the names we give to the different ways we are positioned

---

[28] Khachig Tölölyan, 'The Role of the Armenian Apostolic Church in the Diaspora', *Armenian Review* 41.1 (1988), pp. 58–62.

[29] Andrée Tabouret-Keller, 'Language and Identity', *The Handbook of Sociolinguistics*, ed. Florian Coulmas (Oxford: Blackwell, 1998), p. 324. See also Asif Agha, *Language and Social Relations* (Cambridge: Cambridge University Press, 2007). Agha argues that language is not simply a tool for social conduct, but an effective means for creating models of conduct.

[30] Kum-Kum Bhavnani and Anne Phoenix, 'Shifting Identities, Shifting Racisms: An Introduction', *Feminism and Psychology* 4.1 (1994), p. 9; see also Aneta Pavlenko, 'Bilingualism, Gender, and Ideology', *International Journal of Bilingualism* 5.2 (2001), pp. 117–51.

[31] Tabouret-Keller, 'Language and Identity', pp. 319–24.

[32] Anne Woollett, Harriette Marshall, Paula Nicholson and Neelam Dosanjh, 'Asian Women's Ethnic Identity: The Impact of Gender and Context in Accounts of Women Bringing up Children in East London', *Feminism and Psychology* 4.1 (1994), p. 120. See also Michele Koven, 'Two Languages in the Self/the Self in Two Languages: French Portuguese Bilinguals' Verbal Enactments and Experiences of Self in Narrative Discourse', *Ethnos* 26.4 (1998), pp. 410–55.

[33] Jean Mills, 'Connecting Communities: Identity, Language and Diaspora', *International Journal of Bilingual Education and Bilingualism* 8.4 (2005), p. 260. See also Jerzy Smolicz, 'Language Core Values in a Multicultural Setting: An Australian Perspective', *International Review of Education* 37.1 (1991), pp. 33–52.

by, and position ourselves within, the narratives of the past'.[34] Thus, language is a highly significant identity marker that can maintain group boundaries and a group's sense of its unique ethnic identity. Nonetheless, ethnic groups vary in the degree of importance that they place on language as an identity marker, with some groups more language-centric than others.[35]

The positioning of oneself in narratives of the past can become more intense when Iranian Armenians visit their ancestral homeland, only to hear a proliferation of non-Armenian languages. In his short story 'Hayots' Yerge' (The Armenian Song), Khach'ik Khach'er recounts the tale of a family visiting Yerevan, Armenia, from Iran. On the nineteenth day of their stay, the family hears someone singing an Armenian song while dining in a restaurant. The men of the family, greatly excited, walk up to the stage and thank the confused singer, who cannot understand why someone would thank him for singing a regular song. One of the men explains:

> There's nothing to be surprised – You sang the song 'Carousel' very beautifully. We have been in Yerevan, the three-thousand-year-old Armenian capital, for three weeks now; and in fact, this is the first Armenian song that we've heard, so we're excited. Thank you so much for singing an Armenian song. Because we listen to songs of other languages all the time. How can we explain to our children that we're in Armenia, and we are non-stop listening to songs in English, Turkish, French, Spanish etc.[36]

Khach'er's story captures the significance of the diasporic family unit in teaching and maintaining the Armenian language. The Armenian language and its importance become a source of frustration for the family, as they realise that their ancestral language is less prevalent in the Armenian capital than they

[34] Stuart Hall, 'Cultural Identity and Diaspora', *Colonial Discourse and Post-Colonial Theory*, ed. Patrick Williams and Laura Chrisman (London: Wheatsheaf, 1993), pp. 392–403.

[35] See Susan Gal and Judith T. Irvine, *Signs of Difference: Language and Ideology in Social Life* (Cambridge: Cambridge University Press, 2019); Kira Hall and Mary Bucholtz (eds), *Gender Articulated: Language and the Socially Constructed Self* (New York and London: Routledge, 1995).

[36] Khach'ik Khach'er, 'Hayots' Yerge' (The Armenian Song), *Im Chakatagri Sove: Patmevatskner Zhoghovats'u* (*The Sea of My Destiny: A Collection of Short Stories*) (Antilias: Printing House of the Armenian Catholicosate of Cilicia, 2011), p. 138.

had imagined. While the polyglot nature of Yerevan draws diasporic Armenians together, in this story it becomes a source of anxiety for the diasporic Iranian Armenian parents who are attempting to emphasise the importance of the Armenian cultural heritage to their children.

The use of the Armenian language and the knowledge of religion are of paramount significance to Armenian identity formation. However, the same language and religious tradition that evokes ethnic pride also creates boundaries that underscore national identity, nation-states and nation-building. Arby Ovanessian's cinematic opus *Ghara Kelisa* or *Lebbaeus Whose Surname Was Thaddaeus*, which documents the annual Armenian pilgrimage to the mausoleum of Holy Thaddaeus, begins with a voice narrating the story of the mausoleum in Armenian.[37] We observe the amalgamation of religion and Armenian language clearly in this documentary, in which Christian motifs abound while the Armenian lingual heritage and the use of black/dark and white/light constructions deepen their meanings. Although seemingly disjointed, the importance of language is first highlighted by its absence in the film's first seven minutes. When voices are finally heard, they are never aligned with the footage of the speakers, and Persian words and phrases are audible and scattered throughout the dialogues. Similar techniques are used in Ovanessian's *Cheshmeh*, although the language in this film is Persian rather than Armenian.[38] In his customary style, Ovanessian's mediation deconstructs several elements of this film, too. Regarding language, Ovanessian's film challenges stereotypical Iranian representations of Armenians, subtly showcasing fluency in Persian without a heavy accent and Armenian, as well as seamless code-switching between both languages.

Using spoken and visual languages to maintain Armenian cultural heritage situates the consciousness of the individual in the past (through the remembrance of images and cultural materials), while their own performance of remembrance and cultural maintenance is situated in the present. Iranian Armenian diasporic communities define themselves by a historical antecedent linked to important cultural markers and shared history, geography and memories. The less transnational cohort harnesses

---

[37] Ovanessian, *Ghara Kelisa*.
[38] Arby Ovanessian, *Cheshmeh* (*The Spring*) (Tehran: National Iranian Radio and Television, 1972).

the sense of belonging established by these shared elements of diasporic heritage, hinging on nostalgia.

In contrast to this non-transnational group, the transnational groups do not base their sense of belonging on a relationship with the nation-state, the homeland. In a move that counterbalances the importance of language, religion, geography, memory and history, transnational diasporic Iranian Armenians look forward to their own 'feeling' of Armenianness. For them, the homeland of Armenia as a nation embodies a large, dynamic diaspora community with a diasporic identity that is in constant flux and redefinition.

Language Instruction and Assimilatory Practices

Amid all the multilingualism and the anxiety about maintaining the mother tongue, the family is the primary vehicle among Iranian Armenians for the intergenerational transmission of language and heritage. Linguist Joshua Fishman agrees that the 'home-family-neighbourhood' nexus is the foundation for the transmission of the minoritised community language. After these social institutions initiate socialisation, school and education become the second domain of socialisation, encompassing possibilities ranging from community-led literacy classes to state-coordinated language instruction.[39] However, host nation schools are tasked with reproducing mainstream culture, ideas and values, which suggests that both majority and minoritised groups have anxieties around language and acculturation. For instance, in the US, the rise of the Latina/o population heightened concerns about the future of American identity *vis-à-vis* English language acquisition, and this led to certain approaches to manage ethno-linguistic diversity. Schools have become crucial tracks for ethno-linguistic identity formation.[40]

---

[39] See Joshua Fishman, '"English Only": Its Ghosts, Myths, and Dangers', *International Journal of the Sociology of Language* 74 (1989), pp. 125–40; Joshua Fishman, 'Language and Ethnicity', *Language, Ethnicity and Intergroup Relations*, ed. Howard Gilles (London: Academic Press, 1977), pp. 15–57; Joshua Fishman, 'What Is Reversing the Language Shift (RLS) and How Can It Succeed?' *Journal of Multilingual and Multicultural Development* 11 (1990), pp. 5–36; Joshua Fishman, 'An Interview with Joshua A. Fishman', *Language Loyalty, Language Planning, and Language Revitalization*, ed. Nancy H. Hornberger and Martin Putz (Clevedon: Multilingual Matters, 2006), pp. 1–28.

[40] Ana Celia Zentella, 'Latin@ Languages and Identities', *Latinos: Remaking America*, ed. Marcelo Suárez-Orozco and Mariela Páez (Berkeley: University of California Press, 2009), pp. 321–38.

In the case of Iranian Armenians, Armenian leadership and community members struggled to establish Armenian language instruction in the Iranian curriculum. In contrast, Armenian language instruction in the US exists largely outside of the US educational structure, as an extracurricular endeavour, with the exception of a few schools that integrate it into the curriculum as an option, and even this is mostly done in Los Angeles, a city that houses the majority of Armenians. Although diasporic Iranian Armenians are encouraged to maintain their cultural identity and heritage by Armenian national, political and elite figures, the host nation's emphasis on integration and assimilation, and desires for upward mobility at the cost of acculturation have restricted these attempts. For instance, Iranian Armenians chafed under Reza Shah Pahlavi's (r. 1924–41) restrictive social and linguistic Persianisation reforms, which demanded that all subjects be instructed in Persian, including those at Armenian schools.[41] In the US, the integrative activities of the Americanisation League (1910s–30s) competed with diaspora parties for the hearts and minds of community members.[42]

In short, diasporic Iranian Armenians were caught between the need to fit into mainstream culture, on the one hand, and the desire to transmit Armenian identity to the next generations, on the other. In Iran, Armenians were mandated to learn Persian, the national language. In a global context, English has increasingly assumed the role of a *lingua franca* for international communication.[43] Hence, Armenians who are scattered all over the world, with English as the dominant language, have had to acquire this linguistic capability as well. In this regard, the emphasis on retaining the mother tongue and the confusion that ensues when attaining bilingual or multilingual fluency illustrate the difficult realities for a hybrid, diasporic transnational individual, in comparison to an idealised life situated within the dominant culture.

The Iranian Armenian school system and curriculum lean towards exclusivity, enrolling only Armenian students and passing through strictly

---

[41] Firoozeh Kashani-Sabet, *Frontier Fictions: Shaping the Iranian Nation, 1804–1946* (Princeton, NJ: Princeton University Press, 1999), pp. 213–14, 220.

[42] Panossian, *The Armenians*, pp. 296–97.

[43] Leigh Oakes, *Language and National Identity: Comparing France and Sweden* (Amsterdam and Philadelphia: John Benjamins, 2001).

Armenian ownership. This, in and of itself, contributes to a separatist sense of Armenianness, even among Armenians, and non-Armenian Iranians.[44] Historian Houri Berberian records that 'Armenian schools have a long tradition in Iran, with formal religious schools aimed at training prospective clergy and the children of merchants having operated in the country since at least the 1630s'.[45] In the early nineteenth century, Armenians from the South Caucasus began establishing western-influenced Armenian schools across Iran. Gradually, these schools expanded their reach from the elite to the masses, teaching both primary and secondary education.[46] Later, they changed into centres that fostered Armenian identity, religion and nationalism. The first Armenian schools in Tehran have been documented as early as in the 1870s, and more than likely they segregated students by sex. However, out of socio-economic necessity, these schools became co-educational in the 1890s.[47]

Reza Shah's Persianisation efforts, which required that instruction in all schools, including minoritised ones, be conducted in Persian, caused a great deal of suffering and Armenian anxieties around language. These themes appear in Vartan Gregorian's *The Road to Home*. Gregorian reminds readers that language and national identity were entwined when the Armenian schools were shut down by Reza Shah and later opened after his abdication and exile in the 1940s. After the re-opening, Russian was taught as a second language, Persian was de-emphasised and, for a brief time-period from 1945 to 1946, following the autonomy of the Republic of Azerbaijan, Azeri Turkish was also included in the curriculum.[48] Of course, the Russian and Turkish instructions mentioned here are only because Gregorian lived in Tabriz. In Tehran, language instruction was different and not necessarily influenced by the Russian

---

[44] Barry, *Armenian Christians in Iran*, p. 64.

[45] Houri Berberian, *Armenians and the Iranian Constitutional Revolution 1905–1911: 'The Love of Freedom Has No Fatherland'* (Boulder, CO: Westview Press, 2001), pp. 43–44.

[46] Annie Basil, *Armenian Settlements in India: From the Earliest Times to the Present Day* (Calcutta: Armenian College, 1969), p. 125.

[47] Hovhannes L. Pahlevanian, *Iranahay Hamayk'e: 1941–1979* (*The Iranian Armenian Community, 1941–1979*) (Yerevan: Armenian SSR Academy of Science Press, 1989), pp. 192, 205–6.

[48] Gregorian, *The Road to Home*, p. 25.

or Turkish languages. Reza Shah's unification agenda did not last long, but it did leave significant marks on minoritised populations' understanding of their precarious social position within the country.

After the Islamic Revolution, although, as before, Armenian schools were immersed in Armenian culture – that is, all the students were of Armenian descent – the teachers and administrative staff were not. The curriculum was inherently anti-Armenian in context, and Armenian was taught for only a few hours weekly – a small concession to the Armenian community's struggles to maintain their curriculum.

Within this environment, both Armenian and Iranian cultural and religious occasions were celebrated. For instance, at school, students celebrated 1 January as the Armenian New Year, but they also celebrated the Iranian New Year, Nowruz, on 21 March. Along with this dual curriculum, Armenian schools as much as possible endeavoured to foster a strong affection for the homeland. For the majority of Iranian Armenians, the homeland was geographically ambiguous, an unvisited space that existed mostly on maps and as an idea.

After the Islamic Revolution, Iran's Pahlavi-era language policies remained virtually unchanged. The 1979 Constitution declared Persian the official language of Iran, and while languages other than Persian were recognised, they were deemed ineligible for educational institutions.[49] In the 1980s, the state extended this restriction to Armenian schools, justifying this with the claim that granting such rights to Armenians would inspire other larger minoritised populations to demand the same. Consequently, in 1981, Armenian schools closed voluntarily for a week, in formal protest to the ruling, with Armenian political leadership struggling at the federal level to restore Armenian autonomy. At the federal level, Armenian politicians emphasised the Armenians' constitutional rights based on Article 13 of the 1979 Constitution, which phrased Armenians as a recognised religious community possessing rights to perform their religious and cultural ceremonies. In response to these challenges, the ministry ruled that all religious education must take place in Persian, and Armenian language instruction was limited to two hours a week. Although this ruling resulted in a coalition between language activists,

---

[49] Barry, *Armenian Christians in Iran*, p. 68.

it caused a rift between the Armenian minoritised bloc and the government, as the ruling violated Article 15 of the constitution. In *Religious Minorities in Iran*, Eliz Sanasarian notes that some schools – often those bearing the names of kings or queens – faced mandated name changes. Many educational institutions resisted this, and some succeeded.[50]

Subsequently, however, the state introduced sex-segregated education policies, with minoritised community leadership reclassifying entire schools for each sex. Following these changes, the Iranian government banned schools on church, synagogue, or temple grounds. Sanasarian posits that this was mainly to protect Muslims from exposure to non-Muslim religions. For instance, the Kooshesh Armenian Boys' School in Tehran constructed a wall to separate the school from its adjacent church building. Shortly after these new rulings, Armenian schools were also ordered to appoint Muslim principals, teachers and clerks, eventually giving way to the elimination or reduction of Armenian language teaching hours. Over time, all these changes accumulated, resulting in state interference in minoritised communities' religious education with the imposition of a single Persian text for religious instruction (based on Islam). Parallel to education, the government began expressing interest in taking over the Armenians' Ararat Sports Complex in Tehran.[51]

These suppressive measures continued, with some Muslim principals attempting to forbid the Bible, administering ministry-imposed curricula and favouring rigid Persian education. This prompted Armenian schools to halt operation in a one-week national strike, followed by a re-opening and a return to schools devoid of instruction, classroom activities and everyday operations. Eventually, Armenian schools refused to comply with the mandates, instead reinstating Armenian language and religious instruction in 1983. It was clear to the Armenian community that their linguistic and curricular authority was under threat. In response to the wave of protest, the ministry announced that religious teaching must take place in Persian and that Armenian language instruction must be reduced or even eliminated from the curriculum in order to avoid overloading the students. To the Armenians, the reasoning was clearly a pretext, as the excuse of 'overloading'

---

[50] Sanasarian, *Religious Minorities in Iran*, p. 77.
[51] Ibid.

had occurred for generations. Following this announcement, the ministry imposed a standardised Persian text, written by state authorities, for all religious instruction among all religious minoritised groups. Schools that wished to conduct religious or other ceremonies required government permission, and female teachers and students were required to adhere to the Islamic dress code. Most importantly, Armenian language instruction would be reduced to two hours weekly.[52]

I vividly remember that, when I was seven years old and in second grade, my elementary school, Arax, closed down to protest this governmental ruling. This closure was not a forced one. We used to go to school every morning, but we would not go to class – instruction was voluntarily halted. We would sit on the grounds of the school in strike against this ruling. I recall sitting on the three steps in front of the school. After weeks of protest, we were ushered back into class, and instruction was restored; however, now our religious education was in Persian and with content that included Islamic teachings for minoritised students. In addition, Armenian language instruction was limited to two hours weekly. This obviously had grave consequences for my generation, since we did not learn about Armenian literature, history, or religion properly. We also lacked fluency in reading and writing Armenian. Even in our everyday conversations, we began using Persian words frequently. This went on until graduation from high school. After high school, I pursued English Literature so naturally I no longer read in Armenian. It was not until February 2020, when I began reading the Armenian works under study here, that I returned to my mother tongue. At first, my pace was excruciatingly slow, and I could not understand many of the sentences clearly, but with time I managed to read, translate and analyse all the poems, novels and stories for this book.

Within Iranian Armenian diasporic cultural productions, Robert Safarian evokes language as one of the determining factors in the setting and tone of a social environment. Safarian believes that language is of utmost importance in the reconstruction of the social context of ethnic communities, as it shapes collective, individual and national identities.[53] This is masterfully illustrated

---

[52] Ibid.
[53] Robert Safarian, 'Qisi-yi farʿi-i khanum-i Nurulahi va Shutayt' (The Secondary Story of Mrs Nurollahi and Shutait), *Haft* 1 (2004), p. 24.

in Iranian Armenian cultural productions that use Armenian language and sounds to establish an ethnic Iranian Armenian setting. These cultural productions are imbued with Armenian names, place names, foods and book titles. The use and repetition of melodies within names and words create a sort of linguistic space, reminiscent of the native language of Armenian characters and personas.

Representing their diasporic consciousness, an author's use of Armenian in proper, grammatical style is one method of conveying the characters' cognitive investment in the promotion of their elusive homeland. Zoya Pirzad's characters in 'A Day Before Easter' have lived in Iran for so long that they are naturally bilingual, fluent in both Armenian and Persian. Linguistic hybridity is a dynamic phenomenon through which a community achieves fluency in two or more languages, which are spoken by the same community for similar purposes. The extent of linguist hybridity is contingent on the frequency and intensity of contact. This can easily be observed in the linguistic contact between the Persian and Armenian languages in Iran, with uninterrupted linguistic, social and cultural contacts. Significantly, both Armenian and Persian are sub-categories of the Indo-European languages and share many linguistic features, smoothing the exchanges and flows between the two languages. The social level of linguistic contact includes various aspects of everyday life and language, providing Armenians with a stock of everyday Persian cognates.

In addition to evoking the Armenian language, cultural productions explore cultural anxieties surrounding the presentation of the Armenian language. In Pirzad's 'A Day Before Easter', we read about Edmond's linguistic exchanges, including several reprimands by Grandmother for his use of colloquial Armenian and Persian words. Edmond is corrected for his use of the Persian word for tulip by Mrs Grigorians, who insists that he replace it with the Armenian word *kakach*.[54] Similarly, in Rosemary Cohen's book *The Survivor*, the narrator – a mother and survivor of the Armenian Genocide who lives in Iran with her toddler daughter – recalls: 'Liana was sitting in front and while I was holding her, we were conversing with each other for the first time. She noticed the birds and animals and plants, and she asked about them. I corrected her words in Armenian, and I tried to teach

---

[54] Pirzad, *The Space Between Us*, pp. 238, 243.

her new ones'.[55] These instances highlight the diasporic Iranian Armenians' anxiety about preserving the Armenian language as an element of ethnic identity, intoning that the more eloquent, formal and perfect the language use, the deeper the speaker's heritage.

The same concept emerges with the characters' use of English and Armenian in *Things Left Unsaid*, where Pirzad reconstructs the everyday linguistic setting of the region through the use of English words and idioms in 1960s Abadan. At various points in the story, Pirzad highlights the importance of maintaining the Armenian language in an environment that integrates English, in addition to Persian, into everyday conversations. In one notable scene, the grandmother teaches Armineh and Arsineh to use proper Armenian words instead of English: 'We heard the brakes of Artoush's Chevy screech, and moments later the twins ran in. "*Hello*, Nanny. *Hello*, Auntie". Mother hugged Armineh. "Again with the *hellos* in English? We're not English. Are we? Say it in Armenian: Barev!"'[56] This exchange affirms the grandmother's desire for the children to favour *barev* over the English hello or the Persian *salaam*. Pirzad weaves English and Armenian phrases throughout the text using words and phrases such as *gata, nazouk, barev* and hello, among others, which narratively underscores the reciprocal influence of the English and Armenian languages. Pirzad's use of multiple languages allows her characters to emphasise the importance of maintaining their cultural heritage, and the narrative features characters who constantly remind each other to speak in Armenian. Other than a handful of words, interactions and dialogue occur in colloquial Persian, with the author interpreting them as colloquial or formal Armenian. While the novel highlights the importance of the Armenian language through complex Armenian characters, the novel itself is written in Persian, depicting the reality that daily interactions among Armenians occur in Persian.

Although subtle, Pirzad's positioning of each language contextualises their social position. Her use of Persian as the novel's primary language signifies the minoritised position of Armenian, conveying dislocation and displacement. Likewise, the typeset used for Armenian words and dialogue is distinguished from Persian with bold or italic letters, further othering the printed aspect of

---

[55] Cohen, *The Survivor*, pp. 76–77.
[56] Pirzad, *Things We Left Unsaid*, p. 71.

Armenian. For Pirzad, language, in both its spoken and written modes, represents a fragmented consciousness, becoming a metaphor for the tension between national belonging and assimilation into Persian culture, both beautifully dramatised in a language that itself marks her Armenian as Other. For a community that is living outside of the immediate homeland, whose first officially learned language is not Armenian; for a community that lives in a host nation with whose people they cannot fully identify, 'what recourse is left to them but to create their own language? A language which they can connect their identity to, one capable of communicating realities and values true to themselves . . .'[57] And that is exactly what Pirzad does in her works. Living in a country with a language different from her mother tongue, she embraces both her mother tongue and the host nation's language and transforms them into an authentic language that is hers – an utterly hybrid language that mimics her lived experiences. This reveals Pirzad's status within the liminal space of *verants'ughi*, where life is difficult but also full of potential.

Typesetting the Armenian language distinctively is a widespread practice for diasporic Armenian writers, with the use of italics and brackets that otherises the language and culture in the context of another. Pirzad applies this linguistic technique in Persian, and Emmanuel P. Vardanyan utilises the same tactic in English, italicising all Armenian words: 'The older people kissed the *garibs* resting on soft mattresses, and the younger ones shook hands with them, almost everyone uttering: "*Baroveck yegel mer achki vra* [Welcome to our eyes]". The expression was the highest courtesy that a person could tender to his friend'.[58] In another passage, Vardanyan makes references to Armenian roots, traditions and religious rituals during a bridal outing: '"That's right", seconded Sarah. "We better finish our business, then go to the café. Which way is the goldsmith's bazaar, Zohrab? My darling Marina – ah, the sweet thing – she must have a pair of *chichags* [a decoration of gold pieces], a gold tiara, and a silver belt"'.[59] The use of italicised Armenian *chichags* followed by a bracketed English definition complicates the linguistic dynamic, using an Armenian term to describe elements of an Iranian ritual within a biography written in English.

---

[57] Anzaldúa, *Borderlands/La Frontera*, p. 77.
[58] Vardanyan, *The Well of Ararat*, p. 16.
[59] Ibid. p. 80.

In the US, Armenian language acquisition and the Armenian school system both operate differently from those in Iran. Armenian students attend either American schools or private Armenian schools, with those youth who attend American schools and who want to foster Armenian culture and heritage attending extra-curricular classes hosted by private Armenian schools. Often, such schools are organised and managed by the Armenian community or nationalist organisations such as the Armenian Revolutionary Federation. Of course, the sense of Armenian identity and belonging is cultivated through other events as well, both in the US and in Iran. For instance, cultural events and celebrations, conferences and publications, as well as annual memorial ceremonies commemorating the Genocide foster a deeper sense of Armenian identity. Language competency concerns, however, fluctuate over time from mother tongue to the host nation's language and back to the mother tongue across generations. According to diaspora scholar Ashod Rhaffi Aprahamian, early Detroit Armenians were not fluent in English, and so the community obtained permission to use some rooms at the downtown YMCA to hold classes in English, arithmetic and American citizenship. However, he recounts, over the years the problem of education shifted from English fluency to problems with Armenian fluency in later generations. The concern now was to educate younger Armenians in the Armenian language.[60]

Evidently, the most celebrated element of Armenian identity is the Armenian language itself. According to James Barry, in cases where Armenian language and culture are not included in the curriculum, particularly in Iran, the Armenian language 'is considered to be continually under threat'.[61] For diasporic Iranian Armenians, knowing, speaking and living with the Armenian language is experienced as loyalty to the homeland and to one's ancestral roots. While living in the diaspora requires Iranian Armenians to maintain

---

[60] Ashod Rhaffi Aprahamian, *Remarkable Rebirth: The Early History of the Armenians in Detroit* ([n. p.]: Author-Publisher, 2005), pp. 31–32. See Shushan Karapetian, 'Opportunities and Challenges of Institutionalizing a Pluricentric Diasporic Language: The Case of Armenian in Los Angeles', *The Routledge Handbook of Heritage Language Education: From Innovation to Program Building*, ed. Olga Kagan, Maria Carreira and Claire Hitchins Chik (New York and London: Routledge, 2017). Karapetian's work focuses on spoken Armenian in Los Angeles, particularly on heritage language fluency.

[61] Barry, *Armenian Christians in Iran*, p. 64.

their heritage through various identity markers, Iranian Armenians face psycho-social pressures to learn English, Persian, or other majority languages of the host nation. Variables such as socio-cultural environment, learner differences, environmental and cultural contexts of learning, and linguistic outcomes all come into play when considering language acquisition and retention. Linguist Bert Vaux's qualitative research indicates that Armenian children who are not immersed in Armenian-speaking environments will not learn to speak it. This is more common in the US than in Iran, where interreligious and interethnic marriages are frowned upon. In the US, both family members and the community play an important role; when parents communicate in English, children do not learn to communicate in Armenian. Similarly, if churches or Armenian clubs use English, then the relationship between language and ethnicity shifts as 'English becomes the language of living Armenianness'.[62]

Armenians in the US take one of the two sides on this matter: on the one hand, a group of Armenians, generally the older generation, maintains that there is a crucial link between language and ethnicity, identity and authenticity; on the other hand, the more Americanised Armenians argue that language is simply a means of communication and that its link to ethnicity is arbitrary. According to this mindset, one can be Armenian without speaking the language.[63]

In keeping with these two attitudes, the two main approaches to second-language acquisition have also been differently described as either integrative or instrumental. In the integrative approach, emphasis is placed on social and interpersonal relations, keeping the need for social affiliation in mind. According to linguist Colin Baker, 'an integrative attitude to a particular language may concern attachment to or identification with a language group and their cultural activities. Wanting to be identified with a defined group of "other" language speakers, or wanting friendship within that group indicates an integrative orientation'.[64] Thus, the integrative method cultivates positive

---

[62] Bert Vaux, 'The Fate of the Armenian Language in New England', *The Armenians of New England*, ed. Marc C. Mamigonian (Belmont, MA: Armenian Heritage Press, 2004), pp. 208–9.

[63] Ibid. pp. 209–10.

[64] Colin Baker, *Attitudes and Language* (Clevedon, Philadelphia and Adelaide: Multilingual Matters, 1992), p. 32.

attitudes and feelings toward the host nation. By contrast, the instrumental approach is associated with utilitarian gains such as finding a job, securing a higher salary and gaining recognition or social and economic standing – all motivations for learning the host nation's language. Scholar of second-language acquisition Jacqueline Norris-Holt focuses on the utilisation aspects of this attitude:

> With instrumental motivation the purpose of language acquisition is more utilitarian, such as meeting the requirements for school or university graduation, applying for a job, requesting higher pay based on language ability, reading technical material, translation work, or achieving higher social status. Instrumental motivation is often characteristic of second language acquisition, where little or no social integration of the learner into a community using the target language takes place, or in some instances is even desired.[65]

The instrumental approach is related to an individual's desire for basic security and driven by a sense of survival. While these two approaches may seem divergent, they are not mutually exclusive. According to Baker, '[i]ntegrativeness is an identifiable factor [only] when analyzed alongside a wide variety of ability, achievement and general variables' that are instrumental in orientation.[66] Hence, each approach should be viewed as one of several variables unique to each learner.

For diasporic Iranian Armenians, while the less transnational group endeavours to maintain their culture in hopes of imparting it to their progeny, their counterparts experience the tension of maintaining the Armenian language or assimilating and integrating into the host nation – each with a distinct relationship to linguistic diversity. As the cohort tasked with bridging past and future and preserving Armenian cultural heritage for future generations, the transnational Iranian Armenians are also an anchor in the host culture. This unique position places the transnational Iranian Armenians in a quandary, as learning the host language is necessary for everyday survival, yet maintenance of the Armenian language is prioritised. This transnational cohort is part of a

---

[65] Jacqueline Norris-Holt, 'Motivation as a Contributing Factor in Second Language Acquisition', *The Internet TESL Journal* 8.6 (2001), http://iteslj.org/Articles/Norris-Motivation.html
[66] Baker, *Attitudes and Language*, p. 33.

broader socio-cultural landscape. The spaces that they occupy have been considered generically as 'third spaces' by Brah or as 'hybridity' by Hall.[67] While the experiences of the less transnational group remain meaningful in terms of cultural maintenance, the transnational Iranian Armenians carve out third spaces where their language maintenance aligns with a hybrid identity – one that is decolonised, and theirs.[68] In a poem titled 'Refuge', evoking Armenian, Persian and English, Iranian Armenian American poet Leonardo Alishan expresses a hybrid identity crafted within a diasporic transnational third space:

I need structure
I need form

When the poet is a mad Armenian priest
When the poet is a drunk Iranian cleric

I need clean English
I need Alexander Pope.[69]

Within Iranian Armenian cultural productions, such third spaces depict the diasporic struggle to maintain a linguistic heritage, while simultaneously learning the mainstream language and culture of the host society. Equally important are the ways in which a sense of belonging is fostered.

In this context, the concept of 'language ideologies' is important. Broadly defined, language ideologies are 'models that link types of linguistic forms with the types of people who stereotypically use them'.[70] In practice, these

---

[67] Avatar Brah, *Cartographies of Diaspora: Contesting Identities* (London: Routledge, 1996); Stuart Hall, 'New Ethnicities', *Race, Culture and Difference*, ed. James Donald and Ali Rattansi (London: Sage, 1992), pp. 252–59.

[68] Joanne Winter and Anne Pauwels, 'Language Maintenance and the Second Generation: Policies and Practices', *Maintaining Minority Languages in Transnational Contexts*, ed. Anne Pauwels, Joanne Winter and Joseph Lo Bianco (New York: Palgrave Macmillan, 2007), pp. 180–81.

[69] Alishan, 'Refuge', p. 51.

[70] Stanton Wortham, 'Linguistic Anthropology of Education', *Annual Review of Anthropology* 37 (2008), p. 43. See also John Haviland, 'Ideologies of Language: Some Reflections on Language and US Law', *American Anthropologist* 105.4 (2003), pp. 764–74; Ann Wennerstrom, 'Immigrant Voices in the Courts', *International Journal of Speech, Language and the Law* 15.1 (2008), pp. 23–49.

models typically stigmatise second-language speakers, not only for their acquisition of the host nation's official language, but also for the loss of their mother tongue. These language models also promote assimilation into monolingualism and mainstream culture. As a result, second-language speakers are marginalised within the host nation, regardless of whether they are born and raised within its borders. This theory defines assimilation as a binary process through which immigrants and their descendants come to disidentify with their previous national identity as they identify with the host nation. For the Iranian Armenian diasporic community, this process entails the diminution of their Armenian roots in order to integrate in the host nation's mainstream society.

Language ideology is an essential belief that defines languages and their appropriate usage. Everyone engages in this ideology and uses different registers where appropriate. A good example for Armenians in Iran is the circumstances of its use. For example, if an Armenian were to start speaking to another Armenian in Persian, it might seem out of place, due to language ideology. However, the state also chooses language ideologies: if an Armenian speaks in Armenian in a US court, it will be translated into English by an interpreter, and only the interpreter's words will be recorded in the court archives because the language ideology holds that what is translated as essentially true to what was said.

Public education institutions play a major role in the language assimilative process for Armenians in the US and Iran. According to Stanton Wortham, 'schools are important sites for establishing association between "educated" and "uneducated", "sophisticated" and "unsophisticated", "official" and "vernacular' language use and types of students'.[71] Furthermore, assimilation is frequently conceptualised as an individual choice based on a personal desire to claim or resist a certain nationality. In this context, language use gets interpreted as a definitive cultural practice by which to gauge the success of any assimilationist project. Frequently, in public schools, the host nation's language hegemony prevails with monolingualism as the norm. Diasporic students' bilingualism or multilingualism is stigmatised, creating cultural and social associations that value fluency in the host nation's language over any form of multilingualism and the mother tongue.

[71] Ibid. p. 43.

Language ideologies allow us to chart a host nation's operating hegemony and, in turn, the nuances contained within the hegemonic language that promote monolingualism as a cultural norm, especially within an educational institution's practices, policies and procedures.[72] The monolingual orientation of some nations stems from ideologies of one nation-one state, a hegemonic ideal tied to the emergence of modern nation-states. Reza Shah's 1930s Persianisation agenda and later the education policies of the Islamic Republic clearly involved these notions. The construction of monolingualism as a national norm obscures the reality of global and local multilingualism and helps secure positions of power for a select cadre of citizens who have allowed assimilation to subsume their own ethnolinguistic diversity. This type of assimilation overlooks the limitations of monolingualism, instead framing multilingualism as a liability and further marginalising the same diasporic communities encouraged to assimilate into mainstream society. Gregorian writes about his experience learning the correct pronunciation of English words in the US and the difficulty of overcoming his Armenian accent:

> He tried desperately to have us differentiate pronunciations of 'the' and 'd', 'w' and 'v', and asked us to go around the campus to pick up unfamiliar English words or expressions and make a list of interesting euphemisms. My list included the expressions, 'It's cool, man', which I found very confusing. I understood when boys and men called each other, 'hey, guys', but did not know why some women called other women 'guys'. Many of us were puzzled by the expression 'funeral homes' and 'funeral parlors'. We had heard of ice cream parlors but 'funeral parlors'? We had not heard the expressions 'passed on' or 'passed away' in lieu of 'dying' or 'deceased' in lieu of 'dead'. Nor had we heard the expression that somebody had 'kicked the bucket', meaning a person had died. Why 'kick the bucket'? What kind of bucket?'[73]

---

[72] Ofelia García and Rosario Torres-Guevara, 'Monoglossic Ideologies and Language Policies in the Education of US Latinas/os', *Handbook of Latinos and Education: Theory, Research, and Practices*, ed. Enrique G. Murillo Jr, Sofia A. Villenas, Ruth Trinidad Galván, Juan Sánchez Muñoz, Corinne Martínez and Margarita Machado-Casas (New York: Routledge, 2010), pp. 182–93.

[73] Gregorian, *The Road to Home*, p. 139.

While scholars of immigration and diaspora posit various models of assimilation, such as the straight-line or segmented model (discussed in Chapter Two), diasporic linguistic practices indicate that both models fall short in their analysis of assimilation. This is due, in part, to an analytical dependence on static, monolithic, idealised identities instead of multiplicity and hybridity.[74] In reality, Iranian Armenian diasporic communities are multicultural, multilingual people who code-switch and draw on multiple systems of language, race and ethnicity to define themselves. The assimilation models fail to capture these non-linear trajectories. Another shortcoming of these models concerns the belief that usage of the host nation's language parallels assimilation, and the unwillingness to learn or use the host nation's language is an assimilation failure. These perspectives depend on a rigid distinction between national identities and linguistic identities and practices. The language ideologies that inform these views obfuscate the host nation's widespread multilingualism, flattening linguistic heterogeneity by advancing the categories of host language and home language as monolithic categories, equating Persian with Iranianness and Armenian with non-Iranianness in the case of Armenians in Iran. In the case of Armenians in the US, English is correlated with Americanness and Armenian with non-Americanness.

Linguist Benjamin H. Bailey's research demonstrates that, often, the host nation's language can function as a unifying element for communities who speak different regional dialects of a single language.[75] In this sense, the host nation's language practices may mediate shared identification among various diasporic national subgroups. This can be true for the different Armenian national sub-groups in Iran as well as in the US – Eastern Armenian and Western Armenian. Armenian does not play a unifying role for these subgroups, although Persian or English can mediate shared identification. In the west, socio-cultural identities are often categorised through race, ethnicity, nation, language, or dialect, among many others. However, referring to an ethnic minoritised group *vis-à-vis* a nation's dominant majority population

---

[74] Benjamin H. Bailey, 'Shifting Negotiations of Identity in a Dominican American Community', *Latino Studies* 5 (2007), p. 178.

[75] Benjamin H. Bailey, *Language, Race, and Negotiation of Identity: A Study of Dominican Americans* (New York: LFB Scholarly Publishing, 2002), p. 12.

effectively otherises them.[76] Discourses about national and ethnic identities describe the coexistence of groups in the language of cohabitation, with a clear demarcation between the majority mainstream and minoritised diasporic people; therefore, speaking of national and ethnic identities that coexist side by side can be a complicated task that goes against the prevailing discourses of ethnic identity.

As languages transform intergenerationally (and trans-generationally), their vitality may diminish over time. This is not to say that these minoritised languages lose their symbolic value altogether, and while they might not be the primary spoken language of the diaspora population, these languages maintain their symbolic value for cultural insiders. The majority language, however, becomes a stigma that marks outsiders.[77] The relationship between language and identity is a dynamic one that has undergone major transnational changes during the twentieth century, as most people no longer identify with just one nation-state. Transnational diasporic Iranian Armenians not only maintain symbolic ties to the Armenian homeland, but they also cultivate affiliations with their host nations. This multiplicity of transnational identities requires the capacity to balance increasing cultural diversity and heterogeneity with a core value of multilingualism.[78]

Diaspora and diasporisation make it possible to consider ethno-diasporic identities as multidimensional, but these concepts can be potentially just as rigid as assimilation theories. When considering diaspora, scholars tend to emphasise cultural maintenance, heritage and traditions, or change and disjuncture. However, Juan Flores, a scholar of socio-cultural analysis, proposes that we should think about diaspora 'from below', which . . .

---

[76] Eugene Roosens, *Creating Ethnicity: The Process of Ethnogenesis* (Newbury Park: Sage, 1989).

[77] Guus Extra, 'Comparative Perspectives on Immigrant Minority Languages in Multicultural Europe', *Maintaining Minority Languages in Transnational Contexts*, ed. Anne Pauwels, Joanne Winter and Joseph Lo Bianco (London: Palgrave Macmillan, 2007), p. 31. See also Jerzy J. Smolicz, 'Minority Languages as Core Values of Ethnic Cultures: A Study of Maintenance and Erosion of Polish, Welsh, and Chinese Languages in Australia', *Maintenance and Loss of Minority Languages*, ed. Willem Fase, Koen Jaspaert and Sjaak Kroon (Amsterdam: Benjamins, 1992), pp. 277–305.

[78] Selma Van Londen and Arie De Ruijter, 'Ethnicity and Identity', *Culture, Ethnicity and Migration*, ed. Marie Claire Foblets and Ching Lin Pang (Leuven and Leusden: Acco, 1999), pp. 69–79.

. . . helps to point up the many diaspora experiences that diverge from those of the relatively privileged, entrepreneurial or professional transnational connections that have tended to carry the greatest appeal in scholarly and journalistic coverage. That approach, guided by a concern for subaltern and everyday life struggles of poor and disenfranchised people, also allows for special insights into ongoing issues of racial identity and gender inequalities that are so often ignored or minimized in the grand narratives of transnational hegemony.[79]

If we do not assume or take as a given ethno-linguistic categories such as Eastern and Western Armenian or subaltern Armenians, then it becomes possible to track the dynamic processes and trajectories by which Armenian diasporic identities are constructed, enacted and transformed. It becomes possible to track the ways in which Iranian Armenian cultural productions fuse various languages, texts, words and proverbs into different narrative styles that signify characters' hybridity, and by extension that of their authors or artists, and their struggles to uphold their Armenian identity or shifting to those of the host nation. Such existence involves remapping identity, transforming borders and socialising differently – often a political choice, rather than a personal one.

Reconfiguring identity through language, artist Garnik Der Hacopian's latticework represents subliminal elements of lettering, calligraphy and symbols. According to Der Hacopian, . . .

In retrospect, I can see the source of my latticework. Once, when I was fifteen, my mom's patches of crochet, which was laid on the table caught my attention. I was tempted to lay them on each other, and rotate them on different directions. The variations of lines and interwoven patterns were fascinating and the beauty of it remained imprinted on my memory.[80]

His symbolism with scattered letters does not convey any specific textual meaning but simply evokes the idea or sensation of written words. This calls

---

[79] Juan Flores, *The Diaspora Strikes Back: Caribeño Tales of Learning and Turning* (New York: Taylor and Francis, 2009), p. 25. This is why I have included my lived experiences in this book. As someone who grew up in the working class and moved up to the middle class, my experiences are very different from those of some of the elite Iranian Armenians.

[80] Der Hacopian and Pakbaz, *The Presence of the Absent Artist*, p. 157.

Figure 3.1 Garnik Der Hacopian, *Disintegration*, mixed media with cement on wood panel, 1995. Courtesy of the artist.

attention to the symbolic aspect of language, which can highlight the meaning of a word or make it appear meaningless and absurd in a different context. This symbolism is clear in his work *Disintegration* (Figure 3.1).

Words are scattered all over the surface of the painting, without any discernible pattern or grouping. The play on the word 'disintegration' is a reminder of diasporic people who are required to shed their heritage, traditions and language in order to fully integrate into the host nation's society. Der Hacopian works with letters, words and language as a symbolic medium that only acquires meaning when society imposes meaning onto it. The work also references his multilingual, hybrid identity, which itself destabilises language, dichotomies, or hierarchies. Der Hacopian's *Disintegration* seems to be taking us . . .

> . . . deep into the political unconscious of a nation that is nominally imagined as a disembodied abstraction [. . .]. What one can describe, however, is its construction of desire in relation to fantasies of power and impotence. [. . .] What the picture awakens our desire to see, as Lacan might put it, is exactly

what it cannot show. This impotence is what gives it whatever specific power it has.[81]

Like other ethnic groups in Iran and the US, Iranian Armenians gradually become symbolic ethnics who do not need to rely on ethnic-specific groups and institutions to conduct their daily lives. Their ethnicity is more of an expressive, voluntary affiliation pursued spiritually, changing in response to their environment and circumstances. As opposed to the less transnational Iranian Armenians where social inclusion depends on affiliation with the Armenian Apostolic church and the spoken Armenian language, the transnational ones manifest Armenianness more symbolically, through an awareness of their origins, a nostalgia for the past and an understanding of a shared history, culture and traditions. They feel no obligation to live in Armenian culture, but endeavour to preserve it. They are symbolically affiliated with the homeland of Armenia regarding their shared history and make this affiliation publicly visible by enacting their ethnicity through rites of passage and the observances of religious holidays with family members, Armenian traditions, dialogues and Armenian food, but they are simultaneously immersed in their host cultures, too.

[81] Mitchell, 'What Do Pictures Really Want?' p. 78.

4

HISTORY, MEMORY AND COLLECTIVE CONSCIOUSNESS

The 23rd April – that particular day in the calendar Iranian Armenian schools every year commemorate the anniversary of the Armenian Genocide. I remember that, when I was an elementary school student, our Armenian teachers would coordinate with the Apostolic Church to take us to the service. My elementary school was the Arax Armenian Girls' School; hence, the closest church to the school was the Surb Sarkis Church on Karim Khan Zand Street. My friends and I would line up together with all other classes and walk from our school to the church. Our teachers would also provide us with flowers to place on the gravestone of some important Armenian figure or the victims of the Genocide in the courtyard of the church. My middle school years were spent in the Kooshesh Girls' School, and we had a church adjacent to our building which made it much easier for us to walk to the service. And my high school was the Tovmasian Girls' High School, also in walking distance from the Surb Targmanch'ats Apostolic Church in Zarkish. This was a routine in all Armenian schools every year.

Building and maintaining collective identity is based on shared consciousness, memory and knowledge. Historical knowledge of the homeland is a major facet of identity for a minoritised diasporic community such as the Armenians. 'Collective consciousness' implies a consciousness that is both internal to the individual and shared by an entire community. Social theorists such as Emile Durkheim and psychoanalysts such as Carl Jung have delineated the ways in which an autonomous individual identifies with their larger community; they believed collective consciousness to be the internal representation of external forces exerted on individuals and assimilated into their consciousness. Following Durkheim's ideas, societies and communities are constantly influenced by people who are no longer alive but who have influenced the consciousness of the society or community. He posits that any given society consists of the characteristics of individuals who compose it; however, the whole may be different from the sum of those individuals. Durkheim postulates that there are certain conditions imposed on members to form a group identity, and that these conditions were established long before the current members of society were born. Hence, group identity and consciousness are always greater than individual identity.[1]

In addition to Durkheim's theories, Jung's notion of the 'collective unconscious' was a major turning point in the development of psychoanalysis. Jung argued for the existence of a pre-experiential set of 'mythological motifs, combinations of ideas or images which can be found in the myths of one's own folk or in those of other races', which yield 'a collective meaning, a meaning which is the common property of mankind'.[2] This means that, although individuals are unaware of their unconscious, it nevertheless exerts control over their behaviours, desires and drives. Hence, the unconscious is intertwined closely with the individual's consciousness. The Jungian 'collective unconscious', alongside the 'collective consciousness', evokes an original set of archetypes common to all members of a group, out of which they formulate meanings, contexts, memories and patterns.

In *The Collective Memory*, philosopher and sociologist Maurice Halbwachs also writes: 'While the collective memory endures and draws strength from its base in a coherent body of people, it is individuals as group members who remember'.[3] According to this definition, collective memory is not an inherent or a mystical group mind; rather, it is a socially constructed notion. There can

---

[1] See Emile Durkheim, *Rules for the Sociological Method and Selected Texts on Sociology and Its Method*, ed. Steven Lukes, transl. William D. Halls (New York: Free Press. 1982).

[2] Carl G. Jung, *Civilization in Transition: The Collected Works of C. G. Jung, Volume 10*. 2nd ed. (Princeton, NJ: Princeton University Press, 1970), p. 322.

[3] Maurice Halbwachs, *The Collective Memory* (Harper and Row, 1980), p. 84.

be as many collective memories as there are groups and institutions – social classes, families, associations and corporations – in a society. While it is true that individuals are the ones who remember, the location of these individuals in a group context is also important in how they recreate the past. According to Halbwachs, '[e]very collective memory requires the support of a group delimited in space and time'.[4] Regarding time and historical memory, individuals do not remember events directly but are stimulated through reading, listening, commemorating, or celebrating common deeds or accomplishments of departed members. Hence, various social institutions or individuals interpret the past differently.

Iranian Armenian diasporic cultural productions explore the shared, collective memories of their community by what cannot be remembered, what cannot be forgotten, and what simply cannot be disavowed. In such a world, a single experience evokes ties to the past, present and future. Trauma transcends the bounds of physical space and time in these works. Such representations of a traumatic past surface in Sato A.'s poetry where she weaves together Armenian history, Christianity and a call for justice:

Armenian history,
Unrepeatable,
Full of heroic pride,
Patiently patience,
You are full of bloody pages
My history.

Unseen and ignored
My existence,
You are sanctified by the ruins
My holiness,
You, still bearing the cross of strength
Crucifixion
Awakened with the smell of May
My resurrection.

[4] Ibid.

A call for justice,
An unwavering claimant,
My history full of triumph.

You, my undefeated
Sacred history.[5]

These works in all aspects are products of unique configurations of reality as contextualised by the diasporic Iranian Armenian individual. Living in a host nation with limited rights, Iranian Armenians in their diasporic practices are shaped by their ethnic and cultural affiliations and shared experiences, all of which help them survive.

With various moments of relocation and dispersion, Armenians have defined their identities in accordance with their new environment's norms. In this process of self-definition, some assimilated into the new norms of their host nation, while others attempted to resume their Armenian identity. In some cases, Iranian Armenians perceived Muslim Iranians as the other, while the opposite was also true. Cultural assimilation and alienation became the two choices Iranian Armenians faced and with which they continue to struggle. Incorporating details about Armenia – its history and its cultural traditions – into narrative and art became the practice by which authors and artists preserve Armenian culture. As Armenian author Lorne Shirinian writes, '[m]emory is not only an individual, collective, and social phenomenon; it is a cultural one as well'.[6] As a diasporic Armenian writer, Shirinian feels that it is his responsibility to write 'this absence of memory', even though this 'relationship to [the] past is one of disconnections'.[7] However, amid disconnections and displaced stories, Iranian Armenian diasporic authors and artists recover the past, imagine and recreate it. This re-imagination is not devoid of the host nation's influences.

---

[5] Sato A., 'Hayots' badmutyoun' (Armenian History), *Hrajeshtits araj* (*Before Farewell*) (Tehran: Nayiri Publishing House, 2002), p. 10.

[6] Lorne Shirinian, *The Landscape of Memory: Perspectives on the Armenian Diaspora* (Kingston, ON: Bule Heron Press, 2004), p. 35.

[7] Ibid. p. 38.

Shared Memories and Folktales

In Iranian Armenian cultural productions, diaspora is more than just a biographical context or social setting. It constitutes a common ground among members of the Iranian Armenian community. Diasporic Iranian Armenian artists and writers frequently refer to historical moments, folk music and art, traditions, rituals and writings that shape Armenian cultural heritage and collective consciousness. As they keep reaching back to the past, they also reshape their present. Creating their personal narratives, they recreate the collective story, too. A notable example is Arby Ovanessian's *Ghara Kelisa* or *Lebbaeus Whose Surname Was Thaddaeus*, which incorporates Armenian church music and folk songs as its background score.[8] The film also engages other images and motifs central to Armenian cultural consciousness: the church bells tolling, Armenian traditional architecture, Armenian symbols, traditional Armenian folk song and dance, Armenian language, kebabs over the fire, Armenian coffee and a woman in traditional Armenian costume. In his film *Cheshmeh* (1972), Ovanessian features similar music – church music, church bells and the music of Komitas (Soghomon Soghomonian, 1869–1935, from the Ottoman Empire), an ethno-musicologist and composer who created the basis for a distinctive national musical style in Armenia.

Within Armenian cultural heritage, one of the most significant songs that has shaped Armenian communities for many decades is 'Yerevani sirun aghjik' (Beautiful Girl from Yerevan). The composition has been recorded by many Armenian singers in various styles, including the Iranian Armenian American singers Vigen Derderian and Andy Madadian. The original music is by Arno Babajanyan and the lyrics by Vladimir Harutyunyan:

> Beautiful girl from Yerevan, with your arched eyebrows,
> I know for sure that you were born just for me,
> The wine in my hand with sweet games, I call you,
> Come on with your coquettishness, with your dance, why are you torturing me?
> You have a sweet young lover like me,
> Beautiful girl from Yerevan, what else do you have to worry about?

---

[8] Ovanessian, *Ghara Kelisa*.

I became an *ashugh* [troubadour], calling you, where are you my precious,
I am always waiting for you in the flower garden of my love.
The wine in my hand with sweet games, I call you,
Come on with your coquettishness, with your dance, why are you torturing me?
You have a sweet young lover like me,
Beautiful girl from Yerevan, what else do you have to worry about?

While both Vigen and Andy sang many of their songs in Persian, they also adopted and adapted songs from the Armenian homeland, including this one. This clearly indicates their loyalty to their homeland, but more importantly it manifests shared history, culture and folk music in the works of diasporic Iranian Armenians and within the homeland. Interestingly, Vigen alternates the word 'Yerevan' with 'Armenia' in his adaptation, invoking the homeland as a whole in a pop rendition of the folk song. Following Vigen, Andy also uses a guitar in his dance-pop rendition.

Similarly, creating the busts of two prominent and influential figures for Armenian identity and history, Lilith Terian (1931–2019), an Iranian Armenian sculptor referred to as 'the mother of modern Iranian sculpture', honours her Armenian ancestors by evoking the collective shared consciousness. Drawing on the significance of important figures in Armenian cultural heritage, Terian has created a memorial of Mesrop Mashtots', the inventor of the Armenian alphabet, that was installed in the Surb Targmanch'ats (Holy Translators) Church in Tehran in 1992 (Figure 4.1). Mesrop Mashtots' as the teacher who gave Armenians their alphabet and primary language tool, the cornerstone of Armenianness, is celebrated annually in Iranian Armenian schools.

Terian has also sculpted Yeprem Davitian (known as Yeprem Khan), an Iranian Armenian revolutionary who was active during the Constitutional Revolution of 1905–11 (Figure 4.2). This sculpture was installed in the Surb Astvatsatsin (Holy Mary) Church of Tehran in 1968. Yeprem Khan is known as a hybrid and bicultural figure. In sculpting his bust and honouring his endeavours in Iranian history, Terian acknowledges her own Iranian Armenianness, as well as his. For his contribution to the Constitutional Revolution, Yeprem Khan was made the Chief of Police of Tehran, an unusual role for a Christian in a Muslim country (technically forbidden under custom of Islamic law). Yeprem Khan was also

Figure 4.1 Lilith Terian, *Mesrop Mashtots'*, installed in the Surb Targmanch'ats Church in Tehran in 1992. Courtesy of the author's uncle and cousin, Vanik and Argin Nazari.

promoted by the Dashnaks as an exemplary martyr for the constitutional revolution, even though he had left the party in the years leading up to his assassination.[9] Yeprem Khan advocated for the global class struggle and encouraged Iranian Armenians to think of themselves as Iranian first and foremost. He emphasised that he held his Iranian identity above his Christian Armenian identity, especially when opponents questioned the legitimacy of non-Muslims holding such high office.[10] After his death, his

[9] Berberian, *Armenians and the Iranian Constitutional Revolution of 1905–1911*, p. 156. Another important figure is Mirza Malkum Khan; although this is controversial because he converted to Islam and also did not play an active role in the constitution, he was certainly a major influence on the constitutionalists, and his activism over many decades led to the constitutional movement.

[10] Ibid. p. 150. It is important that he was from Ganja, not modern Iran. That he called himself Iranian may have been because many Azerbaijanis (then called Muslim Tatars) in Russia still called themselves Iranian as well, despite nearly a century of Russian rule, and it points to the non-rigid nature of identity at the time.

Figure 4.2 Lilith Terian, *Yeprem Khan*, installed in the Surb Astvatsatsin Church in Tehran in 1968. Courtesy of the author's uncle and cousin, Vanik and Argin Nazari.

property was donated to the Armenian community, and it now hosts the Surb Astvatsatsin Church on Mirza Kuchik Khan Street in Tehran. The compound encompasses two schools and a monument of Yeprem Khan at the entrance, yet only the church is open at this time.[11]

Terian was born in old Tehran but traced her ancestral roots back to the Armenians deported to Iran by Shah Abbas in the seventeenth century. She introduced the modern art of sculpture to the Iranian educational system and was one of the founders of the Faculty of Decorative Arts, where she served as professor for twenty-three years. Some of today's famous Iranian sculptors were her students. Her works can be seen everywhere in the country, and they are almost obligatory on the terrain of Armenian churches and

---

[11] Barry, *Armenian Christians in Iran*, p. 83.

cultural centres. She was a sculptor and painter whose worldview drew on the traditions of Armenian, Persian and European cultures.[12]

This dedication and connection to Armenian heritage can also be found in literature. In Zoya Pirzad's short story 'A Day Before Easter', the protagonist Edmond would hear 'the soft shooshing static of Radio Armenia' during evening as he rested in his bedroom.[13] For Edmond's father, the homeland is evoked by a sense of shared political belonging, cultivated by listening to Radio Armenia as well as other factors such as myth, symbols and cultural markers. In this story, Iranian Armenians endeavour to maintain their heritage in an exclusionary context. Such anti-Armenian attitudes in a predominantly Muslim coastal town can be summed up in a school janitor's declaration: 'I know these people. They take up all the air and then act as though we don't even exist'.[14] This comment represents many societies' natural predisposition to reject and alienate minoritised cultures.

Rosemary H. Cohen also explores the theme of shared intergenerational memory and connections to the homeland in *The Survivor*. In one scene, Cohen recounts her father's return to Iran from business in Russia and Armenia, telling them about their homeland and Mount Ararat.[15] She also recalls her brother, Nicola, bringing her small flat stones from the shores of Armenia's Arax River whose 'water was so blue and clear that he saw this stone underwater and grabbed it for me. The stone had a soft surface and beautiful lines traced on it. I looked at it and I felt the pure water of my ancestors' river running through my fingers'.[16] Mount Ararat and Mount Masis are two common symbols of beauty, integrity and perseverance that are prevalent in Armenian works. An important aspect of Armenian identity concerns the belief that Noah and his descendants visited the homeland of Armenia and that Noah's Ark landed on Mount Ararat in Armenia. The term 'Armenia' is derived from Armina – a Greek and Persian term – while Armenians call

[12] Ruben Gyulmisarian, 'Irani kandakagortsutyan mayr-e: inch'pes Lilith Terian-e gravets' Tehran-e' (The Mother of Iranian Sculpture: How Lilith Terian Attracted Tehran), *Sputnik Armenian*, 12 March 2019, https://armeniasputnik.am/columnists/20190312/17663989/iran-i-kandakagorcutyan-mayry-inchpes-lilit-teryany-gravec-tehran-y.html

[13] Pirzad, *The Space Between Us*, p. 2; Pirzad, 'Yik Ruz Qabl az 'iyd-i Pak', p. 226.

[14] Ibid. p. 36.

[15] Cohen, *The Survivor*, p. 3.

[16] Ibid. pp. 7–8.

themselves 'Hay' and their country 'Hayastan'.[17] The Arax River is one of the most utilised references in Armenian collective memory and appears in other works such as Leonardo Alishan's 'Armenia Sings to the Black Sea' in his *Dancing Barefoot on Broken Glass*:

> Arax, my bloodstream, sings my life
> To me. Wolves drink from the banks
> Of Arax, when you, my lost lover, my sea,
> Gone with the leaf and the wind,
> Are aeons of annals away,
> The memory of motherhood
> In an ancient woman's leather breasts.[18]

References to wolves drinking from Arax's bloodstream, woven into themes of motherhood, recall the turbulent history of the motherland, histories of relocation and the 1915 Genocide. Moreover, Armenians who were deported in 1603 were forced to swim across the Arax; of course, many drowned.[19] Crossing the Arax River therefore has symbolic meaning in the collective memory of some Iranian Armenians. In the same book, in a poem titled 'Anahit as Armenia', Alishan pays tribute to Anahit:

> Papa broke the bread in
> Half. This aroma. I remembered
> You. A bone, somewhere in me,
> Broke. Hungry, I kissed mama
> Good-night and left. All night
> I tossed in my sleep, dreaming
> Of your scent, of mama's hair.
> I have never known you, Anahit,
> But I know your perfume well.[20]

---

[17] Kimball, *Angle of Vision*, p. 28. The Arax River is also important in Azerbaijani national imagining. This is significant in shared but exclusive national identities and geographies.

[18] Leonardo Alishan, 'Armenia Sings to the Black Sea', *Dancing Barefoot on Broken Glass* (New York: Ashod Press, 1991), pp. 38–39.

[19] See Arakel of Tabriz, *Book of History*, transl. and annot. George Bournoutian (Costa Mesa, CA: Mazda Publishers, 2010).

[20] Alishan, 'Anahit as Armenia', p. 44.

Drawing from mythology, Alishan references the goddess of fertility, healing and wisdom, Anahit. These ruminations remind the reader of Alishan's hybrid identity, as Anahit is most likely borrowed from Iranian mythology by way of the healing goddess Anahita. This also references the intertwining of two cultures – Armenian and Iranian – and their many shared historical junctures. While these cultural entanglements are inevitable, Alishan refers to Anahit as the homeland, Armenia. By drawing a parallel between the present-though-absent Anahit and the homeland, Alishan captures the hope and emotion involved in yearning for the rejuvenation of his community. These references to folktales, geography and mythology indicate that, while diaspora communities rely on their shared memories and knowledge of the homeland, knowledge of the past is insufficient to legitimise present experiences, unless they become performative through commemorative ceremonies and traditions.[21]

References to various Armenian literary, religious and historical texts appear throughout Iranian Armenian diasporic cultural productions. A common historical theme concerns the 1915 Armenian Genocide and the memorial ceremony, which are often presented in character conversations. Likewise, religion and religious texts, ecclesiastical words, phrases and prayers, or references to Jesus Christ and the Virgin Mary are featured in many works. These references are an important counter-tactic to challenge Iranian Armenian representation in Iranian cultural productions. Within many Iranian works, Armenians are stereotyped as the foreigner with an accent, drinking too much coffee or alcohol.

An excellent example of these trends to highlight Armenian traditions is presented in Pirzad's novel *Chiragh-ha ra man khamush mikunam* (*Things Left Unsaid*). After her secret desire for an affair with Emile, Pirzad's Clarice attends church, prays and reads from the Bible. In the English translation, all translated Armenian scripture is rendered in all capitals: 'VIRGIN MARY, MOURNFUL MOTHER / I DID ADJURE THEE BY THE WOUNDS OF THY SON / AND THOU DIDST RESTORE TO ME MY CHILD'.[22]

---

[21] Paul Connerton, *How Societies Remember* (Cambridge: Cambridge University Press, 1989), pp. 4–5.

[22] Pirzad, *Things We Left Unsaid*, pp. 249–50; Pirzad, *Chiragh-ha ra man khamush mikunam*, p. 221.

Among the bold and italic typeset throughout the story, Pirzad places biblical phrases in quotation marks and italicises them.[23] This may imply the otherness of Armenian culture, language and religion, but it also shows that going to church brings peace to Clarice, prompting her to experience Abadan as a beautiful city.[24]

Pirzad's Clarice reads the Armenian national poet-laureate Hovhanness Tumanyan's (1869–1923) poem 'Parvana' to her children.[25] The references to Tumanyan, Sayat Nova (1722–95) and Sardo – with their emphasis on the importance of love – reinforce Clarice's struggles in choosing between love and duty.[26] Pirzad's integration of Armenian literature into her works echoes efforts by other Iranian Armenian diasporic artists and authors. In Nerses D. Mesrobian's poetry, literary, cultural, national and religious icons such as Sayat Nova, Paruyr Sevak, Yeghishe Charents, Narekatsi, Siamanto and Mesrob Mashtots' play a significant role.[27] Similarly, Emmanuel P. Vardanyan sheds light on this concept in his *The Well of Ararat*, where he writes about 'Ashig Jivany', another Armenian troubadour who sang poems at wedding ceremonies.[28]

These Iranian Armenian cultural productions draw on a rich cultural, historical and literary heritage to contextualise the narratives and infuse them with deeper levels of significance. They place their works in conversation with other works through a mosaic of allusions, direct quotations and intertextual references. Intertextuality, as propounded by Julia Kristeva in her essay 'Word, Dialogue, and Novel', refers to how a single work engages in a dialogue with other texts, or intertexts, that creates complex, layered meanings. Intertextuality manifests itself through symbolism, metaphors, allusions and other rhetorical figures. According to Kristeva, 'any text is constructed

---

[23] Ibid. p. 250.

[24] Ibid. p. 244.

[25] Ibid. p. 226.

[26] Anahid Ojakians, '*Chiragh-ha ra man khamush mikunam*', *Namih Farhangistan* 21 (2003), pp. 166–74. Sayat Nova, who was born Harutyun Sayatyan, was an Armenian poet, musician and an *ashuq* (derived from the Persian word *ashiq* denoting troubadour musicianship). Sayat Nova has songs in Armenian, Georgian, Azerbaijani and Persian.

[27] Nerses D. Mesrobian, 'Who has Seen?' *Karot-e Hayi* (*Armenian Longing*) (Glendale, CA: Yerevan Printing, 2014), p. 29.

[28] Vardanyan, *The Well of Ararat*, p. 97.

as a mosaic of quotations; any text is the absorption and transformation of another'.[29] Each text simultaneously retains its original voice and acquires additional resonances in relation to other texts, establishing a multiplication of meaning that Kristeva terms 'ambivalence'.[30] Using intertextual references, writers can transcend the limitations of history and culture and create compound, nuanced meanings.

For instance, Arby Ovanessian's *Cheshmeh* (*The Spring*, 1972) is a free adaptation of Armenian author Megrditch Armin's story 'Cheshmeh Highnar' (Highnar's Spring). Ovanessian's adaptation features an Armenian actor, Aramais Vartan Yousefians (also known as Arman), and Julfa in Isfahan serves as the main cinematic location.[31] As Ovanessian expressed, 'I think my film is in Armin's book, but Armin's book is not in my film. This is only because of the difference in our goals. The same encounters, the same events, and the same acquaintances exist, but the values and valuations differ'.[32] Undoubtedly, the primary level of intertextuality here is Ovanessian's representation of his source material (literature) in his own medium of film. Beyond this, multiple layers of cinematic intertextuality fittingly represent diaspora as an inherently multivocal experience that requires the simultaneous negotiation of two or more cultures.

Kamal Abdel-Malek also analyses diasporic liminality and writers' use of intertextuality in 'Exile and Life on Border Lines'. In his exploration of intertextuality, Abdel-Malek argues that the trauma of war and exile have shaped the individual and collective consciousness of diasporic communities, infusing their writings with a haunting sense of loss.[33] This sense of loss and the subsequent trauma manifests itself in poems about or references to the 1915 Genocide in Iranian Armenian cultural productions. Through their

---

[29] Julia Kristeva, 'Word, Dialogue, and Novel', *Desire in Language: A Semiotic Approach to Literature and Art*, ed. Leon S. Roudiez (New York: Columbia University Press, 1980), p. 66.

[30] Ibid. p. 73.

[31] Ovanessian, *Cheshmeh* (*The Spring*).

[32] B. N., 'Chishmih-yi hamishih jushan' (The Ever-Boiling Spring), *Theater and Cinema of Arby Ovanessian*, ed. Majid Lashkari (Tehran: Ruzanih Publications, 2014), p. 741.

[33] Kamal Abdel-Malek, 'Exile and Life on Border Lines', *The Rhetoric of Violence: Arab-Jewish Encounters in Contemporary Palestinian Literature and Film* (New York: Palgrave Macmillan, 2005), p. 35.

skilful use of intertextuality, Iranian Armenian diaspora authors and artists dialogue not only with past Armenian works but also with Iranian works and ultimately with their own trauma and diasporic identity. In doing so, they lay claim to the diverse literary and cultural streams that feed their own hybridised identity. For diasporic Iranian Armenian authors and artists, intertextuality helps evoke the liminality that diasporic communities experience as they live between cultures, languages and literary traditions. Techniques of intertextuality help convey the layered, nuanced multivocality of diaspora. Intertextuality empowers artists and writers to immortalise their works and to express the legacies of profound trauma and suffering. Similarly, Win-chen Ouyang explores the semiotic significance of intertextuality in 'Semiology of Madness', describing intertextual references as a 'network of signs' that produces intricate webs of meaning.[34] Ouyang argues that diaspora writers employ complex symbolism, metaphors and intertextual references to reconstruct their identities and preserve their ancestral memories and those of their homelands.[35] In this sense, Iranian Armenian diasporic cultural productions explore how a range of texts from diverse perspectives and periods interact with one another to represent multiple layers of meaning about their people's sufferings, trauma and existence.

The Cornerstone of Armenian Diasporic Identity: The 1915 Genocide

Flexibility and adaptability are at the core of Armenian collective memory; however, the 1915 Genocide created a rift in this collective memory, as Aghop Der-Karabetian writes. Armenians, who had survived multitudes of superpowers and conquering armies, failed to prevent this catastrophe, which was (and is) a threat to their existence. This feeling of failure has led to collective self-blame. Armenians lost their historical homeland, art, architecture and culture. They were dehumanised as a disposable and worthless people; they lost their dignity and identity.[36] The Genocide laid the ground for a unified nation-state carved out of a dying empire. To achieve

---

[34] Win-chen Ouyang, 'Semiology of Madness', *Politics of Nostalgia in the Arabic Novel: Nation-State, Modernity and Tradition* (Edinburgh: Edinburgh University Press, 2013), p. 99.

[35] Ibid. p. 96.

[36] Der-Karabetian, *Armenian Ethnic Identity in Context*, 230.

this unification for the emergence of the new nation-state, the eradication of the natives and, consequently, the distortion of history were crucial. According to historian and scholar of Armenian Genocide Ronald Grigor Suny, '[c]oming to terms with that history, on the other hand, can have the salutary effect of questioning continued policies of ethnic homogenization and refusal to recognize the claims and rights of those peoples, minorities or diasporas – Aborigines, Native Americans, Kurds, Palestinians, or Armenians – who refuse to disappear'.[37] To keep this history alive and accurate, the ethnic minoritised populations create art and write the impossible.

Today, Armenian authors' and artists' attempts to make sense of the Genocide can be viewed as a way to cope with this blow to Armenian survival. According to Shirinian, 'Armenian diaspora writers in particular find themselves in a double bind: it is almost impossible to write fiction about Armenian Genocide, yet it is impossible to not to write about it. Being a witness through imagination is perhaps the only world possible for Armenian writers of the second and later generations who did not suffer the Genocide'.[38] Successive generations of Armenian writers 'bear witness for the witnesses'.[39]

In this sense, the most significant performance of collective memory occurs in the annual ceremony to commemorate the 1915 Armenian Genocide. In the post-Genocide twenty-first century, two-thirds of all Armenians throughout the world live in the diaspora, and the majority are either survivors or descendants of the survivors of the Genocide. While the majority of Iranian Armenians belong to the seventeenth-century population uprooted by Shah Abbas, part of the Iranian Armenian community belongs to the post-Genocide displacement, and the rest share it as part of Armenian collective consciousness. Hence, the 1915 Genocide of Armenians within the Ottoman Empire has become the cornerstone and unifying factor of modern Armenian identity, particularly for those in the diaspora. This crisis marks the definitive break from Armenia's ancestral past and homeland, which simultaneously

---

[37] Ronald Grigor Suny, 'Writing Genocide: The Fate of the Ottoman Armenians', *A Question of Genocide: Armenians and Turks at the End of the Ottoman Empire*, ed. Ronald Grigor Suny, Fatma Muge Gogek and Norman M. Naimark (Oxford: Oxford University Press, 2011), p. 42.

[38] Shirinian, *The Landscape of Memory*, p. 41.

[39] Ibid. p. 89.

refigures the past and acts as a lens through which national identity, politics and culture are reinterpreted and redefined.[40]

Therefore, for Armenians, shared history is a foundation for collective memory. This focus on collective consciousness finds its way into Marcos Grigorian's works. Influenced by the events of World War II and the massacre of Armenians and Van immigrants, including his own family, Grigorian created large canvases whose deformed subjects intensified the emotional burden of the artist's grief. Grigorian's painting *The Gate of Auschwitz* (Figure 4.3), part of a series of thirteen, artistically expresses the German Nazi regime's crimes and concentration camps. In this series, Grigorian depicts human relationships and catastrophes. His early works, including the Auschwitz murals, present a visual language that expresses anxiety and despair, conveying potent images of the cruelty of war and the inevitability of death and decay.

Grigorian's early expressionist works incorporate skilful drawing technique with mixtures of paint and ash, depicting deformed limbs and facial

Figure 4.3 Marcos Grigorian, *The Gate of Auschwitz*, *Holocaust* series, 1957–59. © Museum of Art and Literature in Yerevan.

[40] Panossian, *The Armenians*, p. 228.

features to emphasise the tragic fate of immigrants from Van and victims of the Armenian Genocide as well as the Holocaust. Through a constant reinvention of himself via his art, Grigorian 'is able to re-read, reinterpret, re-envision, and reconstruct [. . .] his culture's present as well as its past. This capacity to construct meaning and culture privileges the artist', as Gloria Anzaldúa would argue.[41]

Iranian Armenian identity is sustained through this kind of visual and textual collective awareness of history, cultural markers and roots. Pirzad's Edmond recalls the books that his father used to read, in which 'there was a strange picture. It was a photo of a hill made out of people's skulls. The heads of the Armenians who were murdered by the Ottomans'. His mother forbade him to view those books because he was just a child, but his father believed that 'child or adult, everyone has to know what tragedy befell his people'.[42] The belief that all people should be knowledgeable about their history is a dominant mindset of the entire Armenian community, including the explicit and implicit ways in which the community maintains its ties with the homeland. Because of this, Pirzad's characters make considerable ideological efforts to conceive of their communities as on a continuum of their homeland. In Pirzad's narrative, an important factor is the Armenians' annual global march on the anniversary of the 1915 Genocide (the Iranian state has recently banned this march). During this time, Iranian Armenians lobby the host nation's government on behalf of their homeland for official recognition of the Genocide. Hence, while in the diaspora and locally integrated into the social structure of the host nation, Armenians are involved in an institutional network that symbolically engages their homeland.

The widespread victimisation of the 1915 Genocide intensified a feeling of belonging based on shared suffering. The shared victimhood and collective commemoration are depicted in the poem titled 'Tkhrutyun' (Sorrow) by Leonid Sarvarian:

On the eve of 23 April, I too went to the church.
Some were loud,
Some were silent,

---

[41] Anzaldúa, *Borderlands/La Frontera*, p. 183.
[42] Pirzad, *The Space Between Us*, p. 48.

Some were pensive,
Children were crying in the yard.
Then the church bells tolled,
We felt mournful.

The person next to me greeted
The old sad man passing by us
And in an everyday tone of voice
Asked him about his health.
    The bells, the smell of incense,
    The sad man murmured.
His tears moved from his heart
Toward his eyes and voice.
A woman complained to me.
    My clothes were not suitable,
    She had come to lay flowers at the monument.
There was a touching music in the church yard,
There were conversations in the church yard,
And grief, there was grief in the church yard.
The complaining woman was in the church yard,
From the church bells,
Crying from the smell of the incense,
The sad man was in the church yard.
And overflowing with fresh flowers
The sad monument
Was silently listening to the children's cries.[43]

The annual commemoration of the Genocide – the church bells, the rituals, the flowers and the grief – all function as parts of the collective Armenian diasporic identity, regardless of whether individuals were directly impacted by the Genocide. This sense of victimhood became the cornerstone of Armenian identity and an imaginative Armenian collective consciousness. This continued until the 1970s, when another wave of Armenian radicalism emerged. Genocide publications and commemorations were major factors in advancing this

[43] Leonid Sarvarian, 'Tkhrutyun' (Sorrow), *Sirt-e Gravor* (*Written from the Heart*) (Tehran: [n. p.], 1997), p. 18.

victimhood mentality, decades after it had first developed. Four main themes dominated Armenian Genocide literature: the sense of victimhood, the notion of suffering and injustice, the experience of loss following expulsion from the homeland, and the demand for justice.[44] This shared sense of victimhood created by the Genocide transformed the diaspora into a community that identified as Genocide victims. In an attempt to lyrically address this trauma and its associated resilience, Nerses D. Mesrobian writes in his Genocide poem dated 24 April 1915 and titled 'Aprilyan sev oreri 95-amiyak' (The 95th Anniversary of the Dark April Days):

> April Days
> Days of slaughter,
> All humanity
> A living witness,
> With no guilt, builders,
> And intellectuals,
> Walked toward Golgotha
> But endured, and lived,
> Because they were born
> To live . . .
> And so
> They lived,
> They live,
> And will live . . .[45]

Before 1915, Armenians experienced various waves of migration and forcible relocation. Although the pre-Genocide diaspora had been linked to exile and hardship, these concepts were magnified and multiplied in the post-Genocide diaspora. For post-Genocide Armenians, diaspora was no longer based on a history of merchants, intellectuals, or political exiles, but on one of refugees and survivors. Diaspora and the homeland were no longer two parts unified within the same notion. Instead, the homeland was lost and/or decimated,

---

[44] Panossian, *The Armenians*, pp. 236–38.
[45] Nerses D. Mesrobian, 'Aprilyan sev oreri 95-amiyak' (The 95th Anniversary of the Dark April Days), *Karot-e Hayi* (*Armenian Longing*) (Glendale, CA: Yerevan Printing, 2014), p. 64.

with no option to return – a destruction of the earlier *nostos*. Western Armenia was intensely impacted by the Genocide. Hence, Western Armenians acquired new layers, not only as victims of the Genocide, but also as victims condemned to live in the diaspora.[46]

For diasporic communities, in Kath Woodward's words, '[t]he place left retains importance in shaping collective and individual identities'.[47] This is the mythical, imaginary, furtive homeland to which the diasporic individual is tied, while living the everyday local life in the host nation.[48] These multiple affiliations abate the construction of multiple identities. Stuart Hall notes:

> Diaspora refers to the scattering and dispersal of people who will never lit-erally be able to return to the places from which they came [. . .] and who have succeeded in remaking themselves and fashioning new kinds of cultural identity by consciously or unconsciously drawing on more than one cultural repertoire [. . .] They are people who belong to more than one world, speak more than one language (literally and metaphorically); inhabit more than one identity [. . .] They speak from the in-between of different cultures, always unsettling the assumptions of one culture from the perspective of the other, and thus finding ways of being both the same as and different from the others amongst whom they live [. . .] They represent new kinds of identities.[49]

As a dispersed community that can never return to the same home due to catastrophic loss, Armenians craft new identities in the diaspora by draw-ing on their shared history, memories and cultural markers. For them, the Genocide was a turning point. Living in the diaspora is seen as an effect and simultaneous continuation of the Genocide. For many Armenians, the Genocide signifies the loss of homeland followed by the loss of identity due to the threat of cultural assimilation in a foreign nation. This experience of losing the homeland and, by extension, deeply-rooted ancestral identities is

---

[46] Panossian, *The Armenians*, p. 239. Its tenuousness is symbolic in Western Armenian, such as UNESCO's listing of Western Armenian as an endangered language, reflecting the lasting and ongoing impact of the Genocide for some Western Armenians speakers.

[47] Kath Woodward, *Understanding Identity* (London: Arnold, 2002), p. 48.

[48] Brah, *Cartographies of Diaspora*, p. 192.

[49] Quoted in Mills, 'Connecting Communities', p. 253.

a process that Razmik Panossian terms 'the white massacre'.[50] While Armenian provinces and territories were at the centre of political nationalist programmes before 1915, the existence of the land itself was taken for granted. A renewed focus on the repossession of any properties tied to the ancestral homeland occurred after the Genocide. In this respect, Armenian identity became synonymous with a lost homeland that needed to be recovered. This impacted Armenian political identity, particularly after the 1970s.[51] Consequently, nation, sovereignty and territory acquired new meanings – often disappointing and always frustrating. In a poem titled 'What Shall We Do?' Nerses D. Mesrobian writes about his frustration with the constant forced and voluntary migrations of Armenians:

> They leave the country
>> Our sons, what shall we do?
> It is gloomy, and cloudy
>> The universe, what shall we do?
> We dreamt across oceans and seas.
>> We didn't even have a river,
> Left discarded, the wind blew
>> Armenian lands, what shall we do?[52]

The post-Genocide generation of Armenians focused further on the Genocide as they aged. Their younger years had been focused on basic survival; yet, as time passed, they began reliving the pain of their youth and childhood. They realised the fullness of their losses once they married and had children, remembering their own childhood as orphans, or the sacrifices of their parents. Some responded to this trauma with internal repression – attempting not to think about or discuss the Genocide – in hopes that the past would not threaten the stability of their present emotional well-being.[53] In addition,

---

[50] Panossian, *The Armenians*, p. 239. In the context of US racial politics, white massacre may have a subtle racial element to it.

[51] Ibid. pp. 240–41.

[52] Mesrobian, 'What Shall We Do?' p. 30.

[53] Donald E. Miller and Lorna Touryan Miller, *Survivors: An Oral History of the Armenian Genocide* (Berkeley, Los Angeles and London: University of California Press, 1993), pp. 155–58.

there was no proper framework for them to talk about it until the 1960s, when they began to mention the Genocide as they spoke of *medz yeghern* (literally, the great evil crime). It was only after the word 'genocide' was coined in the 1940s that Armenians were really able to make some sense of the organised and systemic nature of what had happened. The 1965 protest in Yerevan was a catalyst and remains a central moment in the cause of Genocide recognition, a full two generations after the event.

Armenians in Iran were not directly targeted in the 1915 Genocide, but there were exceptions. Vartan Gregorian's 'grandmother was among those who fled with her three remaining children. Her two sisters, Manooshag (Violet) and Sophia, were part of the exodus. [His] grandmother and her sisters never spoke about their husbands and their fate. Were they killed? Had they abandoned them?'[54] While this group, including Gregorian's grandmother, felt outrage, anger and the fires of resentment burning deep within their conscience, their anger did not manifest itself in political action to redress the injustice and pain.[55] Instead, they intentionally tried to avoid more pain as a survival tactic – a very common approach among people who are caught between worlds.[56] Gregorian illustrates these conflicting emotions beautifully in the following passage:

> Even though she was a churchgoing, fervent Christian, my grandmother seemed dazed by the calamities visited upon her by the loss of her husband, loss of six of her seven children, loss of her home and village, loss of a grandson. I had the impression, as I grew up, that she was angry at God or mystified by His actions, and that she lived to protest against Him. Her rudimentary argument with God was that since He is the Author, or at least it is with His consent that events take place in this world, He could have preserved at least some of her children, since she was not so sinful to deserve such a severe punishment. Her grief was private. She never complained; she cried for her sorrow, she cried for her children only in private. Her plight broke my heart.[57]

[54] Gregorian, *The Road to Home*, p. 11.
[55] Miller and Miller, *Survivors*, pp. 158–160.
[56] Anzaldúa, *Borderlands/La Frontera*, p. 61.
[57] Gregorian, *The Road to Home*, pp. 11–12.

This passage highlights Gregorian's grandmother's coping mechanism of rationalising the Genocide within a religious context. Believing that the Genocide was a punishment from God, many post-Genocide Armenians found consolation in knowing that at least they no longer had to suffer, due to the resulting exodus from Turkey.[58]

Another important dimension of the Genocide highlighted in Gregorian's writing is its impact on women and children. While the entire population suffered, women's experiences were significantly different. Early on during the deportation, many men were killed, leaving their wives and children behind. Faced with brutal and violent deaths, women also suffered the physical and psychological traumas of being raped, losing their children and being forced to make excruciating decisions; for example, whether to value their own lives over their children's, making decisions about who had a greater chance of survival, or which child should be preferred, and whether it was possible to live with the guilt of sacrificing their children. Faced with such hardships, many women drowned themselves in the Euphrates River, often after giving their food and water rations to their children. These women, bearing the overwhelming burden of defeat, gave up the struggle and took their own lives in anticipation of being killed. These tragic decisions embody the Genocide's grotesqueness.[59]

This shared collective consciousness about children and women's predicament emerges in Alishan's poetry. In 'An Armenian Nightmare', he touches on the calamity that befell the Armenian population during the Genocide:

Women wrapped in black
Wail on the shore,

Old men stare at the sea
And the driftwood:

Remains of the offering
The sea received with raised hands.

---

[58] Miller and Miller, *Survivors*, p. 160.

[59] Ibid. pp. 94–104.

My mother pregnant with me,
My wife pregnant with my son,

Both wrapped in black,
Both wailing on the shore.[60]

In contrast to the group experiencing a more private grief, another group of furious Armenians responded to their own rage and resentment with political or retaliatory expressions that often involved a return to the home-land – voluntary return migration. Others have chosen reconciliation and forgiveness, and while they do not deny the horrors of the Genocide, they have come to terms with their childhood trauma. Finally, there is a popula-tion of Armenians who despair over the violence that shattered their lives, yet they yield to resignation. Emotionally, they lack the strength to rise above their past.[61] In her book *The Survivor*, Cohen chronicles the story of an Armenian family in Iran during the Genocide. She writes about Nazan, who took refuge in Masht Agha's household for one and a half years but was abused and raped. In response, Nazan talks about the Genocide with great resignation:

> While listening, I was amazed at how she had changed. How could she retell the story so indifferently? Was the savagery a contaminating disease? Had we caught a virus from the Turks? Were these men and women like this before the massacre or did the massacre change them? I remembered her as a nice person but now I saw a stranger in front of me. Then I remembered the Chief of the Turks that I had met. He seemed to be a good person. What the soldiers did, was it human nature or was it from orders coming from higher up?[62]

Cohen also recalls hearing about the horrors of the Genocide happening to Armenians in the Iranian city of Khoy. However, the Iranian government did not heed notices about what was happening to its Armenian minoritised

---

[60] Alishan, 'An Armenian Nightmare', p. 65.
[61] Miller and Miller, *Survivors*, pp. 158–60.
[62] Cohen, *The Survivor*, p. 108.

population. This occurred during the reign of the last Qajar king who 'cared little for his subjects, much less for the Armenians'.[63] Cohen writes:

> The Turks attacked all the Armenian houses. They separated the men from the women. Some of the local Muslim businessmen had taken the women to the bazaar so that the Turks would not harm them. Although these brave people were trying to help them, in time the women were left in the open-air court of the bazaar, with almost no food or no hygienic facilities. There were many epidemics and the older women and children were dying fast. Some friendly Muslims either took all the young and beautiful girls into their homes, or the Turkish army abducted, raped, and killed them. The men, however, were immediately taken away. Most were taken to the mountains and killed, one by one, or en masse. Most of the time, when they found a man in a house, they first killed him in front of his family and then they took the women and children away.[64]

Gregorian explores the Genocide as the cornerstone of Armenian identity, especially for those in the diaspora, and how it is commemorated by survivors' descendants in many western and Middle Eastern countries in *The Road to Home*. When he arrives in Beirut to continue his studies, faced with the post-Genocide shantytowns that housed Armenian refugees, Gregorian is surprised: 'This one housed Armenian refugees, the remnants of the World War I Armenian Genocide, and their offspring, who had survived the death march to the Syrian desert and found refuge in hospitable Arab countries, including Syria and Lebanon'.[65] While these Arab countries became a safe haven for survivors and refugees after the Genocide, the fact that they resided in the ghettos of the city demonstrates their social position. In a sense, no

---

[63] Ibid. p. 56. This part might not be historically accurate as the Ottoman Empire invaded this part of Iran early on, in October 1914, before the Ottomans had officially entered World War I and in violation of Iran's neutrality. In other words, the invasion was part of a land grab that resulted in ethnic cleansing and genocide over the next four years. However, Iran did not have an effective central government at the time – the shah was a figurehead and the majlis had been rendered redundant in 1912 when the Russians invaded. The country was effectively divided between British and Russian spheres of influence, and the shah himself was only sixteen years old.

[64] Ibid. p. 57.

[65] Gregorian, *The Road to Home*, pp. 67–68.

matter the wave of refugee displacement, each wave's minoritised position is highlighted even in the spaces where they live.

Iranian Armenians are politically and culturally connected to the Genocide. Iranian Armenian organisations promote Armenian culture and history to community members from a very young age, creating kinship along ethnic lines so that their anger equals that of the post-Genocide diaspora. In the diaspora, the recognition of the Genocide unifies Armenian communities that are otherwise divided by political, religious and cultural differences.[66] This unification and the Armenian resilience manifests itself in Almin's poem, addressed to the Turks:

> Your Turkish dynasty is a three-headed monstrous beast,
> Ottomans, Young Turks, Kemalists,
> They all massacred the Armenian race,
> And occupied my Western Armenia,
> But know and understand that the Armenian fight is eternal,
> Armenia is ours from sea to sea and with all its lands,
> Witness to the million and a half Armenian forget-me-nots immortal,
> Our Armenian history is proof of our existence.[67]

The shared collective consciousness of the Genocide unites the community, helping them manage the anxiety of living in a foreign country, away from the homeland. In a poem titled 'Aryamb yev poghpatov' (With Blood and Steel), Grish Davtian extrapolates this shared memory and how the past results in the courageous survival of Armenians in the present:

> Darkness covered the Armenian world,
> Genocide and mourning enveloped Armenia,
> The storms were roaring,
> The great hopes were living in the womb.
>
> Moments were hastily avoided,
> Firearms [cannons] were howling obituaries,
> To anyone courageous in the mountains
> The fight was bloody, the fight was unstoppable.

---

[66] Barry, *Armenian Christians in Iran*, pp. 87–88.
[67] Almin, 'Turkerin' (To the Turks), *Shk'egh Banasteghtsutyun* (*Rich Poetry*) (Tehran: Alik Publishers, 2018), p. 32.

And stone men, with hearts of stone,
With hearts of stone and wills of stone,
Bending on the mountains of Armenia
The metal song of life and death . . .

It was the end of the world with infinite chaos,
The forces ravaging the abyss and the mountain top,
The earth erupted and lava was flowing,
A volcanic eruption accumulated for centuries . . .

The clash of the good and the bad
The indestructible in the last war.
People and lands merged invincibly
Overflowing with triumphant vigour . . .

They were creating with the courage of survival,
Achieving authority and ownership.
With the mixture of blood, steel, and stone
Embarking on life from height to height.[68]

During World War I, Turkey violated Iran (particularly in the region of Azerbaijan), attacking the Armenian and Assyrian communities. Approximately 50,000 refugees from Turkish territory escaped to Iran after the Genocide.[69] Gregorian discusses this exodus: 'Following the outbreak of World War I and Ottoman and Russian invasions into northern Iran, Kurdish and Turkish fighters and brigands had looted the Armenian and Assyrian villages of Karadagh and elsewhere. Thousands of Armenians and Assyrians left their villages for Tabriz'.[70] At least 25,000 Armenians and 15,000 Assyrians entered Iranian Azerbaijan from the Ottoman Empire in 1914 alone.[71] Many of these

---

[68] Grish Davtian, 'Aryamb yev poghpatov' (With Blood and Steel), *Norjughayakan* (*Of New Julfa*) (Yerevan: Antares Publishing, 2016), p. 12.

[69] Nicola Migliorino, *(Re)Constructing Armenia in Lebanon and Syria* (New York: Berghahn Books, 2008), p. 32.

[70] Gregorian, *The Road to Home*, p. 11.

[71] Emil Hakopian, *Artazi kam Azerpayjani Hayots' T'eme* (*The Armenian Diocese of Artaz and Azerbaijan*) (Tehran: Nayiri, 2013), p. 73.

refugees did not remain in Iran, as approximately 60,000 Armenians and Assyrians were transplanted to Iraq in 1918 by the British.[72] As a result, a majority of Genocide-affected Armenians were moved out of Iran, creating a situation where the majority of post-Genocide Iranian Armenians do not have a direct lineage connection to the Genocide. Nevertheless, Iranian Armenians view the Genocide as a violent attempt on their lives and ancestry, even though most were not directly affected by it, did not live through it and did not have family members who did.[73]

This type of symbolic connection is clear in the work of the Iranian Armenian American author Khoren Aramouni; his novel *Dznhal: Veb* (*The Thaw: A Novel*) tells of a young woman who grew up in Diyarbakır, Turkey, embedded within Turkish culture yet unaware of her Armenian roots. Susan, a college student, lives with her mother, Gozal, in Turkey. The context of Diyarbakır is historically significant to diasporic Armenian readers: in 1895, an estimated 25,000 Armenians and Assyrians were massacred in this city, a population that mainly consisted of Armenians and Syriac Orthodox Christians at the time. Twenty years later, in 1915, it became the site of ethnic cleansing against Armenians and Assyrians, with 150,000 deported and driven out of the city. In Aramouni's novel, these historical trials gain meaning as we learn that Susan's mother is a descendent of the Armenian Genocide's survivors. As part of her survival, Susan's great-grandmother was forced to convert to Islam to live in post-Genocide Turkey. Susan's mother was forced to keep this life-long secret to protect her daughter, so she lived as a disguised Muslim Turk. Another important factor in Aramouni's novel is that the author himself is an Iranian Armenian; however, he is writing about the precarious post-Genocide conditions of Armenians in Turkey, which speaks to the impact of the Genocide on Armenians beyond those directly impacted by it.

As the story begins, a group of Armenian students from Armenia and UCLA travel to Turkey to explore their ancestral town. At that time, Susan meets the group and asks to join, as she is planning to move to the US to attend UCLA. When Susan tells her mother about this encounter, Gozal

---

[72] Alan Stewart, *Persian Expedition: The Australians in Dunsterforce 1918* (Sydney: Australian Military History Publications, 2006), p. 143.

[73] Barry, *Armenian Christians in Iran*, p. 91.

becomes concerned that a group of Armenians showed interest in a Turk. Susan explains that the students are looking for Turkish Armenians, to which the mother responds that there are no Armenians here. Susan relays: 'The UCLA professor says, there are, mom, many, disguised Armenians, converts to Islam. [. . .] These Armenians are very interesting people. Nothing other than World War I interests them'. Gozal tells Susan: 'And you think they've come to visit Turkey. No, they've come to their homeland, their ancestors lived in this area, they are looking for their lost roots . . .'[74] The story includes many moments of dramatic irony, where Gozal or Susan talk about something the significance of which is clear to the reader but not to the pair.

After being exposed to the history of the events following the 1915 Genocide, the uprooting of many Armenians from their capital city of Diyarbakır and the conversion of churches into mosques, Susan feels lost and doubtful. Although Gozal is fully aware of the history, she is apprehensive to tell her daughter, prompting her to say:

> They insist on their story, we insist on ours. We write our history, they write theirs. We both write what's to our benefit. Neither I am a historian, nor are you. Finish your studies, graduate from the university, then you can go dig deep into it to find the truth. There aren't just Turkish or Armenian books, each nation writes what benefits them. You better work on your graduation. Yes, I don't disagree. In our city, we had Armenians at some point, but the circumstances and World War I have caused them to emigrate, but where, neither do I know, nor you.[75]

Interestingly, Gozal comments on the process of writing history and the significance of its authors. More often than not, historical narratives and the narratives of minoritised communities are authored by individuals within those nations guilty of atrocities, and hence these atrocities tend to be normalised. The same is true in the case of Turkish official narratives about the 1915 Genocide. In these Turkish narratives, the story emphasises Armenians as enemies of Turkey, claiming that Armenians and Russians killed hundreds

---

[74] Khoren Aramouni, *Dznhal: Veb* (*The Thaw: A Novel*) (Yerevan, Armenia: AHA Polygraph, 2014), p. 22.

[75] Ibid. p. 27.

of Turks.[76] Later, we read that even talking about the 1915 Armenian Genocide in Turkey is a taboo topic, imbued with many ambiguities. The novel
seems to be implying that, if Armenians were the betrayers, then why is
Turkey living under such a heavy cloud of ambiguity regarding the topic?

We learn in the novel that the American Armenians are pilgrims: 'They've
come to their ancestors' country'. A priest accompanies the group, and we
also hear the story of the priest's grandfather and that the group is going to
visit the priest's 'ancestral home, fortunately, it is standing, the Kurds are
living there . . .'[77] When they visit the town, there is a multitude of symbols
and remnants of Armenian life. For instance, there are khachkars, indicating
that the building once was either a church or an Armenian cemetery.[78] After
the 1915 events, Turkey drove the remaining Armenians into the deserts.
During this time, the priest's grandfather, Karapet, had a friendship with a
Kurdish shepherd with whom he left his young daughter as the family was
fleeing the massacres. The Kurdish family raises the child, calling her Asna
(originally Sona), but a few years later, she suddenly disappears. The family
realises that they cannot search for the child, because they would risk impris-
onment if they revealed that they deceitfully gave refuge to an Armenian.[79]
This contradicts what Susan has learned in school about Armenians. This also
shows interpersonal interactions between Armenians and Kurds and that,
while Turks were killing Armenians, this Armenian father trusts a Kurdish
shepherd with his daughter's life. These types of relationships among various
ethno-religious groups in Iran, in the US and in Turkey are significant, as
they contradict mainstream narratives pitting different ethnic groups against
each other.

Aramouni's novel comments on the cultural genocide that accompanied
Turkey's Genocide of Armenians and the ways in which this cultural erasure
affects any efforts to recover ancestral traditions. Name changes, conversion
to Islam and the use of language are all tools that majority populations use
to erase ethnic minoritised existence. Hearing the priest's story from Susan,
Gozal writes a letter to the priest, asking to meet with him. At the end of

[76] Ibid. p. 49.
[77] Ibid. p. 31.
[78] Ibid. p. 33.
[79] Ibid. p. 36.

the letter, Gozal writes: 'I kiss your right hand'[80] – a phrase that describes the Christian practice of asking for a blessing, which would be taboo for a Muslim. Although this makes the priest suspicious of Gozal, he decides to meet with her and realises that her real name is Geghuhi – an Armenian name. She tells him the story of her life as a disguised Armenian living in Turkey, concluding with the request that he baptise her.[81] Aramouni aptly comments on important elements in the construction of ethnic identity. Not only is one's name part of their identity, but so too are their language, their traditions and their religion.

After this interaction, Geghuhi/Gozal shares her grandmother's diary with Susan. Reading the diary, Susan realises that the young Armenian girl in the priest's story, whom the Kurds harboured before she suddenly disappeared, was also Susan's grandmother. The diary explains that the child, Asna, was so beautiful that a Muslim man kidnapped her to marry her, without realising that she was, in fact, Armenian. Asna survives a very violent and turbulent marital life and loses a child, but survives with her daughter, Gozal, with the help and protection of the gospel left for her by Karapet, her father.[82] After reading her grandmother's diary, Susan experiences inner turmoil:

> I wonder which one of my genes is stronger, the Turkish or the Armenian one. No, this is not possible. I must become as much Armenian as I am a Turk. Should I let them fight against one another now? It's not a fair fight, fair battle though. But the only thing I know about Armenians is that they are very aggressive, backwards, slaughterers, and vindictive people, in addition to being nomads. I don't know anything else.[83]

Later she goes through more internal battle, thinking that not only is she of mixed race and mixed genes, but also immersed in multiple religions and cultures. She remembers how at school she was taught to 'hate these non-Muslims; how proud were we of our ancestors' bravery'.[84] After her mother's

[80] Ibid. p. 40.
[81] Ibid. p. 47.
[82] Ibid. pp. 71–76.
[83] Ibid. p. 95.
[84] Ibid. p. 106.

death, Susan leaves for the US to attend UCLA. There, she meets a group of Armenian students, including a man named Karen, with whom she begins spending time. During these meetings, Susan becomes preoccupied with the cultural differences and historical enmity between Armenians and Turks.

Karen's family, however, is from Armenia; his grandmother is a survivor of another uprooting and has lived a difficult life in Siberia. Rooted in the past, Karen's grandmother describes it this way:

> I give meaning to my present through my past. Would they let us leave freely? The presence of the past is perhaps because I'm lonely and only the dead understand me. I am living so you wouldn't count me as absent, so you wouldn't feel lonely before the time comes. [. . .] If I had buried them, had the seventh- and fortieth-day rituals, the anniversary and all [. . .] My child, they didn't die, they were killed. Where should I look for their bones? In the deserts? [. . .] my sorrow is not just mine; it's a whole nation's misery. A misery that's like a cloud on our nation. How can I tolerate it? I've had the life of a dog, just the years in Siberia [. . .].[85]

Through the character of Karen's grandmother, Aramouni illuminates the shared memories and traumas of Armenians. Karen's grandmother's fragmented memories, her insistence on living in the past and reliving her traumas, point to the ways in which past and present are enmeshed in a uniquely diasporic consciousness. This layered Armenian consciousness lives in the individual and at the collective level, and it is built upon several waves of forced and voluntary migrations, losses, traumas and shared histories.

Similar to Aramouni, Gregorian explicitly draws on all the collective histories and memories of the Armenian people as influenced by folktales, history, the Genocide and so on. When he visits Armenia, he finds himself again and again wandering through the church, questioning the role of Christianity and the Armenian Apostolic Church in shaping Armenian national identity and consciousness. He visits the most significant church in Armenia, Etchmiadzin Cathedral, and watches the congregation, struck by the diversity of Armenians– native Armenians; immigrants from Egypt, Iran, Greece, Lebanon, Syria and France; visitors from Russia and Soviet

---

[85] Ibid. pp. 163–64.

Union nations; and visitors from the US, Ethiopia, France and Lebanon. He writes:

> All kinds of languages were spoken in that courtyard and I wondered what it was that had brought all of us together. Faith and religion? Cultural and moral ties to past generations? A commitment to tradition as an anchor of stability? Craving for individual and collective historical community immortality? Paying homage to our national heritage? I did not have clear answers to those questions and to many others I had met in Armenia. History, language, culture, and religion? Race, ethnicity, nationality, common genes, national consciousness, intellectual and moral ties to the dead, the past? Collective suffering? Discrimination, massacres, and genocide? How about the fact that I was also an Iranian and American?[86]

As many other Armenians do, Gregorian finds himself comparing the many categories of Armenians in the diaspora and native Armenians, wondering what the common bond between them is: 'Were we a virtual nation, held together by memory, language, and faith? Had we become the first transcendental nation? How about the Jews? I spent some time reading and rereading William Saroyan's observation on Armenia and Armenian'.[87] This virtual nation is dynamic, suspended within a constant flux in its definition of national and cultural identity. Being in the diaspora, this definition of many identity factors is constantly being reinterpreted, rediscovered and reconstructed.

This reconstruction of identity for diasporic Iranian Armenians, according to James Barry, involves performing Armenianness for a presumed audience to position their identity, including communication and body language such as official or impromptu speeches, stories and jokes. This repertoire of Armenianness is regularly enacted during community education events centred on Armenian identity. Armenian symbols such as the Armenian tricolour or Mount Ararat are utilised to evoke a collective historical identity. Hence, cultural events are centred within Armenian identity performance. Of great significance to Armenian identity performance is the commemoration of the Armenian Genocide, for which observants gather every 24 April.

---

[86] Gregorian, *The Road to Home*, p. 189.
[87] Ibid. p. 189.

On 24 April, Iranian Armenian schools do not hold classes. On this day, the anniversary of the 1915 Genocide, no Armenian in Iran works, but it is not a national holiday. Everyone participates in the commemoration of the Genocide in one way or another. Many participate in the long march (now banned by the Iranian government) which lasts for hours, lobbying for the Iranian government and the world to officially recognise the Genocide. For us school children, however, 24 April came with an automatic penalty in our report cards for that specific quarter. Every year, the school principal (usually a Muslim Iranian) would take away four or five (out of twenty) points from every student's 'behavioural discipline' grade (*numri-yi inzibat*). Yes, this was implemented in Iranian schools, which mainly meant that you have been a quiet, subservient student, followed the Islamic dress code and obeyed the rules of the school. In short, for commemorating our ancestral loss and observing religious traditions, we were penalised – this can only happen to minoritised populations. We were not even given a day to mourn our collective loss, while for Islamic religious occasions instruction was paused for days, if not weeks. Recently, the Islamic Republic has forbidden the 24 April March in commemoration of the Armenian Genocide; hence, Armenians gather in churches to commemorate the victims (Figure 4.4).

Other significant dates centre on the adoption of Christianity and the creation of the Armenian alphabet. History, language and religion are critical elements of Armenianness.[88] The use of the Armenian language is an important performance of Armenianness, as most Armenians resonate with the Armenian language as their primary language.[89] For Iranian Armenians, past and present are interwoven with collective consciousness and memory. Iranian Armenian cultural and historical heritage is transmitted across generations with specific commemorations.

Enmeshing the past within the present establishes a dynamic whereby a collective consciousness oriented towards the past is constantly placed under scrutiny.[90] Transnational Iranian Armenians are conscious of balancing the present with a self-defined, constructed past through commemorative

---

[88] Barry, *Armenian Christians in Iran*, pp. 207–11.
[89] Ibid. p. 217.
[90] Halbwachs, *The Collective Memory*, p. 80.

Figure 4.4 Armenians commemorate the Genocide in a church in Tehran, 24 April 2022. Courtesy of the author's uncle and cousin, Vanik and Argin Nazari.

occasions within diasporic communities that recreate and reimagine a past susceptible to disappearance over time. Collective memory largely relies on individual group members' knowledge of the past. The present is causally connected to past events, and references to those events in the present evoke sensations and memories linked to a collective history. Just as the present is distorted by a remembered past, a collective history can distort or influence experiences situated within the present, making it nearly impossible to separate past from present. In this way, images of the past lend credibility to the present social order, based on group members' shared memory.[91] When comparing intergenerational notions of shared Armenian history, we can see that memories vary in detail from generation to generation. While the conceptual basis of nationhood changes, the collective sense of identity may remain stable. However, the ideological bases of national belonging shift across generations. As these background narratives of collective memory transform between progenitor and progeny, different generations maintain their physical solidarity with the diasporic community, yet they are emotionally and mentally distant from their culture.

---

[91] Connerton, *How Societies Remember*, pp. 2–3.

5

TRANSNATIONAL DIASPORIC IDENTITY

The idea of 'home' has recently become more nebulous for me. Wherever I go, home goes with me – I mean I do not even know where home is, other than what is inside of me. Following the 1979 Revolution and the Iran–Iraq War, many from the Armenian community, including members of my family, emigrated from Iran to US cities with already large Armenian communities such as Glendale, California, where my parents and siblings now reside. Before landing my current academic position in Chapel Hill, I taught at Georgia College and State University in Milledgeville, Georgia, for three years. Despite my professional success, living in the US has not always been easy. When I first moved to Chapel Hill, without any support system or friends, I learned that some of my next-door neighbours were white supremacists. Initially laughing off the overt displays of racism and bigotry, I soon felt that I was becoming a target for my brazen neighbours. I had never been exposed to that kind of extremism and hatred, even in Iran. But I quickly learned how to deflect the taunting questions about my origin, by responding that 'I came from Georgia'. These volatile incidents of hostility were moments of opportunity for me to begin thinking about origins, identities and the malleability of our dependence on time and space.

Diasporic individuals inherently navigate a dual challenge – the everyday implications of their kaleidoscopic identity in a new environment and the task of piecing together an identity rooted in a fragmented, idealised home and an often-hostile host nation. As they attempt to resolve these challenges, their cultural identity takes root. Cultural theorist Stuart Hall defines cultural identity as a focus on one's shared culture and the vectors of multiple cultures.[1] Because diasporic individuals experience multiple consciousnesses, the establishment of a cultural identity is often full of challenges, including the suffering arising from fragmented memories, the weight of solitude and constant roaming between borders of two or more worlds. New and old environments coexist, placing life in the diaspora 'outside of habitual order [. . . in a] nomadic, decentered, contrapuntal' sphere.[2] Focusing on the idea of dignity inherent in 'multiplicities' rather than on attempts to belong, political philosopher Frantz Fanon describes how diasporic multiplicities often contradict one another as a 'way of being'.[3] To become is a never-ending journey; they cannot seek approval in either the majority or minoritised group and must create an amalgam of all identity factors, firmly establishing a diasporic multiplicity in all aspects of life.[4]

In this chapter, while I revisit the experiences of diasporic Iranian Armenians to maintain cultural heritage, I mainly focus on how transnationalism manifests itself in cultural production. This is achieved by investigating how Iranian Armenian characters and creations are presented as diasporic transnational people who are culturally anchored in the host nation, yet simultaneously maintaining symbolic and spiritual ties with their homeland. In addition to assimilation and separation, I will discuss another option that potentially might reframe the Iranian Armenian diasporic transnational story – one that cultural theorist Gloria Anzaldúa calls a 'new tribalism': diasporic Iranian Armenians have the opportunity to make a conscious choice, where '[their] resistance to identity boxes leads [them] to a different tribe, a different story [. . .] enabling [them] to rethink [themselves] in more global-spiritual terms [. . .]. In this narrative national boundaries dividing us from the 'others' (nos/otras) are porous and the cracks between the worlds serve as gateways'.[5] This new tribalism is in

---

[1] Stuart Hall, 'Cultural Identity and Diaspora', *Colonial Discourse and Post-Colonial Theory: A Reader*, p. 226.

[2] Said, 'Reflections on Exile', p. 149.

[3] Frantz Fanon. *Black Skin, White Masks* (Paris: Editions du Seuil, 1952), p. 14.

[4] Homi Bhabha, 'Foreword', *Black Skin, White Masks*, by Frantz Fanon (Paris: Editions du Seuil, 1952), p. vii.

[5] Anzaldúa, 'now let us shift', pp. 560–61.

direct contrast to the notion of 'new nationalism' (discussed in the previous chapter) and constitutes the essence of transnationalism, multiple consciousnesses and *verants'ughi*.

Within the Iranian Armenian diasporic community, this new tribalism is achieved by sifting through representations of identity – sometimes through traditions, shared memories and religion, and at other times through language, art and literature. Since collective identity is forever being (re)defined, its physical representations are constantly reformulated, too. On occasion, some past representations are completely cast aside for new ones. Social psychologist Henri Tajfel defines socio-cultural identity, generally, as 'that part of an individual's self-concept which derives from [the] knowledge of [the] membership of a social group or groups, together with the value and emotional significance attached to that membership'.[6] According to this definition, social groups represent a crucial link between social environment, collective identity and individual identity. It would logically follow that shifts or changes in the social environment and the culture at large have profound consequences for socio-cultural identity.[7] The identity effects of cultural change are frequently addressed in the context of acculturation or assimilation in Iranian Armenian diasporic works, as cultural shifts evoke associated identity changes. Diasporic Iranian Armenian authors and artists aim to determine those identity formations that are most adaptive and that yield long-term psychological adjustment for their diasporic communities.

However, there are various ways to respond to cultural change. Cultural psychologist John W. Berry proposes four types of changes, dependent on an individual's relationship with both native and non-native cultures: integrated, assimilated, separated and marginal. Each of these responses involves a shift in behaviour, as well as an associated response within cultural identity.[8] Similarly,

---

[6] Henri Tajfel, *Human Groups and Social Categories: Studies in Social Psychology* (Cambridge: Cambridge University Press, 1981), p. 255.

[7] Ibid. p. 239.

[8] John W. Berry, 'Social and Cultural Change', *Handbook of Cross-Cultural Psychology, vol. 5: Social Psychology*, ed. Harry C. Triandis and Richard Brislin (Boston: Allyn and Bacon, 1980), pp. 211–79. See also John W. Berry and U. Kim, 'Acculturation and Mental Health', *Health and Cross-Cultural Psychology*, ed. Pierre Dasen, John W. Berry and Norman Sartorius (London: Sage, 1988), pp. 207–35.

in the discussion of his social skills model of cultural adjustment, Stephen Bochner points out that the most adaptive response would implement a structure for promoting 'multicultural attitudes, skills and self-perception'.[9] These models imply that identity is acquired alongside social skills, cultural knowledge and norms. In other words, if a person successfully functions in multiple cultures, understands values and norms, and speaks the language of the nation or of the community, they are assumed to have acquired a bi- and multicultural identity. If, on the other hand, the person only operates well in one culture, then they exhibit a monocultural identity. However, an individual's successful acquisition of cultural skills and norms is not necessarily an indicator of that individual's cultural identification.[10] Individuals may obtain new skills, competencies and behaviours without affecting their sense of cultural identity. Nevertheless, the overwhelming consensus argues that the development of bicultural or multicultural competence ultimately allows for a successful life in a bicultural or multicultural context. Bicultural or multicultural competence involves both the adoption of social skills and cultural knowledge and the acquisition of at least some aspects of non-native cultural identity. This view implies that individuals living in the diaspora for an extended period of time, who gradually learn aspects of the host culture, will experience a shift in their cultural identity.[11]

Biculturalism is how Armenians survive in Iran, and multiculturalism is how Iranian Armenians function in the US. Armenians in Iran who already experience multiple consciousnesses move to the US, only to be faced with the quandary of yet more dimensions of consciousness. These multiple consciousnesses and multiculturalism are artfully presented in Arby Ovanessian's

---

[9] Stephen Bochner, 'Social Stereotypes and Social Identity', *Social Identity Theory: Constructive and Critical Advances*, ed. Dominic Abrams and Michael A. Hogg (New York: Springer, 1986), p. 350.

[10] Teresa LaFromboise, Hardin L. K. Coleman and Jennifer Gerton, 'Psychological Impact of Biculturalism: Evidence and Theory', *Psychological Bulletin* 114 (1993), pp. 395–412. See also Teresa LaFromboise and Wayne Rowe, 'Skills Training for Bicultural Competence: Rationale and Application', *Journal of Counseling Psychology* 30 (1983), pp. 589–95.

[11] John W. Berry, 'Psychology of Acculturation: Understanding Individuals Moving Between Cultures', *Applied Cross-Cultural Psychology*, ed. Richard Brislin (London: Sage, 1990), pp. 232–53.

Cheshmeh (*The Spring*, 1972, 100 minutes), a black-and-white Persian-language film with a handful of professional actors (Jamshid Mashayekhi and the Armenian actor Aramais 'Arman' Vartan Yousefians).[12] While some of the locations, such as Julfa in Isfahan or *Bagh-i Firduws*, are explicitly named, the film unfolds in generic and generalisable terms that extend the film's context beyond specificities of time and space. In this sense, the film is part of the larger discourse of 1970s New Wave Iranian Cinema – influenced by Italian Neorealism and French New Wave. The film is an adaptation of Armenian author Megrditch Armin's story 'Cheshmeh Highnar' (Highnar's Spring); yet, Ovanessian has a distinctive and recognisable influence on the narrative.

In the film, various types of music heighten its cultural meaning. The film begins with church bells tolling and church music, later featuring Armenian ethno-musicologist and composer Komitas' music as a background score to scenes of a town in mourning for someone. During this solemn composition, we hear this sentence from the Apocalypse of St John IX:6: 'And when those days come, men shall seek death and not find it. And they shall desire to die: and death shall fly from them'. This passage prepares the viewer for a cinematic life-and-death journey. For the film's first ten minutes, there is no audible dialogue. According to Iranian Armenian artist Lida Berberians, '[a]t first glance, the dark hole (opening) in the thatched wall of a house looks like an empty grave at the beginning of the film. [. . .] For the soundtrack of such an atmosphere, the use of a quartet was appropriate with the four characters in question, but the director wanted to use the music of Komitas, which was accompanied by a piano for singing'.[13] The film has no direct plotline – it is non-linear. Instead of a plot-driven film, Ovanessian tries to craft the film's form through its content. For instance, the architecture of the buildings reflects the inner psyche of the characters. The story revolves around a love affair. The master spring-maker dies after building his fortieth spring. The master spring-maker's friend falls in love with the master spring-maker's wife, but when he realises that she is his friend's wife, he commits suicide. The woman has a young lover, too, whom she secretly meets in an

---

[12] Ovanessian, *Cheshmeh*.

[13] Lida Berberians, 'Musighi dar film-i *Cheshmeh*' (The Soundtrack in the Spring), *Theater and Cinema of Arby Ovanessian*, ed. Majid Lashkari (Tehran: Ruzanih Publications, 2014), p. 452.

abandoned house. The women in the neighbourhood begin feeling jealous of this woman's love and start disgracing her in various ways. Thus, the woman kills herself and is buried in an abandoned house. The young lover leaves town and goes into the wilderness (like Majnun). Ovanessian endeavours to portray the cultural differences between Iranian Armenians and Muslim Iranians, the importance of the family unit and the significance of love; he also shows that these cultural differences evolve over time.

Portraying both Armenians and Muslims, Ovanessian has been criticised for depicting Armenians as more beautiful and cleaner than their Iranian counterparts. According to Iranian Armenian film critic Robert Safarian, this kind of representation of the two cultures probably has its roots in Ovanessian's nationalist (Armenian) ideology, his love of Armenian culture and his attachment to global avant-garde art. It is interesting that, although Ovanessian was fluent in both Iranian and Armenian languages and cultures, he retained his Armenian identity over his Iranian identity when he relocated to France.[14] While the film might be influenced by Ovanessian's nationalist ideology, he includes elements from both cultures. In an interview, Ovanessian commented on his depiction of Armenians and Iranian Muslims:

> First, the fact is that the tribes are not positioned against one another, they are together. This is different. They are two things that go in parallel, not in collision. I see one in the form of its family relationships and related issues that gradually generalises that group relationships start with the family, but in the other culture that runs parallel to it, we only see communities, not individuals. Naturally, these two affect each other. That is, none of them are apart from the other.[15]

Ovanessian's images, symbols and metaphors attempt to move beyond social constructs by actively deconstructing them for the viewer, an unprecedented act at the time, solidifying *Cheshmeh* as an important voice in Iranian New Wave cinema. In comparison to later Iranian Armenian cultural productions, *Cheshmeh* is not completely transnational, and the film is often understood as a pioneering opus of the 1970s; however, one way in which it negotiates

[14] Safarian, *Sakin-i du farhang*, pp. 108–10.
[15] B. N., 'Chishmih-yi hamishih jushan' (The Ever-Boiling Spring), pp. 743–44.

these deconstructions is through the inclusion of a *film Farsi* actor (Arman) in the adaptation of a serious literary work with lyrical expression and rhythm.[16] In contrast to Iranian films' stereotypical representation of Armenians with a thick Armenian accent, Ovanessian engages in a second moment of deconstruction when the film's Armenian characters speak fluent Persian. Ovanessian's film represents his attempts at moving beyond the national world and towards a transnational existence that amalgamates elements of multiple cultures.

Similarly, Lilith Terian's (1930–2019) sculptures exhibit both traditional sculptural detail and abstract constructions. Terian's busts of Mesrop Mashtots' and Yeprem Khan (discussed in Chapter Four) reflect her mastery of a realistic technique that embraces her Armenian and Iranian cultural aspects. However, her more cosmopolitan modernist figures exhibit characteristics of surrealism and cubism; they have been compared to the work of sculptor and painter Alberto Giacometti. The majority of these sculptures are large and reinforced and plastered with wire and thick linen threads, and many present three figures (Figure 5.1). The figures' larger-than-life scale makes them seem real and tangible, yet fragile, imaginary and inaccessible. The quick strokes of the hand and the knife give the surface of the work a rough texture replete with spongy cavities. These hard yet porous figures allude to the decay and gradual deterioration of the human form and, by extension, to the hardships and suffering of modern people, compounded by the fragility and roughness of the human condition, both physical and existential. The themes of decay and loss are heightened by the sculpture's materials, the way in which they allude to fullness by shaped cavities. As part of Terian's modernist works, these were meant to function as a reflection on the emptiness of modern life.

These modernist works are inspired by Terian's multiplicity and cosmopolitanism – embodying neither Armenian nor Iranian ethnic features, but more neutral global ones. On the day of Terian's funeral in 2019, the famous Iranian Armenian musician and conductor Loris Tjeknavorian expressed:

I am very sad that we have lost this great master. Sometimes when they [the officials] talk about Armenians, it is as if Armenians have fallen from the sky

---

[16] Film Farsi is used to describe a low-quality film copied from the Bollywood cinema, featuring poor plots and singing and dancing arrangements.

Figure 5.1 Lilith Terian, *Three Figures*.

[like aliens]. Armenians are part of the nations that formed Iran with Cyrus [the Great]. Iran is one nation and it is for all of us. But there are narrow-minded people who say, Armenians are a minority. Armenians have done a lot for this country, for their country. You cannot find more Iranian than Armenians.[17]

Consistent with Tjeknavorian's comment about the ways in which Iranians otherise Armenians, Trinh T. Minh-ha would agree that identity is commonly shaped through an 'us' versus 'them' framework; however, she also suggests a third space 'of hybridisation which, rather than simply adding a here to a there, gives rise to an elsewhere-within-here/-there that appears both too recognizable and impossible to contain'.[18] Terian's works appear to be creations within this 'third space' of 'elsewhere-within-here/-there'. Her hybrid identity allows her to introduce the us-within-them framework.

---

[17] 'Lilith Terian Was One of the Pillars of the University, But They Expelled Her', *ISNA*, 16 March 2019, https://www.isna.ir/news/97122513455/

[18] Trinh T. Minh-ha, 'Other Than Myself, My Other Self', p. 38.

A contemporary of Terian, graphic designer and cartoonist Arapik Baghdasarian (1939–85) was another outstanding figure whose work embodied global and transnational humanity. Baghdasarian's work is a paradoxical combination of aesthetic tendencies and an attention to social justice. As a member of the Institute for Intellectual Development of Children and Young Adults (Kanun) in Tehran, Baghdasarian directed two animated films titled *Vaznih-bardar* (*The Weightlifter*) and *Giriftar* (*Stuck*), as well as a short film called *Hozih-yi Istihfazi* (*The Guarded Territory*). He was an apprentice to the prominent Iranian director Abbas Kiarostami when Kiarostami produced his short film *Nan va Kuchih* (*The Bread and the Alley*, 1970). Baghdasarian was very sensitive to the plight of the working class, which he portrayed in many of his works. For instance, in one of his works, he compares an overcrowded public bus with a wealthy family's expensive luxury sports car. Attuned to social justice, he also frequently questioned the era's dominant capitalism and consumerism. However, Baghdasarian does not reference his Iranian or Armenian identities in his works, making him the example of an artist who moves from ethnic identity to transnational consciousness.[19]

Baghdasarian created humorous images through which he unravelled the truth. In addition to graphic design, Baghdasarian excelled in animation, and his first filmmaking experiences earned him international accolades. Towards the end of his short life, he translated works in the field of design. Baghdasarian drew many political cartoons that were published, with his signature, in the monthly magazine *Nigin*. The only hallmark of his works was the black five-winged star that functioned as his signature. Baghdasarian never resorted to symbolism but engaged characters in a story full of social commitment and devoid of intellectualism – a critique the artist had of his own medium. His images were akin to shocking statements that denounced stupidity, illusion and oppression. His cartoons are bitter, sad warnings about the socio-political atmosphere. His works are an attempt to raise awareness about everyday injustices occurring around us. Poignant examples include the image of a farmer holding harvested bunches of rice in one hand and a sickle in the other, while in the background we see a wealthy landowner next

---

[19] Safarian, *Sakin-i du farhang*, pp. 126–33.

to a luxury car, a caricature of patients tangled with each other in a medical office's crowded hallway, or the image of poor people searching for food in a trash heap amid the hustle and bustle of a city. Instead of humorous, grotesque, or terrifying caricatures, Baghdasarian's works contain simple and clear messages. In Figure 5.2, an opulent and bulky figure sits on a carriage pulled by a slight, impoverished figure. This labourer is reaching for a car suspended in the air by a conception that the wealthy figure controls. Here, Baghdasarian critiques oppressive systems in a pseudo-modernised capitalist society that exploits the masses. On a deeper level, the image is hinting at the plight of the working class mired in corrupt power dynamics bolstered by classism, prejudice and social stratification. This image is reminiscent of George Hegel's master-slave dialectic, where the interaction between the master and the slave results in the emergence of a unique self-consciousness for subjects. The recognition of each other's self-consciousness causes them to realise their interdependence, but this knowledge is only possible when they mutually recognise the other's self-consciousness.[20]

In this sense, Baghdasarian's works utilise the contrast between two viewpoints within mundane situations to elicit new meanings that vacillate between humour and sadness. Baghdasarian's outspoken, bitter and

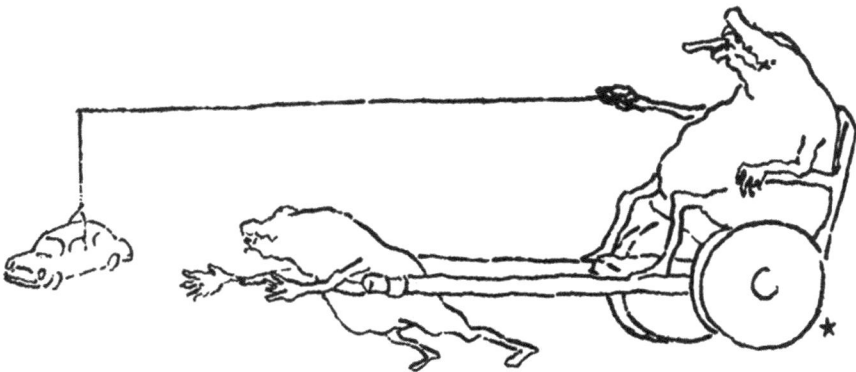

Figure 5.2 Arapik Baghdasarian (1939–85).

[20] Georg W. F. Hegel, *Phenomenology of Spirit*, trans. Arnold V. Miller and foreword by John N. Findlay (Oxford: Clarendon Press, 1977).

straightforward critique of his surroundings challenged aesthetic precon-
ceptions. Instead of adhering to political or ideological policies and ideals,
he refused to accept ideologies that presented inhumane rules, exploitative
dominance, or limits on freedom and humanity. Rather than situating these
critiques within ethnic identity or experiences, his motivations concerned
his dissatisfaction with the coercive and unjust mechanisms of the world.
The atmosphere of the city streets – the bureaucracy, the consumerism and
the conformity to larger power structures presented in his works – reflect an
identity constructed from cosmopolitan ideas and the tangible environment
around him.

While Terian's and Baghdasarian's works are more global, Marcos Grigorian's
global works advance ethnic Iranian and Armenian elements and modern concepts. Grigorian is revered as a pioneer of Iranian conceptual art. At a time when
the nation had not developed an art that featured a combination of different
tools, media and the integration of photos, slides, film, music, paintings and
mundane objects into artworks, Grigorian successfully opened a conceptual art
exhibition. Some of his works, especially a number of his collages and patches,
are influenced by his proximity to street and market life. His collages – borrow-
ing everyday objects such as cups, saucers, or Sangak bread – establish a unique
rendering of Iranian pop art.[21]

Grigorian's works are of universal interest without being derivative and
inflect local identity without referencing the ethnic. In Figure 5.3, in the collage
Abgousht Dizy (which translates as 'meat broth'), a bowl and a *Sangak* or *Barbari*
bread, along with a cup, saucer and sugar, are all placed against a background
of Iranian soil, gathered from a life led in close proximity to bazaar and street
life, conveying his authentic Iranianness. As a hybrid individual, Grigorian paid
much attention to the folk arts of Iran by collecting a 'coffee house' style of art,
in which the artists sing as they show their work to the assembled audience,
prompting Grigorian to term them 'coffee house' (*qahvi-khanih*) paintings that
invoke religious and epic themes, engaging Iranian visual memory as well as the
artists' attempts at minimalism to represent a belief system. Since Grigorian's
work transcends the pictorial, baring not only his own but also his Iranian and

---

[21] 'Zindigi-namih: Marco Grigorian (1925–2007)', *Hamshahrionline*, 17 June 2011,
hamshahrionline.ir/x3bnR

Figure 5.3 Marcos Grigorian, *Abgousht Dizy*, 1968. © Leila Heller Gallery.

Armenian community's soul, it can be viewed as 'autohistoria', which tells both his personal story and integrates his cultural history, too.[22] Using minimalistic ethnic elements from Iranian culture and Armenian heritage, Grigorian resists duality by inhabiting the traditions, cultures and heritage of two or more nations – a binational, trinational, transnational space. His status within a permeable, fluid and liminal space lends itself to a metamorphosis that crosses binary boundaries of existence.

While Grigorian's Genocide murals and dried earth works reference a layer of his Armenian identity (discussed in the previous chapters), his collages and coffee house paintings depict his Iranian identity and the influence of Iranian culture – food, bazaars and street life. Living in the borderlands where every line and boundary is flexible and permeable, Grigorian grounds himself in a hybrid work of art. In Gloria Anzaldúa's words, such borders are

[22] Anzaldúa, *Borderlands/La Frontera*, p. 183.

'the locus of resistance, of rupture, implosion and explosion, and of putting together the fragments and creating a new assemblage'.[23]

Similarly, when asked in an interview with *Courrier International* about her Armenian heritage and how she combines Armenian and Iranian cultures, creative writer Zoya Pirzad expressed the complexities of a hybrid identity:

> Armenian culture is very different. Armenians have been living in Iran for 400 years, but they have maintained their culture, even if they have also adopted much from Iranian culture. I embody both cultures and have been confronted with problems related to both cultures. Armenians are very sensitive about their culture and language. Initially, I was against this low tolerance, but I had to personally experience it to fully understand it. My mother is 100 percent Armenian; she married a Muslim Iranian and converted to Islam. This was very difficult for her; she was rejected by her family. I was always bullied in Armenian schools because my last name did not end in 'ian'. Since I had not traveled to Armenia, I was not close to Armenians. When I traveled there, I realized that if Armenians were not like this, they would not have a community today.[24]

In her works, Pirzad draws on her own and her mother's experiences in Iran to create hybrid characters, exploring the conflicts and contradictions of identity in a style that incorporates forced dislocation and attempted assimilation. Iranian Armenian cultural identity reflects common Iranian Armenian historical experiences as well as shared cultural codes that contextualise them as 'one people'. This unity is advanced as a stable, unchanging, continuous frame of reference and meaning beneath the vicissitudes of history. This 'oneness' is part of the essence of the Iranian Armenian diasporic experience.[25] Identities arise from 'belonging' to distinctive ethnic, racial, linguistic, religious and, above

---

[23] Gloria Anzaldúa, 'Border Arte: Nepantal, el Lugar de la Frontera', *Gloria Anzaldúa*, ed. AnaLouise Keating (Durham, NC: Duke University Press, 2009), p. 177.

[24] Zoya Pirzad, 'I Look for Simplicity and Accuracy', *Courrier International*, 11 March 2009, http://www.courrierinternational.com/article/2009/10/30/je-recherche-la-simplicite-et-la-justesse

[25] Stuart Hall, 'Cultural Identity and Diaspora', *Identity: Community, Culture, Difference*, p. 223.

all, national cultures.[26] However, they also embody factors rooted in the host nation's culture.

In Pirzad's 'Yik Ruz Qabl az 'iyd-i Pak' (A Day Before Easter), the Iranian Armenian community is one whose major and featured characters 'had only seen Armenia on a map; old maps in textbooks or in the bulky tomes that older people kept in their homes'.[27] The protagonist Edmond's grandmother has one of these big maps of Armenia on her living room wall – a gift from Mrs Grigorian, the only person among them who had really seen Armenia.[28] This emotional connection to the homeland creates a dilemma for the characters who struggle between glancing back and moving forward, or what Denise Aghanian describes as being Janus-faced, which casts doubts on sustaining their individual identities.[29] Mrs Grigorian recounts her memories for the community, although the details constantly shift, which captures the fragmented nature of a diasporic consciousness and how a diasporic individual negotiates disparate histories and culture by constructing a hybrid interior identity. Mrs Grigorian's fractured memory creates a multiplicity of stories, histories and identities, although the memory is rooted in two cultures: nostalgia for Armenia and knowledge of Iranian culture. Looking towards the country of her settlement for acceptance and involvement, yet simultaneously yearning for her Rushdiean 'imaginary homeland', Mrs Grigorian is caught between identity crisis and cross-cultural communication, much like other Armenian characters in the story.[30] Through Mrs Grigorian's fragmented recollections, Pirzad's characters consciously maintain a collective identity, finding solace in their common origin, historical experience and geographic location.

Mrs Grigorian is also one of the main characters in the story, who constantly reminds Edmond to use pure Armenian, as opposed to a mixture of colloquial Armenian and Persian words, which signals the metamorphosis towards the

[26] Stuart Hall, 'Introduction: Identity in Question', *Modernity and Its Futures*, ed. Stuart Hall, David Held and Tony McGrew (Cambridge: Polity Press, 1992), p. 274.

[27] Pirzad, *The Space Between Us*, p. 17; Pirzad, 'Yik Ruz Qabl az 'iyd-i Pak', p. 237.

[28] Ibid. p. 17.

[29] Denise Aghanian, *The Armenian Diaspora: Cohesion and Fracture* (Lanham, MD: University Press of America, 2007).

[30] Rushdie, *Imaginary Homelands*, pp. 9–21.

diversity of transnational generations. While some of Pirzad's Iranian Armenian characters consciously perceive themselves as a geographically dispersed community that must preserve its heritage, the transnational generation is not as invested in such ideas or practices. The less transnational individuals try to maintain their religious and ethnic boundaries; they 'have developed a "diasporic subjectivity"'.[31] However, the transnational cohorts of Iranian Armenian characters represent a community of 'diasporic transnationals' – diverse and cosmopolitan – locally settled in an Iranian seaside township and open to a fluid identity, but symbolically invested in Armenianness and the weight of their homeland. The latter are 'diasporic transnationals' precisely because they live in a 'third space' between their homeland and their host nation. By the end of Pirzad's story, even Edmond, who struggles with his own understanding of Armenian identity, reconfigures his attitude towards the homeland by embodying the concept of multiplicity, incorporating a new set of ideas and practices into his consciousness.

While there are many components to the process of identity formation, geography plays a large role, allowing individuals to pull from traditions provided by a given location. This is particularly important for the less transnational generations who conform to the idea of one nation with its borders and territories. The importance of this shared geography is evident in Soukias Hacob Koorkchian's (also known as Varand) poem 'Linelutyun' (Being), where he discusses his own (im)mortality:

> There is a continent in the universe,
> Asia the continent, there Caucasus,
> In the Caucasus, an Armenia,
> In Armenia, a capital city,
> A city
> Called Yerevan.
>
> There is a statue in Yerevan,
> Next to the statue

---

[31] Janine Dahinden, 'The Dynamics of Migrants' Transnational Formations: Between Mobility and Locality', *Diaspora and Transnationalism: Concepts, Theories and Methods*, ed. Rainer Baubock and Thomas Faist (Amsterdam: Amsterdam University Press, 2010), p. 54.

A pool,
In the pool, an image,
Whose owner is not there yet.

> There, I left my hopes
> And since then
> I have no shadow.

I have no shadow,
I'm a ghost,

> I don't reach my
> Being –
> In Caucasus
> There is an Armenia,
> In Armenian, a capital
> > City,

A city
Called Yerevan,
Where the universe bridges my

> Immortality . . .[32]

Varand's poem draws a geographical map of the world, beginning with a larger map and ultimately centring on Armenia and its capital city of Yerevan. On the one hand, this common geography aids the development of a sense of national identity and shared consciousness. On the other hand, when a geographic location is revoked, as in the case of the Armenian diaspora, national, social and cultural identity are reconstructed to function as shared memory – here, the statue, the pool and the reflection. Traditions and experiences are often forgotten due to the physical loss and absence of the geography tied to one's heritage – the nation, the homeland. Varand attaches meanings and significance to the statue and the pool, which signify his hopes. He is not concerned with the global map, as long as he is able to locate Armenia on it. While Varand longs for homecoming, he certainly recognises the importance of the global map, too. For being, existing, living, he only needs Yerevan in

---

[32] Soukias Hacob Koorkchian (Varand), 'Linelutyun' (Being), *An-veradardz* (*Irreversible*) (Tehran: Alik Publishers, 1999), p. 82.

lieu of a homeland (or the western part of it) that is lost. This trauma of losing the physical homeland results in diasporic people's struggle to form an
identity; as a result, they combat the absence of the homeland by attaching
meaning to physical objects or shared experiences.

The less transnational Iranian Armenian diasporic individuals/charac-
ters/personas understand that their cultural identity is not inherently tied to
the past, but instead to the potential posed by the future. However, they are
simultaneously wary of cultural death. As Stuart Hall states, cultural identity
'belongs to the future as much as to the past [. . .] like everything which is historical, [diasporic subjects] undergo constant transformation. Far from being
eternally fixed in some essentialised past, they are subject to the continuous
"play" of history, culture, and power'.[33] Living in a culture different from the
homeland's, the host nation's culture naturally becomes a part of 'the continuous "play" of history, culture, and power' that pulls diasporic people's cultural
identity towards assimilation into the host nation. The fear of cultural death
motivates the less transnational Iranian Armenians to eschew anything that
can lead their counterparts astray from the homeland's cultural identity; however, this effort to avoid fluidity creates monoculturalism and monolingualism, and it centres everything about identity on a single nation. In philosopher
and literary critic Edouard Glissant's words, '[t]he root is monolingual', but
'[t]he root is not important. Movement is'.[34] Glissant emphasises the relationship between mobility and transnationalism, calling it 'the Poetics of Relation'.
This is a space where identities are extended via their relationships with the
other, rather than with their roots and heritage. This is what transnational
generations of diasporic Iranian Armenians strive for. The relational mentality materialises out of a deconstruction of national identity that occurs while
living in a space of uncertainty about one's future identity.[35] This is a space of
verants'ughi, one of growth and transformation. While living in the diaspora
may result in the disintegration of identity, relationality bolsters identity.

Generally, identity formation is a life-long effort. For diasporic Iranian
Armenians, it is an effort compounded by the many factors that influence

---

[33] Stuart Hall, 'Introduction: Identity in Question', p. 225.

[34] Edouard Glissant, 'Exile and Errantry', *Poetics of Relation*, transl. Betsy Wing (Ann Arbor:
University of Michigan Press, 1997), pp. 14–15.

[35] Ibid. p. 20.

their consciousness and process of identity formation, including upbringing, family heritage and religious, racial, cultural and national roots. Growing up in the diaspora, notions of homeland and identity become entwined and interdependent for transnational Iranian Armenians. The lack of a homeland exacerbates identity formation, making it difficult for these individuals to connect to themselves. While these might be true for most diasporic communities, for Armenians the loss of the physical homeland and the history of the Genocide exacerbate their feelings of guilt if they lose ties with the homeland and their heritage. Edward Said describes this lack of a connection between the self and the homeland as 'the unhealable rift forced between a human being and a native place, between the self and its true home: it's essential sadness can never be surmounted'.[36] Having a physical location that represents the collective identity is integral to shaping self-identity, establishing a relationship between individuals and nation, and fostering a sense of belonging. When a homeland is taken away and a person cannot connect to a physical homeland, a part of their identity is thrust into the unknown. For Iranian Armenians, in addition to the lost lands during the Genocide years, the existing nation of Armenia is distinct from the nation from which their ancestors fled or were relocated, which establishes a dual homeland – the geographic nation with which they must identify and the imaginary homeland. As Salman Rushdie states, they yearn to craft an identity by a conviction that they 'had a city and history to reclaim'.[37] Reading Varand's poem in this context, we can interpret it as Varand's attempt at reclaiming (hi)story. Even when physically distanced from the homeland, there is a need to cultivate connections in order to form a diasporic identity. Whether via collective memories or physical objects, the melancholic loss of the homeland overwhelms Varand, pushing him to establish new ways of self-cultivation that integrates the past. In this sense, his identity can be defined as the basic image of the self and the other that provide him with some kind of order, belonging and unity.[38]

---

[36] Said, p. 137.

[37] Rushdie, p. 428.

[38] Rinus Penninx, Kraal Karen and Maria Berger (eds), 'Identity, Representation, Interethnic Relations and Discrimination', *The Dynamics of International Migration and Settlement in Europe: A State of the Art* (Amsterdam: Amsterdam University Press, 2006), p. 204.

Although identity seems to be our most personal creation, it is through interactions with external forces that identity is moulded in an extended, lifelong process. The notion, sometimes merely subconscious, that identity has been completely formed is a mirage. Because of this mirage we come to believe that one aspect of our identity remains in process and another aspect of identity formation has been terminated. While all people struggle with this bifurcating notion, few come to recognise it, and diasporic people seem to have a talent for this discernment.[39]

Iranian Armenian diasporic cultural productions are rife with examples of identity construction and characters who sift through the host nation, simultaneously attempting to retain an aspect of the homeland while feeling powerless to resist assimilation into the host nation's culture and traditions. The external forces of assimilation spur Rosemary Cohen's characters to maintain family tradition, Armenian language, their shared history and cultural markers:

> Our grandmothers would tell us stories and sing Armenian songs. Most of the songs were somber and melancholic. But we were used to these songs. Sometimes I could see little tears falling from my grandmother's eyes; she would always answer that we had a sad history and that she would have preferred to live in the land of our ancestors, in Armenia. For us Persia was our country; we were born there and we loved it. We were aware that most of the population was Muslim and that we were Christians. But we accepted each other and lived peacefully side by side. My parents had many prominent Muslim friends who used to come to our house. We spoke Armenian at home, Persian and Turkish outside. All our family members spoke at least three languages. But my father also spoke Russian and French perfectly, and later my brothers learned Russian, too.[40]

The multiplicity of the Iranian Armenian diasporic experience is nowhere clearer than in Cohen's rendition of her experience receiving an ID card to

---

[39] For instance, Amin Maalouf talks about his identity as a French Greek Orthodox Arab Lebanese man as having 'genes of the soul' which are 'indivisible' in his *On Identity* (New York and London: Random House, 2000).

[40] Cohen, *The Survivor*, p. 3.

teach at the Iranian Air Force base and Tehran University. On the ID card, underneath nationality, was written the word 'Christian'. Cohen's protagonist found it offensive and declared: 'I always considered myself a true Iranian [. . .] But it seems they do not forget that I am not Muslim. They will always remain the same. Why would I spend my entire life in a country where I always would be considered a second-class citizen?'[41] Within this story, Cohen's colleagues also propose that she change her name (a coded phrase indicating conversion to Islam) so that she could attain higher positions. While Cohen feels the urge to assimilate into Iranian culture, she is not recognised as part of the host nation's citizenship. The host nation requires her to change her name – an integral part of her identity – as Armenian names are quite different from Iranian Muslim names.

Although similar to Cohen's experience in an Iranian context, legal name changes manifest themselves differently in the US or Europe for diasporic Iranian Armenians. In Henry A. Sarkissian's *Tales of 1001 Iranian Days*, the narrator describes how the story's protagonists were inventing methods of transforming the 'funny-sounding and curious names that had been given us in elaborate baptism ceremonies' such that they would sound palatable to 'Americans, with their practical manners, [who] have an easy way to deal with that by shortening the most unusual local and foreign names, and do that sometimes arbitrarily with non-English names'.[42] Names shape identities; they are a crucial factor in crafting an individual's sense of self. It is through our names that we place ourselves in the world, and our name is the first personal possession we share with the world in presenting ourselves. When forced to change names, individuals are being asked to shift identities; the fact that host nations force minoritised groups to change their names indicates that host nations harbour feelings of superiority over minoritised populations, attempting to forcefully assimilate the minoritised members into the dominant culture by manipulating important cultural markers, including names. Although diasporic minoritised groups may cultivate their roots, it is often the hostility and ethnocentrism of the host nation that impedes their complete assimilation into the host culture.

[41] Ibid. pp. 143–44.
[42] Sarkissian, *Tales of 1001 Iranian Days*, p. 8.

My last name, Yaghoobi, is indicative of one of these instances. My actual last name in Iran was Yaghoobi Massihi – Massihi is a suffix which means Christian. I dropped Massihi in the US after becoming an American citizen since, in America, Yaghoobi was taken as my middle name. In the US, my last name is pronounced with a variation of Yahoobi or Yagoobi – the 'gh' sound (similar to the French 'r') is lost. My ancestral last name was Hacopian whose translation is Yaghoobi – Yaqub, Jacob, Hacop. In Iran, at some point the office of birth registry translated our last name into one more palatable for Iranians but at the same time added the suffix Massihi to mark us as Christian. In Iran, I had a Muslim colleague whose last name was also Yaghoobi. When colleagues wanted to distinguish between us while we were both present in the same room, they would mark us with our religion – the Christian Yaghoobi or the Muslim Yaghoobi.

Throughout, the Iranian Armenian diasporic narratives accentuate that fewer transnational generations strive to maintain Armenian heritage with an almost monolithic definition of Armenianness. These efforts seem sensible given their predicament. The characters juggle family, complex national histories and their own tumultuous lives in the diaspora. They grow entrenched in the past as they struggle to unravel their present identity. Physically distant from their heritage, they feel groundless in the diaspora. As a result, they spend most of their lives in search of their identity. While adapting to life in the diaspora, they feel that they may lose a part of their identity or, in other words, are displaced from their past selves. Often, integration involves total erasure of the past, their cultural heritage and even their names. The forced dislocation from the homeland has been translated into a form of emotional displacement. In this state, diasporic Iranian Armenians describe how the homeland shifts from being a memory to something closed off, something the essence of which they can hardly even recreate in their new environment. This is true for Iranian Armenians in the contexts of both Iran and the US. In Iran, the shift occurs in relation to Armenia, while in the US it is in the context of both Iran and Armenia.

In this limbo, they engage in a process of loss that entails the sublimation of their old self; in reducing their identity, some parts of the core identity are lost forever, further transforming diasporic identity through imposed loss. Changes in the way in which their names are written and pronounced evoke emotional displacement – a distinct change that leads to a path of blurring memories and blotting out the past. Simply by existing in another place, aspects of their past are blotted out, forcing them into a different iteration of their identity; hence, they are preoccupied with celebrating rituals, traditions and ceremonies related to their homeland's history. In essence, their life becomes a series of constant, irreversible rebirths in a *verants'ughi* space, and while there is a sense of joy in birth, rebirth and creation, there is also pain in the loss of the old and the trauma of the past. What remains common between the two is a surrender to the unknown, the uncertain and the multiple.

The surrender to the multiple is discernible in Iranian Armenian poet Sonia Balassanian's *Yerku Girk Banasteghtsutyun* (*Two Books of Poems*), where she is writing about wars, calamities and the Genocide:

We are standing invincibly
Missiles around
With sweaty foreheads
And our fists hardened
Squeezing a bunch of flowers.

Our view is clear
Our words short.
We do not have a sinister laughter
But a simple demand.

With the ashes of the martyrs' bodies
We have anointed our souls
We stand straight
Look into your eyes
We demand
   Ownership,
   Land.[43]

---

[43] Sonia Balassanian, *Yerku Girk Banasteghtsutyun* (*Two Books of Poems*) (Yerevan: The Armenian Center for Contemporary Experimental Art, 2006), 192.

Balassanian wrote this poem on 15 April 1986 – an important date for understanding the poem's context. We can interpret that this is a poem about the demand for the lost homeland of Armenia and recognition of the Armenian Genocide (24 April 1915) since it was written in the month of April. However, the year of the poem, 1986, falls during the Iran–Iraq War (1980–88), which can also speak to lost Iranian lands and souls to the atrocities of the war. If we disregard the date, the poem can be read in a global context that may apply to any lost land. The fluidity within this poem through which the reader can form multiple interpretations speaks to Balassanian's transnationality and multiple consciousnesses.

Multiplicity of consciousness within identity formation is an important theme in works that study identity, otherness and majority-minority relations. According to Stuart Hall, '[t]he fully unified, completed, secure and coherent identity is a fantasy. Instead, as the system of meanings and cultural representations multiply, we are confronted by a bewildering, fleeting multiplicity of possible identities, any one of which we could identify with – at least temporarily'.[44] Cultural identity was once defined in terms of 'one, shared culture, a sort of collective "one true self", hiding inside the many other, more superficial and artificially imposed "selves", which people with a shared history and ancestry held in common'.[45] This definition, however, severely limits the individual, who is construed as a non-autonomous being experiencing an imposed unification. By this definition, identity 'bridge[ed] the gap between the "inside" and the "outside" – between the personal and public worlds'.[46] Although this definition became a refrain in studies of cultural identity, it has shifted and metamorphosed over time. Today, the individual, earlier viewed as a stable identity, is approached as fragmented, due to contradictory and unresolved aspects of their identity. In Hall's words, this new 'post-modern subject' has no permanent identity and is constantly transforming in accord with cultural systems in their milieu.[47] This 'post-modern subject' is what Zoya Pirzad presents through the character of Clarice Ayvazian in *Chiragh-ha*. In Pirzad's

---

[44] Hall, 'Introduction: Identity in Question', p. 277.
[45] Hall, 'Cultural Identity and Diaspora', p. 223.
[46] Hall, 'Introduction: Identity in Question', p. 276.
[47] Ibid. p. 277.

novel, Clarice's character nullifies this concept of 'a unified and coherent identity' and demonstrates her multiple consciousnesses. Clarice represents this incoherent subject. Living in her small Armenian community in Southern Iran, Clarice experiences an intense internal struggle when she tries to reconcile her multiple, conflicting identities.

At the beginning of the novel, Clarice's cognitive representation of 'the self' adheres to the characteristics of Armenian community members, the most salient group to which she belongs. The feeling of belonging to this community does not allow her to separate her individual 'self' from the collective Armenian consciousness.[48] This orients her in a situation of 'depersonalization of self-representation', since Clarice cannot separate herself from the collective.[49] When individuals categorise themselves within a social context and view themselves as indistinguishable from their community members (the in-group), they may also view other in-group members as interchangeable, suggesting that depersonalisation takes place collectively.[50] The representation of the in-group is embodied in a 'prototype', defined by those features deemed most salient by the group. Such prototypical features (and the ideals that construct them) capture in-group similarities and intergroup differences that distinguish the in-group from comparative outgroups. Perceptions of the self and other in-group members are then assimilated into this prototype. In-group members are perceived as more alike, and relatively homogeneous.[51]

Some recent developments in social identity theory, however, have focused on how groups are internally differentiated with regard to prototypicality. Some member characteristics are deemed more prototypical than

[48] See Marilynn B. Brewer and Wendi Gardner, 'Who Is This "We"? Levels of Collective Identity and Representations'. *Journal of Personality and Social Psychology* 71 (1996), pp. 83–93.

[49] John C. Turner, Michael A. Hogg, Penelope J. Oakes, Stephen D. Reicher and Margaret S. Wetherell, *Rediscovering the Social Group: A Self-Categorization Theory* (Oxford: Blackwell, 1987), 50.

[50] Masaki Yuki, 'Intergroup Comparison versus Intragroup Relationships: A Cross-Cultural Examination of Social Identity Theory in North American and East Asian Cultural Contexts', *Social Psychology Quarterly* 66. 2 (2003), pp. 166–183.

[51] Bertjan Doosje, Naomi Ellemers and Russell Spears, 'Perceived Intragroup Variability as a Function of Group Status and Identification', *Journal of Experimental Social Psychology* 31 (1995), pp. 410–36.

others; prototypicality is associated with differential influence within the group and with processes of leadership and marginalisation.[52] This system implies a depersonalised perception of the in-group since group members are construed either as interchangeable or as different, based on their prototype-derived position in the group. This 'depersonalization' makes Clarice perceive her 'self' as a fungible exemplar of the group rather than as a unique person. For Clarice, this occurs in a comparative context between in-group Armenian members such as her mother, her sister Alice and her friend Nina, and out-group Iranians (Shiite Muslims) such as Mrs Parvin Nurollahi. However, in truth, in-groups and out-groups are interdependent – Iranian Armenians and Muslim Iranians – and they cannot be defined in isolation from one another. Hence, by the end of the novel, Clarice breaks with her Armenian community and the ways in which it has shaped her identity, and she reconstructs her subjectivity in the context of interactions with the Shi'ite Iranian Muslim community. Her split from the shared culture of Armenian identity makes it possible for her to construct a new non-unified and incoherent subjectivity.

The role of community in shaping one's diasporic identity is of the utmost significance. The strongest and most frequent recollections occur among community members. For Clarice, however, this reliance on shared history only deepens the 'us' versus 'them' dichotomy. Her diasporic experience leads her to identify solely with her homeland and her Armenian community in order to find a place of belonging. Living in the diaspora contributes to the potential for bifurcation, causing one's identity to become 'plural and partial'; yet, this bifurcation helps to form a transnational and multifaceted identity.[53] Within this plurality, there is no need to choose between cultures; instead, the hybrid individual must embrace different aspects of each culture and create a new, diverse and plural identity, dependent neither on the original nor host culture, but encompassing both and establishing multiculturality.

Throughout the novel, Clarice displays many personas. At times, she appears to be accepted and admired by her Armenian community; however,

[52] Dominic Abrams, Jose M. Marques, Nicola Bown and Michelle Henson, 'Pro-Norm and Anti-Norm Deviance Within and Between Groups', *Journal of Personality and Social Psychology* 78 (2000), pp. 906–12.

[53] Rushdie, *Imaginary Homelands*, p. 431.

she later realises that she is, in fact, hiding her true 'self' behind these variations and is on the verge of losing her individuality. Hiding her true self and
believing that this is who she really is makes Clarice's life banal.[54] One of
Clarice's personas is dutiful and obliging. She does what is expected under
that rubric so effectively that she can no longer detach herself from it. Clarice
also correlates a variety of statements with specific personas to indicate her
moods. While she formulates most of her statements in the predicative to
convey her stream of consciousness, she also interjects interrogatively. This
questioning implies that she is critical of herself and her milieu.[55] We hear
Clarice saying: 'Then I will finally have time for the things I want to do,
I thought. My critical streak started in, "Like what things?" I opened the
door to the living room and answered, "I don't know". It was a depressing
thought'.[56] Later, she continues: 'My penchant for self-criticism meant that I
had challenged myself on this more than once: What does locking the door
have to do with being alone? To which I always answered: I don't know'.[57]
Clarice's self-criticism is prompted by the communal pressure to conform to
the mould of the perfect Armenian housewife. However, Clarice's rational
side subverts the prescribed Armenian mould. Clarice's struggles suggest that,
like Edmond in Pirzad's other work, she has tendencies of non-conformity
within the Armenian hegemony's in-group.

Clarice defines herself based on the features that she shares with her Armenian
community or based on her Armenian prototypicality. These features maintain
a type of continuity among members of the Iranian Armenian community and
simultaneously distinguish group members from the non-Armenian community
in Iran through constant comparison. According to social psychologist Henri
Tajfel, this type of cultural identity is defined as 'that part of an individual's self-
concept which derives from [their] knowledge of [their] membership of a social

---

[54] Vajihih Turkamani Bar-anduzi and Sanaz Chamani Gulzar, 'Persona az didgah-i Zoya Pirzad'
(Persona in Zoya Pirzad's View), *Baharistan-i Sukhan: Adabiyat-i Farsi* 26 (2015), p. 147.

[55] Muhammad Reza Pahlavan-nijad and Faizih Varzi-nijad, 'Barresi-yi sabk-i roman-i *Chiragh-
ha ra man khamush mikunam* ba ruykard-i fara-naqsh mian fardi nazari-i naqsh-girayi' (The
Study of the Style of *Things Left Unsaid* with Interpersonal Theory of Metafunction), *Adab
Pazhuhi* 7–8 (1388/2010), pp. 51–78, 72.

[56] Pirzad, *Things We Left Unsaid*, p. 13; Pirzad, *Chiragh-ha ra man khamush mikunam*, p. 19.

[57] Ibid. p. 64.

group or groups, together with the value and emotional significance attached to that membership'.[58] We see that, when there is a change in her mother's attitude or her sister's behaviour, Clarice's self is impacted. In response to these changes, Clarice tries to indulge her mother constantly and prove to her that she is a perfect Armenian wife, mother and housewife. In response, Clarice's mother continuously compares Clarice to a status quo, a by-product of the assumption that all Armenian women are the same. In Clarice's case, for example, she critiques her unwashed curtains. In comparison, Clarice's sister, Alice, is never made to observe that same modus operandi. As she gradually loses her individuality in the process of pleasing her mother, Clarice's self becomes increasingly 'depersonalised'. By the end of the novel, however, Clarice accepts Mrs Nurollahi's invitation to participate in a lecture on Iranian women's activism, which illustrates Clarice's tendency to move beyond her Armenian in-group.

Clarice's true self tries to find a way to emerge from behind her masks and personas, a desire for freedom exemplified when she notices Mrs Nurollahi's talk on 'Woman and Freedom' on the amphitheatre's bulletin board and decides to attend. By presenting the parallel life-styles of Clarice and Mrs Nurollahi, Pirzad introduces a catalyst that modifies Clarice's Armenian-based subjectivity. This agent of change, however, is contextualised within Iranian Muslim identity. Because of this, Clarice for some time feels conflicted about accepting this change. As opposed to Clarice, Mrs Nurollahi's relationship with society is not organic but cultural. Mrs Nurollahi is the epitome of a pluralist person. She has moved beyond the borders of self, religion, culture and nationality while maintaining her individuality. Like Clarice, she is married with children, yet also employed and involved with women's rights issues in her milieu. She does not evaluate the world based on her interests or ideologies. Instead, Mrs Nurollahi accepts it as a whole and aspires to make a difference.[59] This sense of transcendence beyond social expectations is absent within Pirzad's Armenian community – probably a comment about the isolation of ethnic minoritised communities in Iran. Immediately after reading the announcement of Mrs Nurollahi's talk, Clarice

---

[58] Tajfel, *Human Groups and Social Categories*, p. 255.

[59] Navid Sahami, 'Naqdi bar kitab-i *Chiragh-ha ra man khamush mikunam*' (A Study of *Things Left Unsaid*), *Chista* 200 (2004), p. 825.

recalls the last time she had a conversation with her husband, Artoush, and their family friends Garnik and Nina about getting involved in Iran's socio-political activism. While Garnik had questioned Clarice's need to be involved and Nina had been absolutely oblivious to what was happening, Artoush, her husband, had expressed: 'We are Iranians, are we not?'[60] Garnik, Artoush and Nina's various responses about women's rights and voting are emblematic of the different responses to Armenian acculturation within an Iranian cultural context. Even though Armenians have lived in Iran for over 400 years (with some over a millennia) and some have been integrated and assimilated, yet others have remained marginal. Those who have adapted to the new culture have also acquired 'multicultural attitudes, skills and self-perception'.[61] Artoush, whose understanding of Iranian culture, values and norms differs from those of other Armenian community members, seems to be functioning successfully in both worlds. Artoush's acquisition of knowledge about Iranian culture has not affected his sense of Armenian identity, however. Having lived in Iran for such a long time, he has learned aspects of Iranian culture, which have led to a bicultural shift in his cultural identity. Clarice's sceptical view of activism in Iran is also reflected in her disapproval of Artoush's political activism. When Clarice confronts him for forgetting about the Armenian Genocide, Artoush explains that tragedy is everywhere; if anyone wants to do something about it, it is better to act for those who are still alive. He does not participate in the ceremony commemorating the Armenian Genocide because he believes that people are suffering from tragedies today near the Shotait neighbourhood – and they need help more urgently than those killed years ago.[62]

By contrasting Artoush's self-perception and Clarice's progress towards self-awareness, Pirzad shows that there is an indubitable solidarity between humans that transcends notions of nationality, religion and culture. Artoush's political tendencies, his opposition to barriers such as ethnicity and his sympathetic view of all human plights around him are indicative of Pirzad's view, as are Mrs Nurollahi's efforts to understand the structure of Armenian social

---

[60] Pirzad, *Things We Left Unsaid*, p. 80.
[61] Bochner, 'Social Stereotypes', p. 350.
[62] Pirzad, *Things We Left Unsaid*, pp. 147–48.

life and her sympathy with the Armenian Genocide.[63] When Clarice asks Mrs Nurollahi why she attended the Armenian Genocide commemoration, Mrs Nurollahi responds similarly to Artoush: 'A tragedy is a tragedy, it's not a Muslim or Armenian thing'.[64] As a result of her exposure to Mrs Nurollahi, we begin to see a gradual shift in Clarice's identity.

Mrs Nurollahi's social activism and Clarice's interest in her illustrate the relationship that the Armenians of Iran experience within extended Iranian society. When Clarice goes to Mrs Nurollahi's lecture on women's rights, she questions herself about the extent to which minoritised populations should get involved in social matters. In contrast, Nina's indifference towards social activism and women's rights is indicative of Armenian women who are confined to their homes, domestically acclimated. Nina's oblivious questioning is, in fact, the bridge that carries Clarice beyond her constraints and into participation in social life and groups addressing social issues. Contradictions and doubts occur when issues of national scale arise. Mrs Nurollahi tells Clarice:

> I wanted to ask if you would be so kind as to attend the next meeting of our society? The Armenian ladies have not been inclined to join in with us. I know that you have your own society, a very active one, but as you know, the Majles elections are coming up, and as you are also no doubt aware, because of the suffrage issue, the coming year will be an important one for Iranian women . . .[65]

This invitation comes as Clarice feels shame for her social estrangement. Clarice is not pleased with her ethnically exclusive surroundings and its consequential constraints. She was not aware of the Majlis (Parliament) elections and had only recently heard about women's voting rights; she reproaches herself: '[Y]ou, and most other Armenian women, act like you are not living in this country!'[66] While the Armenian women in this novel insulate themselves within ethnically exclusive cliques, Mrs Nurollahi believes that '[t]he problems of women apply

[63] Ojakians, 'Chiragh-ha ra man khamush mikunam', p. 172.
[64] Pirzad, Things We Left Unsaid, p. 221.
[65] Ibid. p. 117.
[66] Ibid. p. 117.

to all women, it's not a Muslim or Armenian issue. Women must join together, arm in arm, and solve their problems. They must each teach one another and learn from each other'.[67] This revelation awakens Clarice not only as a woman but also as an Armenian. Mrs Nurollahi's assertions and inclusive views become a catalyst for Clarice to take the first step in getting involved in Iranian women's rights. Fighting for those rights helps Clarice to not only regain her 'sovereignty' as a woman, but also to craft a self that can integrate both her Armenian and Iranian identities – a diasporic transnational subjectivity.

Iranian Armenian cultural productions demonstrate how the less transnational generations strongly reject the idea of an identity rooted in anything other than their homeland's heritage. This experience pushes them towards their culture, as a way for them to compensate and preserve their heritage. Meanwhile, transnational Iranian Armenians find themselves in an independent territory, not belonging to either ancestral or host cultures, but simultaneously belonging to both, much like the 'perilous territory of not-belonging', as described by Said.[68] The experience of balancing the original and the host and national identity changes for the transnational generations as they learn more about the host nation's culture and often experience no other choice but to assimilate. They quickly learn how to adopt multiple nationalities and identify with multiple identities. The struggles of being stuck in-between alludes to the possibility of integrating into the host nation's culture. Diasporic Iranian Armenian individuals are held in this space of *verants'ughi*, a space in transition from being someone who experienced a static and singular identity to a person who must embrace multiplicity along with rebirth and growth.

In a short story titled 'Hakasutyun' (Contradiction), creative writer Khach'ik Khach'er astutely demonstrates the contradictions of this hybridity and in-betweenness. The story begins with the following paragraph: 'The Armenian land (soil) is sacred. This is not something that only Armenians say, but the entire world says so. What battles have been fought and what bloods have been shed to defend the homeland of Armenia'.[69] The story

---

[67] Ibid. p. 221.

[68] Said, 'Reflections on Exile', p. 140.

[69] Khach'ik Khach'er, 'Hakasutyun' (Contradiction), *Im Chakatagri Sove: Patmevatskner Zhoghovats'u* (*The Sea of My Destiny: A Collection of Short Stories*) (Antilias: Printing House of the Armenian Catholicosate of Cilicia, 2011), p. 135.

follows this reflective patriotic statement with a contradiction. The narrator recounts the story of a family visiting Armenia over the summer break. Geghani, the daughter, is playing in the yard with another Armenian child. Geghani's mother notices that the children are playing with soil and furiously calls out to her daughter: 'Do not soil [dirty] yourself. I have just changed your clothes. Don't you know that the soil is dirty, you'll get sick'.[70] Rather than being a simple command, the mother's admonition engages symbolic language rich with metaphors. In this context, soil indicates territory, a homeland that is the object of adoration and martyrdom, or an object that is capable of causing illness, evoking revulsion and aversion. This contradiction is the Iranian Armenian diaspora population's predicament. On the one hand, they are loyal to the homeland, one nation, Armenia; on the other hand, diasporic Iranian Armenians acknowledge that limiting oneself to territories and borders is an archaic practice that can be detrimental. The majority of diasporic Iranian Armenians live in the liminal space of *verants'ughi*, until they realise that their position must change. In order to bridge their divergent cultures, they develop multiple consciousnesses, requiring them to move into transnationalism, where they cannot help but (re)create, (re)birth, (re)define.

Cultural productions examine Iranian Armenian identity in ways that reveal the inevitable cultural clashes and consequences of the diasporic consciousness. As these works explore, hybridity produces tensions for cultures and histories founded on racial, national, religious, linguistic and ethnic divisions. Khoren Aramouni's *Dznhal: Veb* (*The Thaw: A Novel*) reflects these cultural clashes in the characters' inner struggles and desires to trespass (discussed in the previous chapter). Aramouni's protagonist, Susan, was raised as a Turkish Muslim and is unaware of her Armenian heritage as the granddaughter of a 1915 Genocide survivor. When she falls in love with the Armenian man Karen, she faces several internal battles, questioning herself: 'I knew it. How many generations do we need for this mentality, this stigma to be wiped off of our foreheads? What's my fault? Karen is scared [. . .] but what do I want from Karen? I don't know it myself either'.[71] Similarly, as an Armenian man with a patriotic family history, Karen confesses his struggles:

---

[70] Ibid. p. 135.
[71] Aramouni, *Dznhal*, p. 152.

'My conscience, [. . .] I mean my family, my grandma, my roots. . . Every time I meet you, I feel like my grandfather pulls me back from my collar [. . .] Don't be offended. I was raised like this. My grandfather was a great patriot, sworn anti-Turkish Dashnak. If my grandma hears about this . . .'.[72] While Aramouni's novel is a love story between two Armenians, one of whom was raised as a Muslim Turk, it is nonetheless very similar to Pirzad's 'Yik Ruz Qabl az 'iyd-i Pak', where the characters, particularly Edmond, want to trespass boundaries and borders and struggle to reconcile their dual or multiple consciousnesses.

As it transforms from a diasporic subjectivity to a transnational one, Iranian Armenian identity becomes diverse and heterogeneous, spanning generations. The reality of life for Iranian Armenians in the diaspora changes over time, and transnational generations embrace a heterogeneous definition of 'Armenianness'. This transcendence and transnationalism are crystalised in Susan's comment that in today's world for understanding the truth, we need communication rather than the borders that the older generation maintains.[73] Karen also critiques how the less transnational generation has dictated his identity:

Do you want to know the truth? I am a lost generation. Whoever's born in the U.S. is an American. You've forced me, yes dad, forced, the same way they've forced Suzi [Susan] into being a Turk. Forced into the Armenian school, Armenian music, dance, food, market, Khash, Khorovats, [. . .] All these during my happy carefree childhood and teenage years. Dad, I am very different from Armenian youth of my age, I am a different type, as if we are from different nations.[74]

This embrace of heterogeneity is at times isolating for those who cannot adhere to fixity and its strictures. For Armenians, this comes with an additional burden of the memories of the Genocide. Identities are constructed through an interaction with exclusive, specific modalities of power, and in that regard these cultural productions, through their exploration of diasporic

---

[72] Ibid. p. 162.
[73] Ibid. p. 181.
[74] Ibid. p. 214.

otherness, highlight the construction of Armenian identity as the other.[75] However, these writings also emphasise that, in the current world, hybridity and multiculturalism rather than a binary are essential to foregrounding notions such as togetherness-in-difference, rather than separateness.

Hybridity and multiplicity equip Iranian Armenians to reject the divisions of 'us' and 'them'. With these concepts, Iranian Armenians can claim their differences. Non-heterogeneity is transformed into a source of cultural power to reject marginalisation and exclusion. Garnik Der Hacopian's works embody the art of togetherness-in-difference; according to art historian Ruyin Pakbaz, 'he uses different sources, such as western modern art, and Persian traditional arts, and the Armenian cultural heritage; specifically, cubism's geometrical methods of spatial organisation and expressionistic exaggeration of colors and shapes, and also Persian motifs and Armenian ornaments'.[76] His still life paintings emerged out of long-standing attachments from the earliest years of his professional life. His alluring object compositions, in his familiar style of scratching and painting on concrete surfaces, have recurred over the years. Der Hacopian demonstrates how the subjective representation of the world plays in his mind and is eventually transformed into abstract motifs. He emphasises the tension between classical elements of design, geometric composition and modern elements in real life. The object arrangement in his paintings takes the viewer into a simple and unadorned space that includes elements from Armenian and Iranian cultures, revisiting his cultural roots and displaying his own hybrid existence.

In Figure 5.4, an Armenian coffee pot stands in as a staple of Armenianness, the pomegranate as a symbol of fertility associated with both Armenia and Iran, and some latticework frames in the background inspired by the artist's mother's crochet work and embroidery are reminiscent of an Armenian khachkar. These symbols coalesce to illuminate a concern with traditions, roots and heritage. At the same time, the inclusion of the frames that say 'water' and 'juice' in English seem jarring and disruptive. However, this illustrates the amalgamation of the classical and the modern, disintegration and integration, Armenian, Iranian and English. Such combinations grant

---

[75] Stuart Hall, 'Introduction: Who Needs Identity?' p. 4.
[76] Der Hacopian and Pakbaz, *The Presence of the Absent Artist*, p. 155.

Figure 5.4 Garnik Der Hacopian, *Still Life*, mixed media with cement on wood panel, 1996. Courtesy of the artist.

diasporic Iranian Armenians the symbolic power to transcend and reach beyond their ethnic minoritised status, all the while conveying a community that has both historical roots and ancestral heritage outside of the host nation's time and space.

With an emphasis on their 'feeling' of Armenianness, transnational Iranian Armenians are truly part of a 'diasporic transnational' community. This diasporic transnationalism, in turn, provides insight into Iranian Armenians' struggle with multiple consciousnesses, multiple identities and multiple forms of existence. While boundaries are constantly being established, reinforced and modified, these Iranian Armenians also want to free themselves from one culture, one community and one nation. In this sense, the self and the other exist in the same space. In Minh-ha's words, 'it is always over here, between Us, within Our discourse that the "other" becomes a nameable reality. Thus, despite all the conscious attempts to purify and exclude, cultures are far from being unitary, as they have always owed their existence more to differences, hybridities and alien elements than they really care to acknowledge'.[77] Transnational generations of diasporic Iranian Armenians acknowledge these differences and hybridities. They recognise one another's differences, fractured identities and fragmented memories, yet also connect with others cross-culturally. This disrupts positions of privilege because it reveals multiple affiliations. The transnational diasporic Iranian Armenians soften the boundaries of 'us' versus 'them' through exchanges and mutual connections. While not always harmonious, these exchanges allow them to negotiate their social differences and positions. Of course, these exchanges follow and develop out of a tradition of centuries of similar exchanges and negotiations by Iranian Armenians that have made these boundaries porous today. Cultural permeability, which is essential in a world where individuals live together in their differences, is the result of their transnational, liminal, hybrid position today.

In this way, diasporic transnational Iranian Armenians challenge earlier understandings of diaspora, immigration and assimilation; they subvert hegemonic identity formations by insinuating the marginalised other into the fabric of the dominant. This re-articulation decolonises hegemonic notions that we have one unified national identity and destabilises power relations between the ethnic and the native. Through their transnational boundary-blurring within the space of *verants'ughi*, they become – in geographer Michael Smith's words – not only transnational, but also translocal; that is, 'situated yet mobile subjectivities', both here and there.[78]

---

[77] Minh-ha, 'Other Than Myself, My Other Self', p. 45.
[78] Michael Peter Smith, 'Translocality: A Critical Reflection', *Translocal Geographies: Spaces, Places, Connections*, ed. Katherine Brickell and Ayona Datta (Farnham: Ashgate, 2011), pp. 181–98.

CONCLUSION

Negotiating Identity via Creativity

I too create, write and paint. Art and writing allow me to reinterpret borders and identities. When I write/create, I am not limited to the set borders that define places and distinguish 'us' versus 'them'. The realm of artistry is a liminal space, just like *verants'ughi*, where there is no prohibition, nothing is forbidden; hybridity and transnationalism dominate. This creative space is vague and undetermined, a constant state of transition, growth and transformation. Nation-states and political belonging have less significance than the present moment. When I am creating, there are no territories to demarcate my existence; all spaces are de-territorialised, and boundaries are blurred. In the world of creation, I can cross any lines – this is liberating, non-judgmental, transnational. In this empowering state of diasporic transnational hybridity, I can allow for authentic exchanges, crossings and entanglements, softening categorical boundaries between people, cultures, identities. This is where I negotiate differences in order to avoid conflict, the result of which is a profoundly hybridised world where boundaries are porous. My transnationalism in the realm of creativity provide me with moments when I can confront and problematise boundaries, although I cannot erase them. While this involves some degree of ambivalence regarding my social position where it becomes a source of cultural permeability and vulnerability, it is a necessary condition for living as someone in a constant state of *verants'ughi*.

The fields of psychology and medicine have amply documented that patients' symptoms begin to drastically improve as they remember and speak about their trauma and emotions with a psychoanalyst.[1] Talking about one's traumatic past has always been a useful tool for overcoming it – take, for instance, Holocaust survivors sharing their survival stories. For Iranian Armenian writers and artists in the diaspora, this healing space is found in what I call their 'writing/showing cure' – a space where they process through disordered memories of the past. Through their medium of storytelling and reflection on fragmented memories, these artists and authors centre themselves in their diasporic reality. In this chapter, I examine the ways in which Iranian Armenian writers and artists come to terms with their fragmented thoughts and memories through their creativity.

The shifts, changes, traumas and insecurity of a life lived in displacement disorganise thought processes. Diasporic Iranian Armenian authors' and artists' memories appear to lack some connections or details that would make them complete, but each fragment helps to piece them together in order to tell a richer story, making every recollection or fact more significant to the reader. For them, the homeland does not have to be ultimately lost – there is hope in returning to a homeland that is mentally recreated. The physical separation between themselves and the homeland creates two distinct forms of homeland: as it currently exists, and as it is remembered. Salman Rushdie explains this in the context of Indian writers when he notes: 'It may be that when the Indian writer who writes from outside India tries to reflect that world, he is obliged to deal in broken mirrors, some of whose fragments have been irretrievably lost'.[2] Their incomplete memories in the diaspora can be assembled to create a picture of the homeland that is simultaneously whole and fractured.

Literature and art serve as 'writing and showing cures' for authors and artists, not only because they allow them space to process past trauma, but also because they give them an opportunity to construct a kind of home through cultural productions. Addressing the important and complicated aspects of what it means to be in the diaspora, permanently estranged from one's

---

[1] Sigmund Freud, *The Standard Edition of the Complete Psychological Works of Sigmund Freud*, ed. Josef Breuer, James Strachey, Anna Freud and Angela Richards (London: Vintage, 2001).
[2] Rushdie, *Imaginary Homelands*, p. 429.

homeland, or with no choice to return, Edward Said employs the 'writing cure' in his essay 'Reflections on Exile'. While Said uses this space to process the many layers and complexities of exile, he also discusses the role of writing in the life of Theodor Adorno, a German exile and one of Said's principal influencers. Said writes: 'Theodor Adorno, the German-Jewish philosopher and critic, wrote his autobiography while in exile. Adorno's reflections are informed by the belief that the only home truly available now, though fragile and vulnerable, is in writing . . .'[3] In several of the entries throughout his collection *Minima Moralia*, Adorno questions the true meaning of home, where home lies for the diasporic subject and the safety of different kinds of homes. Adorno used writing to heal himself from feelings of homelessness and loss tied to his exile.

Similarly, in his book *Outlandish*, Nico Israel discusses displacement as a predicament explored in writing. He analyses the work of three writers (including Adorno) and discusses twentieth-century diasporic writing. In discussing Adorno's symbolic use of the house, Israel includes Adorno's writing, allowing the theorist to demonstrate an exploration of the 'home-in writing:' 'In his text, the writer sets up house. Just as he trundles papers, books, pencils, and documents untidily from room to room, he creates the same disorder in his thoughts. They become pieces of furniture that he sinks into, content or irritable [. . .] For a man who no longer has a homeland, writing becomes a place to live'.[4] Israel comprehends Adorno's understanding that many individuals who experience isolation – including diasporic people – feel most at home when they have the freedom to put their fragmented thoughts into creation. In the same way, Said confirms the benefits of poetry and writing for those in exile, but also warns against romanticising exilic literature, or using one's position in exile to fuel creativity without adequately addressing the hardships and loss that define their own displacement. Said provides the example of Irish novelist James Joyce, who repeatedly chose conflict with Ireland in order to remain in exile as his inspiration for his work.[5]

While some artists, like Joyce, strive to keep themselves in the diaspora, self-imposed exile, or separated from what is familiar to them in hopes of

---

[3] Said, 'Reflections on Exile', p. 147.

[4] Nico Israel, *Outlandish* (Palo Alto: Stanford University Press, 2000), p. 84.

[5] Said, 'Reflections on Exile', pp. 147–48.

deepening their work, displacement is never a desirable state. These authors and artists process the trauma of being permanently separated from their homeland, as well as the trauma that accompanies life in the diaspora. For Iranian Armenian diasporic cultural productions, this integration and disintegration are situated in the consistently entwined reflections on the historical and political climate, as well as a combination of other elements that coalesce to capture a life in the diaspora. Up against these walls and living in an uncertain world, they use the power of their style, physical writing and producing, and their lexicon to solidify their existence and identity, protesting those who attempt to destabilise their communities and history as things best forgotten. In a poem titled 'Self-Knowledge', Sato A. ponders her identity as she tries to connect it to her history, roots, ancestry and culture:

> How does a person know themselves?
> By their father, mother, their roots?
> By their history and books?
> By the sound of their blood and ashes?
> So, who am I?
> I have thought about this issue a lot
> And I have often replied to myself:
>> A poor stranger Armenian.[6]

A few lines later in the same poem, she recognises herself as an individual who has been driven out of her homeland while her roots are still there. She declares that she will only come to know herself fully when she builds a home in the homeland of Armenia. In a sense, Sato A. connects identity to the homeland and knowledge of self to being in Armenia.

In 'Writing Exile: Writing Home', Øyunn Hestetun discusses the significance of borders and the reality that people can only be incorporated into a citizenry if others are excluded. As borders are emphasised, belonging is reserved for some, and the distinction between natives and nonnatives grows. Emphasising the significance of second-language learning

---

[6] Sato A., 'Inknachanach'um' (Self-Knowledge), *Herazheshtits' araj* (*Before Farewell*) (Tehran: Nayiri Publishing House, 2002), p. 11.

in a foreign country, Hestetun discusses the autobiography of the Polish-American Eva Hoffman, who wrote her autobiography while in the diaspora. She explains: 'The overarching focus is directed at how she has to learn to speak, write, think, and even dream in a new language, while highlighting that this process involves constructing a new sense of self'.[7] Through their works, Iranian Armenian authors and artists are similarly provided with a space to understand the inseparability of integration and disintegration.

In *Free Fall: Collected Short Stories*, Iranian Armenian American author Leonardo Alishan recalls how his language choice caused his work to be rejected by publishers, in a poem titled 'Motion Sickness': 'Then she handed him his manuscript and added, "I know it doesn't mean anything but I read it and liked it very much. Unfortunately, they thought the book was a bit too depressing and the language too archaic. I am really sorry"'.[8] This rejection is indicative of the diasporic author's impasse: they can write either in an ethnic language not often published by mainstream publishers, or in the majority hegemonic language, but as a second- or foreign-language speaker with awkward, 'archaic' sentences.

In addition to their language choices, diasporic narratives are often fragmented, with a disjointed format and flow that directly parallels their own fragmented identity, further illustrating how writing can portray diasporic existence. At other times, they write in a stream of consciousness, jumping from one topic to another, constantly juxtaposing details of the narrator's daily routine with passages of poetry, inner dialogue, political commentary, extensional questioning and seemingly random phrases. This sporadic style is a deliberate choice that reveals personal insights into diasporic life.

In 'Refuge', a poem from *Dancing Barefoot on Broken Glass*, Alishan discusses this quest for identity, the fragmentation of the self and how writing poetry is his refuge in the diaspora.

---

[7] Øyunn Hestetun, 'Writing Exile: Writing Home', *The Borders of Europe: Hegemony, Aesthetics and Border Poetics* (Århus: Aarhus University Press, 2012), p. 236.
[8] Alishan, *Free Fall*, p. 173.

I need structure
I need form

. . . When the poet is a mad Armenian priest
When the poet is a drunk Iranian cleric

I need clean English
I need Alexander Pope.[9]

Alishan is aware of his fragmented memory, existence and writing – he seeks structure; however, he seeks a structure that imitates his multiple consciousnesses. The physical act of writing provides him with an outlet and mechanism to establish memory, history and legacy against forgetfulness, while also allowing him to rewrite the (hi)story. All his life, he struggles to control his situation, connecting with his homeland and understanding his fragmented identity, yet the one constant in his life is writing. In the fight against oblivion, Alishan chooses writing. Writing gives him the ability to be heard, seen and remembered. His personal story is an invitation for a profound conversation about the collective (hi)story that travels from generation to generation. For him, stories are cultural markers as well as artistic quests.

The power of words provides an outlet to explore their existence and identity. Living in the diaspora, triggered by a loss of self, authors grapple with their own being. In a poem titled 'Verjin togh-e' (The Last Line), Soukias Hacob Koorkchian (Varand) equates his being with his writing:

If need be . . . of suicide,
I'll open my vein with a pen.
Let my body become
A large inkpot
I'll write in blood
                    The last line of 'life'
                    Of writing.[10]

Writing is a life-long mission for diasporic authors who are willing to die writing in their own blood – they have to tell their stories, or they will be

---

[9] Alishan, 'Refuge', p. 51.
[10] Soukias Hacob Koorkchian (also known as Varand), 'Verjin togh-e' (The Last Line), *Anveradardz* (*Irreversible*) (Tehran: Alik Publishers, 1999), p. 60.

forgotten. But these authors also see their writing as a refuge. In this sense, writing is an expression of memory that establishes a relationship between safety and comfort and the author. While the physical, geographical home seems unattainable, writing has the capacity to provide both a sense of home and identity by contemplating memories. We observe this in Azad Matian's poem where he, too, finds a home in writing. Writing gives him the power to fight for belonging, the right to remember, while also fighting *to be* remembered. He writes:

I don't have an address.
I've been deported from seven ports.
I carry my home like a turtle.
No, I carry my home like a poem within me.
And I frequently lose my way.[11]

In Matian's poems, the image of the turtle with its house on its back is symbolic, describing the displacement and constant mobility of a diasporic person (this same imagery of the turtle and home has been used by Anzaldúa).

One of the key aspects of living in the diaspora is uncertainty – uncertainty about whether one will be able to return home, or if the homeland will continue to exist as remembered. Nothing is certain; identities are in flux, as are social positions. This is that space of *verants'ughi*, of bridges, of passageways, full of pain but also full of potential and growth. Iranian Armenian diasporic cultural productions capture this uncertainty, in part, through language and structure. These works manifest the artists' existence in a world where their roots are on the edge of extinction. They manipulate the subject of divine, eternal existence to demonstrate the excruciating dissociations that a diasporic author endures, furthering their drive to prove their existence.

As an author in the diaspora, struggling with such existential concerns, Vahe Armen associates his divine beliefs with geographic location and place. In a poem titled 'Golgotha', Armen, using Christian symbolism, refers to his pen as the cross he carries and his poetry as his Golgotha:

---

[11] Safarian, *Dar Fasiliyih du Kuch* (*Between Two Migrations*).

The cross I was wearing on my neck
I sold it yesterday
To the Gold seller

My cross
Is a wooden pen
On the shoulder of a paper
My Golgotha
A short poem
But
Glorious[12]

By actively writing, Armen takes the responsibility of authoring himself and his community into existence, acting as his own creator by establishing a life in the midst of an uprooted state that seems unsustainable. His pen becomes his cross – the burden, the mission – he carries to his crucifixion on Golgotha, in a place of suffering and sacrifice. His written word is crucial to his existence beyond the physical realm because he has no other eternal, spiritual claim of belonging. His poems are like snapshots of his existence. Since his claim to identity is dependent on the written word, he establishes that the pain of his existence is tied to the daily experience not only of living, sacrificing, suffering and dying, but also of resurrection, rebirth and reinvention of the self, themes tied to the symbols of Golgotha and the Cross. In this way, living, dying, rebirth and writing are bound together – the author's body becoming 'the battlefield for the pitched fight between the inner image and the words trying to recreate it. [. . .] a crossroads, a fragile bridge . . . '[13]

Similarly, Sonia Balassanian treats writing as a medium that will save her from drowning and considers *not* writing a sin:

Descended from the gallows
    The faith of the withdrawn eyes of the earth
Makes me write
        The impossible . . .

---

[12] Vahe Armen, 'Golgotha', *Pas az ubur-i Dorna-ha* (*After the Passing of the Cranes*) (Tehran: Nashr-i Adabi, 2015), p. 15.
[13] Anzaldúa, *Borderlands/La Frontera*, p. 96.

Drowned song
>And the deaf blows of the hammer
>Are burying my soul forever in the ground.
My fist
>Creates a future from the ground up.
Bodies in parts
>>Breathing,
>>suffering,
>>Living
>>Under the weight of the stories.
I cannot sin . . .[14]

Balassanian establishes the significance of the body as the ultimate basis for one's sense of identity. In an existence that is outwardly defined by diaspora, Balassanian draws on the imagery of a drowning body to declare a state of internal displacement, creating emotional turmoil about a national existence. More intimately, Balassanian's speaker's detachment from their own body under the hammer blows is an experience that infers the permanent loss of a home, although intensified. By widening the border between psyche and body as well as by amplifying the consciousness that senses the self, Balassanian frees herself from categories that variously delimit or mark her. She knows that something within her must die before something new can emerge. Releasing the old self/body, she frees herself from identities imposed on her, internalised and reinforced. What she thought was fixed and unalterable is a mental fabrication – she realises that everything is fluid and that she must define her identity by looking forward rather than glancing back.

In *Narratives of Identity and Place*, Stephanie Taylor discusses how identity is not necessarily confined by place or geography; rather, it is 'more complex than either "rooted belonging" or "rootless mobility"'.[15] Here, identity and a discovered sense of belonging is paradoxically defined by the ultimate lack of belonging, even to one's own body. Balassanian uses the body as a mode through which she not only gains a sense of identity but also an

---

[14] Balassanian, *Yerku Girk Banasteghtsutyun* (*Two Books of Poems*), p. 85.
[15] Stephanie Taylor, 'The Meanings of Place for Identity', *Narratives of Identity and Place* (Abingdon: Routledge, 2009), p. 2.

understanding of her place in the world and comfort within her solidarity. In *Diaspora, Memory and Identity: A Search for Home*, feminist theorist and race scholar Vijay Agnew explores the formation of identity as it relates to space and time. In an analysis of the self, she claims: 'What is striking about the "mind" [. . .] is not its uniqueness or autonomy, but rather its profound dependence upon intersubjectively shared meanings and its profound vulnerability to the deprivations of the body'.[16] In the diaspora, where one has little external control, the body connects one to others by kinship, thus creating a sense of belonging and home. Balassanian's homeland, her body (and by extension her body of work) must be used to breathe, to live and to exist in order to pass on a sense of home to future generations. In this way, the body and identity are interdependent. Hence, Balassanian deconstructs the imaginary that roots 'home' within place and geography through her realisation that 'home' can reside within oneself – in one's own body and bodily experiences, and in one's writings and creations.

But since stories often emerge from collective trauma that moulds a community, Balassanian's poem can also be a hint at the fear of forgetting the collective trauma of the 1915 Genocide or the Iran–Iraq War, or any atrocity around her, the impossibility of writing it and the impossibility of not writing it.[17] Her poetry is a survival strategy for Armenians collectively. Balassanian poignantly makes the impossible tangible and allows the reader to see the struggles, dreams, longings and aspirations of Armenians. Writing from a

---

[16] Vijay Agnew, 'Wounding Events and the Limits of Autobiography', *Diaspora, Memory and Identity: A Search for Home*, ed. Vijay Agnew (Toronto: University of Toronto Press, 2005), p. 83.

[17] See Inga Clendinnen's *Reading the Holocaust* (Cambridge: Cambridge University Press, 2002), where she discusses the impossibility of representing the horror of genocide in film, literature, art and so on, because of the trivialising effects of plotlines and other essential devices of fiction and representation. Such examples can be found in the representation of Armenian Genocide as well, where the Genocide has been turned into a formulaic film of women coming of age (*The Lark Farm*) or where the filmmaker found the subject so problematic that they chose to distance themselves from story-telling altogether, as in *Ararat* or *The Promise*, which tried to turn the Genocide into a Hollywood blockbuster, and *Mayrig* (*Mother*) where the Genocide is barely depicted and later never spoken of. This is also true in popular music sometimes – for example, System of a Down's attempts to write songs about the Genocide seem forced, as if they want to write about it but do not know where to start.

space of Iranian Armenian representation – one that is politically marked – Balassanian remembers the unforgettable so as to tell and write the impossible. She tells a story that has crossed cultures and travelled generations. While writing trauma is a difficult task, not writing it is not the answer, either. Writing trauma may make the writer sick, since facing one's trauma is debilitating; however, the reconstruction of images that have produced the trauma is crucial to make sense of the particular traumatic incident in order to transform it into healing. Thus, in a way, writing brings healing. In this context, writing (or not writing) becomes a bodily experience because a transformation of the soul is possible only through lived experiences, through the flesh. For Balassanian's creations to have the metamorphic impact of rebirth, she must give birth to them from her own bodily experiences.

Writing and telling becomes the language of trauma for diaspora Iranian Armenian authors and artists, and diction becomes their tool to reach audiences. Without expressing their vulnerability, their experiences of struggling with and overcoming loss and trauma may be lost. Through diaspora cultural productions, these incidents move from the solitary to the collective. After being rejected multiple times for writing poems in English, Alishan published 'Why Write', which explores his purpose, happiness and calling:

> My fairy and I had a wonderful relationship. She has told me, and I concur, that 'happiness' is not within my reach. But I am now at peace and content. I don't drink as much anymore, and I don't get depressed as often. My fairy doesn't give me anything but, at least, I now know for whom I write and why I write these strange Armenian-Iranian-American poems and tales.[18]

Language, and by extension writing, gives Alishan the ability to live beyond the confines of the human lifespan and his current situation. For him, it is as

---

[18] Alishan, *Free Fall*, p. 176. This reminds the reader of the Kafka controversy: the story of a Jewish man (Kafka) who did not practice Judaism or write stories about Jewish people, who was born in one country that no longer exists (Austro-Hungarian Empire) and died in another that no longer exists (Czechoslovakia) and whose legacy has been fought over by countries in which he never lived (the Czech Republic, Germany, Israel) but which all claim him. Reading Alishan reminds one of the fact that authors such as Alishan, Kafka, or Pirzad, who write about the human experience, cannot be reduced to one identity, nationality and the like.

close to immortality as possible. The language used to convey particular experiences is capable of informing later generations, especially around traumatic subjects such as displacement. The importance and usefulness of language stem from its versatility and layered meaning. Words convey more than just their literal meaning and can be used to construct deeply interwoven ideas. Within the context of diaspora, language is the most valuable way to share that experience, not only for contemporary purposes, but also for posterity.

Iranian Armenian diaspora cultural productions show that these authors and artists use the written and spoken word not only to express the paradox of their existence, but also to manifest their existence in physical form. Lacking a definitive position in space and time, writing substitutes as tangible, physical proof of existence for diasporic writers in a state of displacement. They call upon language as a powerful tool to conjure memory and history for those suffering from the symptoms of living in displacement, rampant with fragmentation and manipulation. As a device, language aids this process by grounding history and also by acting as the glue to which memory attaches itself.

The sporadic use of Armenian words and phrases within a text written in the majority language becomes a pillar for Armenian diasporic cultural productions; this convention is the compass that will guide both authors and readers through the turmoil. In consciously using Armenian words, their works bear witness to history, helping to stitch fragmented memories into one coherent fabric. While this might be true for authors, artists' approaches can vary from using the mother tongue or the host nation's language with just a tint of the mother tongue. Arby Ovanessian uses Armenian as the primary language of his documentary *Ghara Kelisa* (*Lebbaeus Whose Surname Was Thaddaeus*), but he uses the Persian language in his 1972 film *Cheshmeh* (*The Spring*).[19] *Cheshmeh*, however, revolves around an interreligious Muslim-Christian love affair. Incorporating elements of both Armenian and Iranian cultures, Ovanessian illustrates the significance of this cultural coexistence, even against cultural differences. By portraying Armenian characters who speak in Persian, Ovanessian recalls his loyalty to the homeland while also settled in the host nation of Iran. Using his bilingualism, Ovanessian

---

[19] Ovanessian, *Ghara Kelisa*; Ovanessian, *Cheshmeh*.

ventures beyond the national to embrace a transnational identity. According to film director Peter Brook, '[h]e is both a man of the East and of the West, open equally to the visible and the invisible worlds'.[20]

Language is rooted in memory, and therefore holds power over it. One can pinpoint when a particular memory was established and how it relates to other fragments based on words and language. However, this memory (and language) for diasporic people with multiple consciousnesses is also rooted in multiple sources from which they draw. For instance, Loris Tjeknavorian does not consider himself, nor wishes to be referred to, as an Iranian minoritised individual. He considers himself both Iranian and Armenian, and he is also a western citizen. According to the Iranian Students News Agency (ISNA), Tjeknavorian was offended when Armenian musicians were described as a minoritised group during a commemorative ceremony for the former conductor of the Tehran Symphony Orchestra, saying: 'It's not Armenians fault that the Armenian part [of the Persian Empire] was seceded from Iran during Fath Ali Shah Qajar's reign. [. . .] We are all Iranians and have worked hard for Iran'.[21] In his interviews, Tjeknavorian has stated he is:

> . . . proud to be a Christian Iranian because, as every Armenian in Iran considers themselves a genuine Iranian, and as an Armenian, I consider my historical origin to be Iranian. My mind has always been occupied with the question of where my homeland is because when I go to Armenia, I feel good, but Armenia has never had a real sense of homeland for me until I travel to my hometown of Boroujerd, then I fully understand the sense of homeland there. On the other hand, like all Iranians, I have fond childhood memories of mourning during the months of Muharram and Safar. I remember how excited I was to mourn with my friends. It may be hard for you to believe that on the eve of my 84th birthday, when I hear the sound of drums and cymbals, the same childhood excitement comes to life for me.[22]

---

[20] Peter Brook, 'Arby Ovanessian', *Theater and Cinema of Arby Ovanessian*, ed. Majid Lashkari (Tehran: Ruzanih Publications, 2014), p. 25.

[21] 'Loris Tjeknavorian: Don't Call Us Minorities So Much', *Fararu*, December 2014, fararu. com/fa/news/214937

[22] 'Loris Tjeknavorian: Imam Abbas Has Helped Me Several Times', *Jahan News*, 25 August 2020, https://www.jahannews.com/news/737934/

As a hybrid individual, Tjeknavorian is a composer with three sources of musical creativity that include the Armenian musical tradition, the Iranian musical tradition (in the general sense of the musical cultures in the region) and the western classical musical tradition. A composer such as Tjeknavorian has borrowed something from each of these creative sources, combining them in most of his works. In the majority of his works, he borrowed thematic and melodic materials from Armenian culture. From Iranian culture, he often borrowed rhythms, melodies and modal materials, and from western culture he derives the art of combining these factors in the form, texture and orchestration of a musical opus. These three influences have found their way into his work due to his determination to embody at least three of his cultures. In this way, by utilising these sources, he inevitably reveals the cultural composition from which he emerged.[23] Tjeknavorian began his adolescence within a world of love for music. His interest in the music of the fifth and sixth centuries of the Armenian Church as well as religious mourning rituals in Iran quickened his enthusiasm for learning music.[24]

While diasporic Iranian Armenian cultural productions are a product of the language's impact on memory, memory is fluid and vacillates among their multiple consciousnesses, and this presents a problem for diasporic subjects. Their life is already in flux due to living in an uncertain world within the diaspora. Without producing, their very existence is at risk. This level of uncertainty and fluidity is what defines diasporic life. Writing his fragmented memories into a poem titled 'Hayi Karot' (Armenian Longing), Nerses D. Mesrobian recalls details from his childhood, to which he wishes to return forever in his imagination.[25] Of course, one may question if the details are accurate, but this is not the fault of language, but of time. In Trinh T. Minh-ha's words, '[d]irecting their look toward a long bygone reality, [diasporic authors/

---

[23] Arvin Sidaghat-kish, 'Rival-hayi mushabih va manabi' si-ganih dar ahang-sazi-yi Loris Tjeknavorian' (Similar Trends and Three Sources of Loris Tjeknavorian's Compositions), *Honar-i Musighi* 23 (2020), p. 8.

[24] Mohamad Javad Sahafi, 'Musighi, 'eshq, va azadi-khahi: barresi-yi zindigi-yi pur faraz va nashib-i Loris Tjeknavorian' (Music, Love, and Freedom-Seeking: A Study of the Ups and Downs of Loris Tjeknavorian's Life), *Honar-i Musighi* 23 (2020), p. 16.

[25] Nerses D. Mesrobian, 'Hayi Karot' (Armenian Longing), p. 14. This is discussed in Chapter Two.

artists] supposedly excel in reanimating the ashes of childhood and of the country of origin'.[26] Memory is the timeline of personal experiences in relation to historical accounts; however, writing memories pushes them forward into the present and future, to the host nation and its images. All that matters is whether writers can get an overall grasp of how their memories relate to one another.

Language is subject to change, mercurial because its survival depends on that evolution, flexibility and change. A change in language does not signify a permanent alteration; in this respect, language is a form of history that is trustworthy because it cannot easily be manipulated and because its roots and stems can always be traced back through etymological records. These two characteristics make written words and creative images the ideal media for those living in the diaspora, as devices to look to their past, present and future to answer questions regarding their identity and memories.

For Vartan Gregorian, the stark reality of his experiences in the diaspora is reflected in his use of the Armenian language as a motif. By doing so, he demonstrates the limitations of language, his own role as a diasporic person and the power of silence. In his memoir, *The Road to Home: My Life and Times*, he writes after being interviewed for a professional position: 'To keep my calm, I wrote my grandmother's name, in Armenian, numerous times in order to give myself the fortitude not to show any emotion. I managed it'.[27] While coping with the struggle of uprooting coupled with rejections and the uncertainty of the future, he expresses a desire for a language that can accurately convey his emotions of loss and ultimately evokes his mother tongue. His relationship with power can be tied to his relationship with language. Yet, as a writer, he values language and the capacity of words. Thus, he yearns for a language that is strong and powerful enough to counter the trauma of diaspora – a language that is dependable and can support him through the feelings of isolation and rejection brought on by displacement.

This is the dilemma of the authors' bilingualism and multilingualism: they cannot judge each language independently of the other, because of the ways in which they are utilised in their own public and private spheres. The mother

---

[26] Minh-ha, 'Other Than Myself, My Other Self', p. 28.
[27] Gregorian, *The Road to Home*, p. 263.

tongue can be inextricable from diasporisation and tends to carry a degree of trauma. The way in which a group of people speaks about themselves shapes their own perspective as well as other people's perspectives toward them – giving them the autonomy to determine their cultural identities. This is crucial to understanding how authors perceive themselves in relation to the Armenian, Persian and American communities. The authors' and artists' Persianised or Americanised education and personal traumas culminate in their projection of properties onto languages that do not necessarily hold space or weight in other people's perspectives. Bilingualism or multilingualism leads them to define each language in contrast to the other and to prioritise one language over the other.

However, the diasporic experience transcends language and becomes much more expansive. Often, authors shift from a muddled and shallow perspective on personal, social and political realities to concise and mature viewpoints that represent their transnationalism. They do this, for example, when they write in the form of a memoir. Through a memoir, authors are able to effectively convey how they obtained these differing perspectives through diasporic experiences. Memoir as a genre allows the freedom to explore personal thoughts and stream of consciousness, compared to a structured autobiographical or fictional space. Henry A. Sarkissian, in his memoir titled *Tales of 1001 Iranian Days*, describes the mental gratification of writing a memoir about his journey as someone who is not a professional author:

> Frankly, I also have a faint hope it may improve my image as someone who has written a book without being a writer or a somebody even if I have to print it at my own expense.
>
> In any case, besides its image-building aspect, this has given me deep mental satisfaction, quite rewarding in itself regardless of what the outcome may be.[28]

Sarkissian oscillates within this work, focusing on both historical accounts and biography from a personal perspective. He sheds greater light on the emotional experience and the impact that events have had on him and his family. He intervenes and states his opinions, giving the reader intimate insight, and

[28] Sarkissian, *Tales of 1001 Iranian Days*, p. 16.

does not follow a strict chronological order. The genre of memoir lends him a strong voice, allowing the readers to share in his emotional journey. By following a pattern of detailing an event, expressing past feelings and including current introspection, he demonstrates the changes and development of his identity. He re-examines the events and people in his life, emphasising their influences and how diaspora exacerbated them. Focusing on a journey of self, he pinpoints the particular instances that helped to develop his identity. In this way, he provides readers with an introspective view of diasporic experiences. While each author and artist present a unique diasporic experience, a (pictorial) memoir gives the audience great context by providing thoughtful relationships and illustrating temporal fluidity. Sarkissian is able to convey his thoughts in a personal, humanised manner. The memoir also provides him with credibility and authenticity, allowing him to speak for the voiceless, ultimately adding his own voice to the growing narrative.

Diasporic Iranian Armenian artists and authors write/create in the same way as other diaspora authors/artists such as Gloria Anzaldúa do, because . . .

> . . . the writing saves [them] from complacency [they] fear. Because [they] have no choice. Because [they] must keep the spirit of [their] revolt and [themselves] alive. Because the world [they] create in the writing compensates for what the real world does not give [them]. By writing [they] put order in the world, give it a handle so [they] can grasp it. [. . . they] write to record what others erase when [they] speak, to rewrite the stories others have miswritten about [them], about you. [. . .] To discover [themselves], to preserve [themselves], to make [themselves], to achieve self-autonomy [. . .] Finally, [they] write because [they are] scared of writing but [they are] more scared of not writing.[29]

Generally, however, for these diasporic Iranian Armenian authors and artists writing and telling stories are means of liberation from the constraints of their minds. They are a form of validation that is as essential as the events they document. Inaction would diminish the validity of their existence. Telling

---

[29] Gloria Anzaldúa, 'Speaking in Tongues', *This Bridge We Call Home: Radical Visions for Transformation*, ed. Gloria E. Anzaldúa and AnaLouise Keating (New York: Routledge, 2001), pp. 166–67.

their stories becomes a means of staving off erasure, whether from forgetting, loss of identity, or death. Creativity in general is indisputably powerful, but what these diasporic productions accomplish is significant and distinctive. Their creations establish existence. Their cultural productions unify their personal lives to the emancipatory power of the individual and the collective. In other words, in this particular context, creativity is the ultimate negation of displacement.

With globalisation, the concept of 'hybridity' has become key in a multicultural world where individuals crave coexistence across difference. The lines between 'us' and 'them' have blurred gradually, and absorption of differences into a hegemony has vanished along with its resulting homogeneity. Through a belief in interdependence and transnationalism, Iranian Armenian diasporic authors and artists claim their differences in order to be included in the mainstream society; they constantly negotiate their minoritised position to move beyond the periphery. In a sense, they liberate themselves from their ethnic status to become transnational subjects. Inevitably, in their works, they reach back to their ancestral roots, to their shared, dispersed historical origins. Simultaneously, they provide a sense of transnational belonging. Regardless of the assimilating forces in the diaspora, these transnational diasporic Iranian Armenian artists and authors manage to bridge emancipation and confinement by accepting their past and acknowledging their present co-ethnic background. Instead of solely using their ancestry to define their identity, they incorporate their contemporary identity into their past in order to blur the lines between Armenianness and non-Armenianness. For them, the homeland is de-territorialised, and they are bound to this de-territorial nation symbolically. Rather than existing in a closed and limited exclusive ethnic world, in a foreign land, in their host nations, Iranian Armenian transnational diasporic authors and artists find a home in their transnational creativity.

EPILOGUE

Where is Home?

My goal in this epilogue is to transform my painful experiences into something beneficial – for myself and the collective – by reclaiming the pain of negotiating between multiple nations, identities and consciousnesses during times of crisis and sharing it with others to empower them, which is the essence of living in the space of *verants'ughi*. In this liminal diasporic space, where different perspectives intersect, I reclaim my multiple consciousnesses and refuse to be categorised into conventional identity labels. Through critical thinking and writing, I embed my personal experiences – both mental and somatic – in the larger collective, creating a bridge between my personal struggles and the public.

As I was working on this book, the global COVID-19 pandemic was raging through the entire world; meanwhile, different forms of turmoil occurred in Armenia, Iran and the US – the countries that have shaped my multiple consciousnesses.

In September 2020, the conflict between Armenia and Azerbaijan over Artsakh (Nagorno-Karabakh), an Armenian-controlled enclave, internationally recognised as part of Azerbaijan for three decades, flared up yet again amid the global pandemic of COVID-19 (Figure E.1). The leaders of the two countries came to ceasefire agreements several times; however, these agreements were breached every single time. This re-ignited a conflict that affected the lives of hundreds of thousands of Armenian and Azerbaijani

Figure E.1 Sato A., *Artsakh*, Glendale, CA, 2020. Courtesy of the artist.

civilians: many lives were lost, and a large number of Artsakh people were displaced from territories captured by Azerbaijan and then sheltered in Yerevan, Armenia. The rise of COVID-19 cases in Armenia only further exacerbated this perilous situation.

Since I have discussed nationalism, nation-state agendas and the importance of religion, language and traditions in this book, I would like to briefly consider some of these points here with specific regard to this conflict. While Armenia is a majority Christian nation and Azerbaijan a majority Muslim one, and while it is believed that religion is the source of friction between the two nations, the conflicts today have deeper roots in nationalist agendas rather than merely religion. In the 1920s, the majority-Armenian region of Artsakh was placed into Azerbaijan after the Caucasus had been conquered by the Red Army. After the Soviet Union had dissolved in the late 1980s, Armenia and Azerbaijan gained independence in 1991. Azerbaijan insisted on the inviolability of its borders, which resulted in a war between the Armenians of Artsakh and Azerbaijanis. Artsakh Armenians fought a bloody war and separated from Azerbaijan. Helped by Turkey since 1991, Azerbaijan has been trying to take back the territory lost to Armenians. In 1992, the Minsk Group, set up by the Organisation for Security and Co-operation in Europe (OSCE), called for a ceasefire to the occupation. By 1994, Armenians had driven the Azerbaijani army from the enclave. Since then, Artsakh and Azerbaijan have fought many a war over the territory. The United Nations considers the territory as belonging to Azerbaijan, while Armenian Prime Minister Nikol Pahinyan called for the recognition of the independence of Artsakh.[1]

When the conflict began in September 2020, the inflamed and violent rhetoric used by Azerbaijani and Turkish officials about wiping Armenians off the face of the earth brought the collective memory of the 1915 Genocide vividly to mind. The entire Armenian population in the homeland and the diaspora quickly switched to survival mode – the conflict became an existential crisis. It was evident that the century-long conflict between Armenia and Azerbaijan (and, by extension, Turkey) is a particular form of nationalism that resulted in hateful violence and dehumanisation on both sides. The same tactics used in stereotyping and dehumanising minoritised ethnic communities have been used by both nations, which speak about ethnic cleansing and historical erasures.

During this time, I witnessed how the Armenian diaspora community from around the world came together in solidarity to fight yet another war in hopes of holding on to the territory called Artsakh as a continuation of the homeland lost in 1915. But more significantly, we came together in support of an end to this war, in the hope of saving lives. The conflict divided diaspora communities of both nations. Stories about enmity among the diaspora communities of the two nations in Moscow and St Petersburg proliferated in news media outlets.[2] Violence broke out in every corner of the world between the diaspora communities of both nations. In San Francisco, in September 2020 an arsonist set fire to the administration building (the offices, Sunday school and library) of the Armenian Apostolic Church of St Gregory the

---

[1] Burhanettin Duran, 'Actors and Perspectives in the Nagorno-Karabakh Conflict', *Daily Sabah*, 12 October 2020, www.dailysabah.com/opinion/columns/actors-and-perspectives-in-the-nagorno-karabakh-conflict

[2] Lucian Kim, '"The Wound Is Very Deep": Azerbaijanis and Armenians in Russia Long For Peace', *NPR*, 6 November 2020, www.npr.org/2020/11/05/931702222/the-wound-is-very-deep-azerbaijanis-and-armenians-in-russia-long-for-peace

Illuminator. The FBI declared it to be an attack on a community rather than just a building.[3] Diasporic Armenians sensed and lived a threat to their very existence.

In times of crisis, Armenians gravitate toward the Armenian Apostolic Church as a centre to keep them grounded. As I have discussed in this book, the Armenian Apostolic Church has always been one of the main Armenian national identity markers, and it has held the Armenians together for over 2,000 years. At times of conflict and struggle, the church has been a place of not only hope and protection but also collective solidarity. The incident in San Francisco followed another act of vandalism against the Krouzian-Zekarian Vasbouragan Armenian School and its community centre in July 2020. Anti-Armenian and pro-Azerbaijani graffiti were spray-painted on the walls. I have also discussed in this book the significance of the Armenian language and the invention of the Armenian alphabet by Mesrop Mashtots' as a national identity marker. Hence, this attack on an Armenian educational institution was another blow to the core of Armenian existence. Historically, every time Armenians come under attack, it is Armenian churches and schools that are targeted first.

Armenians living in the diaspora all around the world similarly came together via the church and Armenian organisations to volunteer and help their fellow Armenians fighting in Artsakh. Many volunteered to help find shelter for the displaced women and children of Artsakh in Yerevan, Armenia. Many raised funds to send help for the displaced. Other examples of organised support included the 'Artsakh Fund' humanitarian organisation which has been operating for years as part of the Armenian Cultural Association of America (ACAA),[4] the donation of the families of the 2020 class of the Vahan and Anoush Chamalian Armenian School and many other institutions that raised funds. Diasporic Armenians raised more than $70,000,000 to help Artsakh, while many men flew from Los Angeles to Yerevan to go to the warfront.[5]

---

[3] 'San Francisco FBI Offering $50,000 Reward in Armenian Church Arson', *CBS San Francisco*, 17 December 2020, sanfrancisco.cbslocal.com/2020/12/17/san-francisco-fbi-offering-50000-reward-in-armenian-church-arson/

[4] Ibid.

[5] 'Chamalian Class of 2020 Donates Funds from Armenia Trip to Displaced Artsakh Armenians', *Asbarez.com*, 12 January 2021, asbarez.com/199777/chamlian-class-of-2020-donates-funds-for-armenia-trip-to-displaced-artsakh-armenians/

As the war came to an end with Armenia losing another piece of land, the struggle for our existence in this world continues. During these few months, I witnessed that the long-term effects of this conflict inspired the younger diasporic Armenian activists, many of them from Southern California, to ensure that Armenia remains safe and that we do not face another blow to our collective existence.

All the while, in the United States, the nation faced a heightened risk of political violence with the looming 2020 general election. In addition to the many hate crimes and killings during the summer of 2020, George Floyd's murder in police custody in May of that year sparked a massive wave of protest across the country. With the COVID-19 pandemic, a disrupted economy, a health crisis, racial injustice and politically motivated violence, the nation grappled with many overlapping risks. Pursuant to George Floyd's murder, demonstrations and protests became widespread in the US. Most significant were those organised by the Black Lives Matter movement. The government and media focused on looting and vandalism to illustrate that the protestors instigated violence. While the US government responded violently to these peaceful protests, demonstrations broke out around the world in solidarity with the BLM movement. Many diasporic Armenians came together with BLM in solidarity, realising how the two communities' historical exposure to genocide and slavery continues to this day. Articles problematised some Armenians' view of themselves as Caucasians, pointing out that this is not only an illusion but detrimental to the collective. BLM became an inspiration for various nations to address their own racial and ethnic inequities, including in Iran. In the US, the situation deteriorated as protestors took to the street to demonstrate over a number of other issues related directly to the COVID-19 pandemic, such as unemployment, evictions and unsafe working conditions. With two months left before the election, the US grappled with deep divisions over racial inequality, the role of the police and economic hardship exacerbated by an ineffective pandemic response.[6] After the elections, the US went through another extreme shock when they witnessed the events of 6 January 2021, propagated by white supremacy.

[6] Roudabeh Kishi and Sam Jones, 'Demonstrations and Political Violence in America: New Data for Summer 2020', *ACLED*, 21 January 2021, acleddata.com/2020/09/03/demonstrations-political-violence-in-america-new-data-for-summer-2020/

As if all these conflicts were not enough, turmoil in Iran was heightened, too. In addition to calamities due to COVID-19, in September 2020 authorities executed the Iranian wrestler Navid Afkari, who was arrested during protests against economic and unemployment issues in Shiraz in September 2018. Regarding Afkari's case, Iranian authorities had obtained from Afkari a confession coerced under torture and had sentenced him to death without a fair trial. After signing multiple petitions and a popular online campaign using the hashtag #Don'tExecute, on 10 July the lawyers representing Afkari announced that the judiciary had halted the execution. Those of us in the diaspora, who had invested time and energy in this matter, felt a ray of hope. However, shockingly, Afkari was then executed on 12 September 2020. Afkari's execution caused a global outcry and condemnation of the Iranian regime, including individual and national statements. Iranians held vigils in the diaspora around the world, including in Toronto, Frankfurt, Paris, London, Rome and Washington DC, among other locales, to commemorate Afkari's life and condemn the regime's violations of human rights.[7]

These events were all happening globally as I was working on this book. Very quickly, it became evident to me that what I was working on as a scholarly book was also my lived experience and an ongoing living struggle for diasporic communities such as mine. Lost lands, blurred borders, multiple identities, transnational activism – they have all become my lived day-to-day experiences. One minute I was invested in US anti-racism protests and the imminent elections, the next I was drawn into Armenia's conflict with Azerbaijan. Immediately, I realised how, as Gloria Anzaldúa astutely puts it, '[n]othing is fixed. The pulse of existence, the heart of the universe is fluid. Identity, like a river downstream, you're not the same person you were upstream. You begin to define yourself in terms of who you are becoming not who you have been'.[8] Yet, this is not the end of it. The universe is ever-changing, and the 'pulse of existence' is transformable – and with the universe, humans change, identities shift, and affiliations become malleable.

---

[7] 'Iran Suddenly Executes Wrestler Navid Afkari', *Human Rights Watch*, 28 October 2020, www.hrw.org/news/2020/09/12/iran-suddenly-executes-wrestler-navid-afkari
[8] Anzaldúa, 'now let us shift', p. 556.

Two years later, in October 2022, as my book is in the copy-editing stage, I once again find myself torn between all these conflicts and turmoil. Azerbaijan attacked Armenia once again. A video and images of an Armenian female soldier who was raped and mutilated by Azeri forces after Azerbaijan's attack on Armenia began circulating on social media. In Iran, protests broke out spontaneously across the country after images appeared on social media of a twenty-two-year-old woman named Mahsa Zhina Amini (#MahsaAmini), unconscious on the hospital bed where she would be declared dead on 16 September, three days after being arrested by a 'morality guard'. Four weeks later, Iranians are still protesting while many have been arrested, kidnapped and murdered on the streets and in prisons. In the US, GOP governors are treating migrants as disposables, the supreme court has banned women's abortion rights (*Roe* v. *Wade*), and the primaries are again looming large. This is the everyday life of a transnational individual with three national affiliations but global belonging. Where do I go from here? What do I do? I have been, I am, trying to remain afloat but . . .

My personal universe, my identity and my narrative are shifting, my multiple consciousnesses metamorphosing and my affiliations oscillating. By creating or recreating this personal narrative, which does not conform to conventional identity labels and cannot be rigidly categorised, I am co-creating the collective narrative, providing alternatives, subverting assumptions and denouncing the old narratives. Reconceptualising the divisive narrative of 'us' versus 'them', I choose to recognise my multiple cultures, views, histories and consciousnesses and redefine myself in global terms rather than traditional identity boxes. In this narrative, national boundaries and borders are porous and no longer hold significance. In this narrative, home is where I go; it is not a geographical location but a spiritual connection. Yet even that spiritual connection is malleable and subject to change. In this narrative, the only thing that makes sense is the life that I have lived in the liminality of *verants'ughi* – full of painful experiences and trauma but also rife with potential and growth, devoid of binaries.

Since identity and the boundaries between self and other are constantly in flux, the meaning of home and host nations, here and there, margin and centre are equally shifting and unstable. It all depends on how we position ourselves in global discourses and how we subsequently define home.

For diasporic Iranian Armenian authors and artists, creating and writing is 'home' to their self; it is the bridge, the threshold, the transformative space, the most uncertain place of *verants'ughi*. For me, home is within myself as I maintain a core version of my Armenianness and Iranianness within my *verants'ughi*. I have built a home in Chapel Hill, North Carolina, in the US; yet, when I want to refer to home, I either say Glendale or Tehran – interesting yet strange. Rebuilding this home is a constant endeavour. Removing the old affiliations and creating new inclusive ones, I aim to build bridges to change and transform within my diasporic, transnational, liminal, uncertain and uncomfortable space of *verants'ughi*.

BIBLIOGRAPHY

A., Sato. *Herazheshtits' araj* (*Before Farewell*). Tehran: Nayiri Publication, 2002.

Abdel-Malek, Kamal. 'Exile and Life on Border Lines'. *The Rhetoric of Violence: Arab-Jewish Encounters in Contemporary Palestinian Literature and Film*. Pp. 35–64. New York: Palgrave Macmillan, 2005.

Abrahamian, Ervand. *Iran between Two Revolutions*. Princeton, NJ: Princeton University Press, 1982.

Abrahamian, Ervand. *Tortured Confessions: Prisons and Public Recantations in Modern Iran*. Berkeley: University of California Press, 1999.

Abrams, Dominic, Jose M. Marques, Nicola Bown and Michelle Henson. 'Pro-Norm and Anti-Norm Deviance within and between Groups'. *Journal of Personality and Social Psychology* 78 (2000): 906–12.

Abrams, Dominic, Jose M. Marques and Michael A. Hogg, eds. *The Social Psychology of Inclusion and Exclusion*. New York: Psychology Press, 2004.

Agha, Asif. *Language and Social Relations*. Cambridge: Cambridge University Press, 2007.

Agha, Asif. 'What Do Bilinguals Do? A Commentary'. *Beyond Yellow English: Towards a Linguistic Anthropology of Asian Pacific America*. Pp. 253–60. Angela Reyes and Adrienne Lo, eds. New York: Oxford University Press, 2009.

Aghanian, Denise. *The Armenian Diaspora: Cohesion and Fracture*. Lanham, MD: University Press of America, 2007.

Agnew, Vijay. 'Wounding Events and the Limits of Autobiography'. *Diaspora, Memory and Identity: A Search for Home*. Vijay Agnew, ed. Pp. 81–109. Toronto: University of Toronto Press, 2005.

Alba, Richard D., and Victor Nee. *Remaking the American Mainstream: Assimilation and the New Immigration.* Cambridge, MA: Harvard University Press, 2003.

Alba, Richard D. *Ethnic Identity: The Transformation of White America.* New Haven, CT: Yale University Press, 1990.

Alinejad, Mahmoud. 'Coming to Terms with Modernity: Iranian Intellectuals and the Emerging Public Sphere'. *Islam and Christian-Muslim Relations* 13.1 (2002): 25–47.

Alishan, Leonardo. *Dancing Barefoot on Broken Glass.* New York: Ashod Press, 1991.

Alishan, Leonardo. *Free Fall: Collected Short Stories.* Gourgen Arzoumanian, ed. Costa Mesa, CA: Mazda Publishers, 2011.

Almin. *Shk'egh Banasteghtsutyun (Rich Poetry).* Tehran: Alik Publishers, 2018.

Anderson, Benedict. *Imagined Communities: Reflections on the Origin and Spread of Nationalism.* London: Verso, 1991.

Ang, Ien. 'Togetherness-in-Difference: Beyond Diaspora, into Hybridity'. *Asian Studies Review* 27.2 (2003): 141–54.

Anzaldúa, Gloria. 'Border Arte: Nepantal, el Lugar de la Frontera'. *Gloria Anzaldúa.* Pp. 176–86. AnaLouise Keating, ed. Durham, NC: Duke University Press, 2009.

Anzaldúa, Gloria. *Borderlands/La Frontera: The New Mestiza.* San Francisco: Spinsters/Aunt Lute, 1987.

Anzaldúa, Gloria. *Interviews/Entrevistas.* AnaLouise Keating, ed. New York: Routledge, 2000.

Anzaldúa, Gloria, and AnaLouise Keating, eds. *This Bridge We Call Home: Radical Visions for Transformation.* New York: Routledge, 2001.

Aprahamian, Ashod Rhaffi. *Remarkable Rebirth: The Early History of the Armenians in Detroit.* [N. p.]: Author-Publisher, 2005.

Arakel of Tabriz. *Book of History.* George Bournoutian, trans. and annot. Costa Mesa, CA: Mazda Publishers, 2010.

Aramouni, Khoren. *Dznhal: Veb (The Thaw: A Novel).* Yerevan: AHA Polygraph, 2014.

Armand. *Shk'egh Merkutyamb (Magnificent Uncovering).* Tehran: Nayiri Publishers, 1982.

Armen, Vahe. *Baran bibarad, miravim (If It Rains, We'll Go).* Tehran: Nashr-i Adabi, 2016.

Armen, Vahe. *Pas az ubur-i Dorna-ha (After the Passing of the Cranes).* Tehran: Nashr-i Adabi, 2015.

Aranda, Elizabeth M., and Guillermo Rebollo-Gil. 'Ethnoracism and the "Sandwiched" Minorities'. *American Behavioral Scientist* 47.7 (2004): 910–27.

Aslanian, Sebouh. *From the Indian Ocean to the Mediterranean: The Global Trade Network of Armenian Merchants from New Julfa.* Berkeley: University of California Press, 2011.

Bailey, Benjamin H. *Language, Race, and Negotiation of Identity: A Study of Dominican Americans*. New York: LFB Scholarly Publishing, 2002.

Bailey, Benjamin H. 'Shifting Negotiations of Identity in a Dominican American Community'. *Latino Studies* 5 (2007): 157–81.

Bakalian, Anny. *Armenian-Americans: From Being to Feeling Armenian*. New Brunswick, NJ: Transaction Publishers, 1993.

Baker, Colin. *Attitudes and Language*. Clevedon, Philadelphia and Adelaide: Multilingual Matters, 1992.

Bakkaer Simonsen, Kristina, and Bart Bonikowski. 'Is Civic Nationalism Necessarily Inclusive? Conceptions of Nationhood and Anti-Muslim Attitudes in Europe'. *European Journal of Political Research* 59 (2019): 114–36.

Balassanian, Sonia. *Yerku Girk Banasteghtsutyun (Two Books of Poems)*. Yerevan: The Armenian Center for Contemporary Experimental Art, 2006.

Barry, James. *Armenian Christians in Iran: Ethnicity, Religion, and Identity in the Islamic Republic*. Cambridge: Cambridge University Press, 2018.

Barry, James, and Ihsan Yilmaz. 'Liminality and Racial Hazing of Muslim Migrants: Media Framing of Albanians in Shepparton, Australia, 1930–1955'. *Ethnic and Racial Studies* 42.7 (2019): 1168–85.

Basil, Annie. *Armenian Settlements in India: From the Earliest Times to the Present Day*. Calcutta: Armenian College, 1969.

Bean, Frank D., and Gillian Stevens. *America's Newcomers: Immigrant Incorporation and the Dynamics of Diversity*. New York: Russell Sage Foundation, 2003.

Berberian, Houri. *Armenians and the Iranian Constitutional Revolution of 1905–1911*. Boulder, CO: Westview Press, 2001.

Berberian, Houri. 'The Dashnaktsutiun and the Iranian Constitutional Revolution, 1905–1911'. *Iranian Studies* 29.1–2 (1996): 7–33.

Berberian, Houri. 'Traversing Boundaries and Selves: Iranian-Armenian Identities during the Iranian Constitutional Revolution'. *Comparative Studies of South Asia, Africa and the Middle East* 25.2 (2005): 279–96.

Berberians, Lida. 'Lebbaeus Whose Surname Was Thaddaeus: A Documentary Film'. *Theater and Cinema of Arby Ovanessian*. Pp. 931–33. Majid Lashkari, ed. Tehran: Ruzanih Publications, 2014.

Berberians, Lida. 'Musighi dar film-i Cheshmeh' (The Soundtrack in the Spring). *Theater and Cinema of Arby Ovanessian*. Pp. 450–55. Majid Lashkari, ed. Tehran: Ruzanih Publications, 2014.

Berry, John W. 'Psychology of Acculturation: Understanding Individuals Moving between Cultures'. *Applied Cross-Cultural Psychology*. Pp. 232–53. Richard Brislin, ed. London: Sage, 1990.

Berry, John W. 'Social and Cultural Change'. *Handbook of Cross-Cultural Psychology, vol. 5: Social Psychology*. Pp. 211–79. Harry C. Triandis and Richard Brislin, eds. Boston: Allyn and Bacon, 1980.

Berry, John W., and U. Kim, 'Acculturation and Mental Health'. *Health and Cross-Cultural Psychology*. Pp. 207–35. Pierre Dasen, John W. Berry and Norman Sartorius, eds. London: Sage, 1988.

Bhabha, Homi. ed. 'DissemiNation: Time, Narrative, and the Margins of the Modern Nation'. *Nation and Narration*. Pp. 291–322. London, Routledge, 1990.

Bhabha, Homi. 'Foreword'. *Black Skin, White Masks*, by Frantz Fanon. Pp. vii–xxv. Paris: Editions du Seuil, 1986.

Bhavnani, Kum-Kum, and Anne Phoenix. 'Shifting Identities, Shifting Racisms: An Introduction'. *Feminism and Psychology* 4.1 (1994): 5–18.

Bochner, Stephen. 'Social Stereotypes and Social Identity'. *Social Identity Theory: Constructive and Critical Advances*. Pp. 230–49. Dominic Abrams and Michael A. Hogg, eds. New York: Springer, 1986.

Bolourchi, Neda. 'The Sacred Defense: Sacrifice and Nationalism Across Minority Communities in Post-Revolutionary Iran'. *Journal of American Academy of Religion* 86.3 (2018): 724–58.

Bonilla-Silva, Eduardo. 'More Than Prejudice: Restatement, Reflections, and New Directions in Critical Race Theory'. *Sociology of Race and Ethnicity* 1.1 (2015): 73–87.

Bournoutian, George. *A History of the Armenian People, Volume One: Pre-History to 1500 AD*. Costa Mesa, CA: Mazda Publishers, 1993.

Bournoutian, George A. *A History of the Armenian People, Volume Two: 1500 AD to the Present*. Costa Mesa, CA: Mazda Publishers, 1994.

Bournoutian, George A. 'Armenians in Nineteenth-Century Iran'. *The Armenians of Iran: The Paradoxical Role of a Minority in a Dominant Culture*. Pp. 54–76. Cosroe Chaqueri, ed. Cambridge, MA: Harvard University Press, 1998.

Bournoutian, George A. *Eastern Armenia in the Last Decades of Persian Rule, 1807–1828*. Malibu: Undena Publications, 1982.

Bournoutian, George A. 'People of Iran: Armenians in Iran' *(Ca. 1500–1994), Iran Chamber*, [n. d.], www.iranchamber.com/people/articles/armenians_in_iran2.php.

Boyajian, Levon Z. *Hayots Badeevuh: Reminiscences of Armenian Life in New York City*. England: Taderon Press, 2004.

Brah, Avtar. *Cartographies of Diaspora: Contesting Identities*. London: Routledge, 1996.

Brewer, Marilynn B., and Wendi Gardner. 'Who Is This "We"? Levels of Collective Identity and Representations'. *Journal of Personality and Social Psychology* 71 (1996): 83–93.

Brook, Peter. 'Arby Ovanessian'. *Theater and Cinema of Arby Ovanessian*. Pp. 20–23. Majid Lashkari, ed. Tehran: Ruzanih Publications, 2014.

Brubaker, Roger. *Ethnicity Without Groups*. Cambridge, MA: Harvard University Press, 2004.

Bucholtz, Mary, and Kira Hall. 2005. 'Identity and Interaction: A Sociocultural Linguistic Approach'. *Discourse Studies*, 7.4–5 (2005): 585–614.

Cainkar, Louise. 'No Longer Invisible: Arab and Muslim Exclusion after September 11'. *Middle East Report* 224 (2002): 22–29.

Cainkar, Louise. 'Thinking Outside the Box: Arab Americans and US Racial Formations'. *Race and Arab Americans Before and After 9/11: From Visible Citizens to Visible Subjects*. Pp. 46–80. A. Jamal and N. Naber, eds. Syracuse, NY: Syracuse University Press, 2008.

Carbado, Devon W. 'Racial Naturalization'. *American Quarterly* 57.3 (2005): 633–58.

Casey, Edward. *Getting Back into Place*. Bloomington: Indiana University Press, 1993.

Casey, Edward, and Tsypylma Darieva. 'Rethinking Homecoming: Diasporic Cosmopolitanism in Post-Soviet Armenia'. *Ethnic and Racial Studies* 34.3 (2011): 490–508.

'Chamalian Class of 2020 Donates Funds from Armenia Trip to Displaced Artsakh Armenians'. *Asbarez.com*, 12 January 2021, asbarez.com/199777/chamlian-class-of-2020-donates-funds-for-armenia-trip-to-displaced-artsakh-armenians/

Chaqueri, Cosroe. 'Armenian-Iranians and the Birth of Iranian Socialism, 1905 to 1911'. *The Armenians of Iran: The Paradoxical Role of a Minority in a Dominant Culture; Articles and Documents*. Pp. 77–118. Cosroe Chaqueri, ed. Cambridge, MA: Harvard University Press, 1998.

Cho, Lily. 'Citizenship, Diaspora and the Bonds of Affect: The Passport Photograph'. *Photography and Culture* 2.3 (2009): 275–87.

Clendinnen, Inga. *Reading the Holocaust*. Cambridge: Cambridge University Press, 2002.

Clifford, James. *Routes: Travel and Translation in the Late Twentieth Century*. Cambridge, MA: Harvard University Press, 1997.

Cohen, Rosemary H. *The Survivor*. Los Angeles: LICO Publishing, 2002.

Connerton, Paul. *How Societies Remember*. Cambridge: Cambridge University Press, 1989.

Coombes, Annie. 'The Recalcitrant Object: Culture Contact and the Question of Hybridity'. *Colonial Discourse/Postcolonial Theory*. Pp. 89–114. Francis Barker, Peter Hulme and Margaret Iversen, eds. Manchester: Manchester University Press, 1994.

Cowlishaw, Gillian. *Blackfellas, Whitefellas and the Hidden Injuries of Race*. Malden, MA: Blackwell Publishing, 2004.

Daftari, Fereshteh. 'Introduction'. *Marcos Grigorian: Earthworks*. Pp. 1–2. New York: Leila Heller Gallery, 2011.

Daftari, Fereshteh. *Marcos Grigorian: Earthworks*. New York: Leila Heller Gallery, 2011.

Dahinden, Janine. 'The Dynamics of Migrants' Transnational Formations: Between Mobility and Locality'. *Diaspora and Transnationalism: Concepts, Theories and Methods*. Pp. 51–72. Rainer Baubock and Thomas Faist, eds. Amsterdam: Amsterdam University Press, 2010.

Darieva, Tsypylma. 'Rethinking Homecoming: Diasporic Cosmopolitanism in Post-Soviet Armenia'. *Ethnic and Racial Studies* 34.3 (2011): 490–508.

Davtian, Grish. *Norjughayakan (Of New Julfa)*. Yerevan: Antares Publishing, 2016.

De Genova, Nicholas, and Ramos-Zayas, Ana Yolanda. *Latino Crossings: Mexicans, Puerto Ricans and the Politics of Race and Citizenship*. New York: Taylor and Francis, 2003.

Deleuze, Gilles, and Félix Guattari. *Kafka: Toward a Minor Literature*. Minneapolis: University of Minnesota Press, 2003.

Der Hacopian, Garnik, and Ruyin Pakbaz. *The Presence of the Absent Artist*. Tehran: Nazar Art Publication, 2016.

Der Hovhanian, Harutun. *The History of Isfahan's Julfa*. Isfahan: Naqsh-i Khorshid Publications, 2000.

Der-Karabetian, Aghop. *Armenian Ethnic Identity in Context: Empirical and Psychosocial Perspective*. Beirut: Haigazian University Press, 2018.

Der Nersessian, Sirarpie, *The Armenians*. New York: Praeger Publishers, 1970.

Dick, Hilary Parsons, and Lynette Arnold. 'From South to North and Back Again: Making and Blurring Boundaries in Conversations across Borders'. *Language and Communication* 59 (2018): 17–27.

Doosje, Bertjan, Naomi Ellemers, and Russell Spears, 'Perceived Intragroup Variability as a Function of Group Status and Identification'. *Journal of Experimental Social Psychology* 31 (1995): 410–36.

Dufoix, Stephane. *Diasporas*. Berkeley: University of California Press, 2008.

Duran, Burhanettin. 'Actors and Perspectives in the Nagorno-Karabakh Conflict'. *Daily Sabah*, 12 October 2020, https://www.dailysabah.com/opinion/columns/actors-and-perspectives-in-the-nagorno-karabakh-conflict

Durkheim, Emile. *Rules for the Sociological Method and Selected Texts on Sociology and Its Method.* Steven Lukes, ed. William D. Halls, trans. New York: Free Press. 1982.

Ehsani, Kaveh. 'War and Resentment: Critical Reflections on the Legacies of the Iran-Iraq War'. *Middle East Critique* 26.1 (2016): 5–24.

Euben, Roxanne L. *Enemy in the Mirror: Islamic Fundamentalism and the Limits of Modern Rationalism.* Princeton, NJ: Princeton University Press, 1999.

Extra, Guus. 'Comparative Perspectives on Immigrant Minority Languages in Multicultural Europe'. *Maintaining Minority Languages in Transnational Contexts.* Pp. 30–56. Anne Pauwels, Joanne Winter and Joseph Lo Bianco, eds. London: Palgrave Macmillan, 2007.

Faghfoory, Mohammad H. 'The Ulama-State Relations in Iran: 1921–1941'. *International Journal of Middle East Studies* 19 (1987): 413–32.

Falian, Hrand. 'Ap'ashavank' (Apology). *Nor Ej Journal* 24 (1999): 11.

Fanon, Frantz. *Black Skin, White Masks.* Paris: Editions du Seuil, 1952.

Fasih, Ismai'l. *Namih-yi bih donya (A Letter to the World).* Bethesda, MD: Ibex Publishers, 1995.

Fazlinijad, Payam. 'Musahibih ba Loris Tjeknavorian' (An Interview with Loris Tjeknavorian). *Shukaran* Programme, IRIB, Channel 4, 2019.

Felski, Rita. 'The Doxa of Difference'. *Signs* 23.1 (1997): 1–22.

Ferdman, Bernardo. 'Literacy and Cultural Identity'. *Harvard Educational Review* 60.2 (1990): 81–97.

Fishman, Joshua. 'An Interview with Joshua A. Fishman'. *Language Loyalty, Language Planning, and Language Revitalization.* Pp. 1–28. Nancy H. Hornberger and Martin Putz, eds. Clevedon: Multilingual Matters, 2006.

Fishman, Joshua. '"English Only": Its Ghosts, Myths, and Dangers'. *International Journal of the Sociology of Language* 74 (1989): 125–40.

Fishman, Joshua. 'Language and Ethnicity'. *Language, Ethnicity and Intergroup Relations.* Pp. 15–57. Howard Gilles, ed. London: Academic Press, 1977.

Fishman, Joshua. 'What is Reversing the Language Shift (RLS) and How Can It Succeed?' *Journal of Multilingual and Multicultural Development* 11 (1990): 5–36.

Flores, Juan. *The Diaspora Strikes Back: Caribeño Tales of Learning and Turning.* New York: Taylor and Francis, 2009.

Flores, Juan. 'Triple-Consciousness? Afro-Latinos on the Color Line'. *Wadabagei: A Journal of the Caribbean and its Diaspora* 8.1 (2005): 80–85.

Foltz, Richard C. *Spirituality in the Land of the Noble.* Oxford: OneWorld Publications, 2004.

Forand, Paul G. 'Accounts of Western Travelers Concerning the Role of Armenians and Georgians in Sixteenth-Century Iran'. *Muslim World* 65.4 (1975): 264–78.

Forney, Rebecca. 'Negotiation/Négation of Double Names in Assia Djebar's "Le corps de Félicie"'. *The Many Voices of Europe: Mobility and Migration in Contemporary Europe.* Pp. 30–39. Gisela Brinker-Gabler and Nicole Shea, eds. Berlin: De Gruyter, 2020.

Fowler, Roger. *Linguistics and the Novel.* New York and London: Routledge, 1989.

Fozdar, Farida, and Mitchell Low. '"They Have to Abide by Our Laws . . . and Stuff": Ethnonationalism Masquerading as Civic Nationalism'. *Nations and Nationalism* 21.3 (2015): 524–43.

Freud, Sigmund. *The Standard Edition of the Complete Psychological Works of Sigmund Freud.* Josef Breuer, James Strachey, Anna Freud and Angela Richards, eds. London: Vintage, 2001.

Gajardo, Lorena M. P. 'Bridges of Conocimiento: Una conversación con Gloria Anzaldúa'. *Bridging: How Gloria Anzaldua's Life and Work Transformed Our Own.* Pp. 19–32. Analouise Keating and Gloria Gonzalez-Lopez, eds. Austin: University of Texas Press, 2011.

Gal, Susan, and Judith T. Irvine. *Signs of Difference: Language and Ideology in Social Life.* Cambridge: Cambridge University Press, 2019.

Garcia Canclini, Nestor. *Hybrid Cultures.* Minneapolis: University of Minnesota Press, 1995.

Garcia Canclini, Nestor. 'The State of War and the State of Hybridization'. *Without Guarantees: In Honour of Stuart Hall.* Pp. 38–52. Paul Gilroy, Lawrence Grossberg and Angela McRobbie, eds. London: Verso, 2000.

García, Ofelia, and Rosario Torres-Guevara, 'Monoglossic Ideologies and Language Policies in the Education of US Latinas/os'. *Handbook of Latinos and Education: Theory, Research, and Practices.* Pp. 182–93. Enrique G. Murillo, Jr, Sofia A. Villenas, Ruth Trinidad Galván, Juan Sánchez Muñoz, Corinne Martínez and Margarita Machado-Casas, eds. New York: Routledge, 2010.

Garsoian, Nina G. *Armenia Between Byzantium and the Sasanians.* London: Variorum Reprints, 1985.

Geertz, Clifford. *Works and Lives: The Anthropologist as Author.* Cambridge: Polity Press, 1988.

Ges, Armen. 'Hayrenadardz' (Repatriate). *Nor Ej Journal* 15 (1967): 74.

Gharabegian, Markar (Dev). 'Ko yergi nman voch mi yerg che ka' (There Is No Song Like Yours). *Nor Ej Journal* 24 (1999): 17.

Gheytanchi, Elham. 'I Will Turn off the Lights: The Allure of Marginality in Post-revolutionary Iran'. *Comparative Studies of South Asia, Africa and the Middle East* 27.1 (2007): 173–85.

Ghougassian, Vazgen. *The Emergence of the Diocese of New Julfa in the Seventeenth Century*. Atlanta: University of Pennsylvania Armenian Texts and Studies Series, 1998.

Giddens, Anthony. *Modernity and Self-identity: Self and Society in the Late Modern Age*. Cambridge: Polity Press, 1991.

Gilroy, Paul. *The Black Atlantic: Modernity and Double Consciousness*. Cambridge, MA: Harvard University Press, 1993.

Glazer, Nathan. 'Is Assimilation Dead?' *Annals of the American Academy of Political and Social Science* 530 (1993): 122–36.

Glazer, Nathan, and Daniel P. Moynihan, *Beyond the Melting Pot: The Negroes, Puerto Ricans, Jews, Italians, and Irish of New York City*. Cambridge, MA: MIT Press, 1963.

Glissant, Edouard. 'Exile and Errantry'. *Poetics of Relation*. Pp. 11–22. Betsy Wing, trans. Ann Arbor: University of Michigan Press, 1997.

González, Norma. 'Children in the Eye of the Storm: Language Socialization and Language Ideologies in a Dual-Language School'. *Building on Strength: Language and Literacy in Latino Families and Communities*. Pp. 162–74. Ana Celia Zentella, ed. New York: Teachers College Press, 2005.

Grigorian, Marcos. *Earthworks*. New York: Gorky Gallery, 1989.

Gregorian, Vartan. 'Minorities of Isfahan: The Armenian Community of Isfahan, 1587–1722'. *Iranian Studies* 7.3–4 (1974): 652–80.

Gregorian, Vartan. 'Minorities of Isfahan: The Armenian Community of Isfahan, 1587–1722'. *The Armenians of Iran: The Paradoxical Role of a Minority in a Dominant Culture*. Pp. 27–53. Cosroe Chaqueri, ed. Cambridge, MA: Harvard University Press, 1998.

Gregorian, Vartan. *The Road to Home: My Life and Times*. New York: Simon and Schuster, 2003.

Gryosby, Steven. 'The Verdict of History: The Inexpungeable Tie of Primordiality – A Response to Eller and Coughlan'. *Ethnic and Racial Studies* 17.1 (1994): 164–71.

Gualtieri, Sarah A. 'Strange Fruit? Syrian Immigrants, Extralegal Violence, and Racial Formation in the United States'. *Race and Arab Americans Before and After 9/11: From Visible Citizens to Visible Subjects*. Pp. 147–69. A. Jamal and N. Naber, eds. Syracuse, NY: Syracuse University Press, 2008.

Guo, Shibao. 'From International Migration to Transnational Diaspora: Theorizing "Double Diaspora" from the Experiences of Chinese Canadians in Beijing'. *International Migration and Integration* 17.1 (2014): 153–71.

Gyulmisarian, Ruben. 'Irani kandakagortsutyan mayr-e: Inch'pes Lilith Terian-e gravets' Tehran-e' (The Mother of Iranian Sculpture: How Lilith Terian Attracted Tehran). *Sputnik Armenian*, 12 March 2019, https://armeniasputnik.am/columnists/20190312/17663989/iran-i-kandakagorcutyan-mayry-inchpes-lilit-teryany-gravec-tehran-y.html

Hakopian, Emil. *Artazi kam Azerpayjani Hayots' T'eme* (*The Armenian Diocese of Artaz and Azerbaijan*). Tehran: Nayiri, 2013.

Halbwachs, Maurice. *The Collective Memory*. New York: Harper and Row, 1980.

Hall, Kira, and Mary Bucholtz. eds. *Gender Articulated: Language and the Socially Constructed Self*. New York and London: Routledge, 1995.

Hall, Stuart. 'Cultural Identity and Diaspora'. *Colonial Discourse and Post-Colonial Theory*. Pp. 392–403. Patrick Williams and Laura Chrisman, eds. London: Wheatsheaf, 1993. [Originally published in Jonathan Rutherford, ed. *Identity: Community, Culture, Difference*. London: Lawrence and Wishart, 1990.]

Hall, Stuart. 'Cultural Identity and Diaspora'. *Colonial Discourse and Post-Colonial Theory: A Reader*. Pp. 227–37. Patrick Williams and Laura Christmas, eds. London: Harvester Wheatsheaf, 1994.

Hall, Stuart. 'Introduction: Identity in Question'. *Modernity and Its Futures*. Pp. 1–12. Stuart Hall, David Held and Tony McGrew, eds. Cambridge: Polity Press, 1992.

Hall, Stuart. 'Introduction: Who Needs Identity?' *Questions of Cultural Identity*. Pp. 1–17. Stuart Hall and Paul du Gay, eds. London, Thousand Oaks and New Delhi: Sage, 1996.

Hall, Stuart. 'New Ethnicities'. *Race, Culture and Difference*. Pp. 252–59. James Donald and Ali Rattansi, eds. London: Sage, 1992.

Hannerz, Ulf. *Transnational Connections*. London: Routledge, 1996.

'Hassan Rouhani Visited Families of Armenian Martyrs Fallen during Iran-Iraq War'. *Armedia.am*, 25 December 2017, armedia.am/eng/news/55931/hassan-rouhani-visited-families-of-armenian-martyrs-fallen-during-iran-iraq-war.html.

Haviland, John. 'Ideologies of Language: Some Reflections on Language and US Law'. *American Anthropologist* 105.4 (2003): 764–74.

Hegel, Georg W. F. *Phenomenology of Spirit*. Arnold V. Miller, trans. John N. Findlay, foreword. Oxford: Clarendon Press, 1977.

Herndl, Diane P. *Invalid Women: Figuring Feminine Illness in American Fiction and Culture, 1840–1940*. Chapel Hill: University of North Carolina Press, 1993.

Herzig, Edmond M. 'The Deportation of the Armenians in 1604–1605 and Europe's Myth of Shah Abbas I'. *Persian and Islamic Studies in Honor of P. W. Avery, Pembroke Papers I.* Pp. 59–71. Charles Melville, ed. Cambridge: Cambridge University Press, 1990.

Hestetun, Øyunn. 'Writing Exile: Writing Home'. *The Borders of Europe: Hegemony, Aesthetics and Border Poetics.* Pp. 231–48. Helge Vidar Holm, Sissel Lægreid and Torgeir Skorgen, eds. Århus: Aarhus University Press, 2012.

Hobsbawm, Eric. 'Opiate Ethnicity'. *Alphabet City* 2 (1992): 8.

Hobsbawm, Eric. *Nations and Nationalism Since 1780: Programme, Myth, Reality.* Cambridge: Cambridge University Press, 1991.

Hogg, Michael A. 'A Social Identity Theory of Leadership'. *Personality and Social Psychology Review* 5 (2001): 184–200.

Hogg, Michael A. 'Intergroup Processes, Group Structures and Social Identity'. *Social Groups and Identities: Developing the Legacy of Henri Tajfel.* Pp. 65–93. William P. Robinson, ed. Oxford: Heinemann, 1996.

Hogg, Michael A., and Dominic Abrams. *Social Identifications: A Social Psychology of Intergroup Relations and Group Processes.* London: Routledge, 1988.

Hogg, Michael A., and Daan van Knippenberg, 'Social Identity and Leadership Processes in Groups'. *Advances in Experimental Social Psychology, vol. 35.* Pp. 1–52. Mark P. Zanna, ed. San Diego: Academic Press, 2003.

Hogg, Michael A., and John C. Turner. 'Intergroup Behaviour, Self-Stereotyping and the Salience of Social Categories'. *British Journal of Social Psychology* 26 (1987): 325–40.

Hooker, Juliet. 'Hybrid Subjectivities, Latin American Mestizaje, and Latino Political Thought on Race'. *Politics, Groups, and Identities* 2.2 (2014): 188–201.

Hovannisian, Richard G. *Armenia on the Road to Independence, 1918.* Berkeley: University of California Press, 1967.

Hovannisian, Richard G. *The Republic of Armenia, Vol. I: The First Year, 1918–1919.* Berkeley: University of California Press, 1971.

Hovian, Andranik. 'Ghara Kelisa'. *Nashri-yi barrisiha-yi tarikhi* 2.5 (1967): 195–210.

Imini, Aliyi, and Muhammad Khazai, 'Naqsh-mayiha-yi tazini dar Ghara Kelisa' (Decorative Elements in Ghara Kelisa). *Nashri-yi ketab mah-i honar* 133 (2009): 42–49.

'Iran Suddenly Executes Wrestler Navid Afkari'. *Human Rights Watch*, 28 October 2020, www.hrw.org/news/2020/09/12/iran-suddenly-executes-wrestler-navid-afkari

Israel, Nico. *Outlandish*. Palo Alto: Stanford University Press, 2000.

Jahanbegloo, Ramin. 'From the Writings, Conversations, and Photos,' *Theater and Cinema of Arby Ovanessian*. Pp. 456–63. Majid Lashkari, ed. Tehran: Ruzanih Publications, 2014.

Jawed, Nasim Ahmad. *Islam's Political Culture: Religion and Politics in Predivided Pakistan*. Austin: University of Texas Press, 1999.

Jetten, Jolanda, Nyla R. Branscombe, Michael T. Schmitt and Russell Spears. 'Rebels With a Cause: Group Identification as a Response to Perceived Discrimination from the Mainstream'. *Personality and Social Psychology Bulletin* 27 (2001): 1204–13.

Joppke, Christian. 'Citizenship between De- and Re-Ethnicization'. *European Journal of Sociology* 44.3 (2003): 429–58.

Jung, Carl G. *Civilization in Transition: The Collected Works of C. G. Jung, Vol. 10*. 2nd ed. Princeton, NJ: Princeton University Press, 1970.

Kaprielian-Churchill, Isabel. 'Changing Patterns of Armenian Neighborhoods in New England'. *The Armenians of New England*. Pp. 17–23. Marc C. Mamigonian, ed. Belmont, MA: Armenian Heritage Press, 2004.

Karapetian, Shushan. 'Challenges with Institutionalizing a Pluricentric Diasporic Language: The Case of Armenian in Los Angeles'. *The Routledge Handbook of Heritage Language Education: From Innovation to Program Building*. Pp. 145–60. Olga Kagan, Maria Carreira and Claire Hitchins Chik, eds. New York and London: Routledge, 2017.

Kashani-Sabet, Firoozeh. *Frontier Fictions: Shaping the Iranian Nation, 1804–1946*. Princeton, NJ: Princeton University Press, 1999.

Keating, Analouise, and Gloria Gonzalez- Lopez. 'Building Bridges, Transforming Loss, Shaping New Dialogues: Anzaldúian Studies for the Twenty-First Century'. *Bridging: How Gloria Anzaldúa's Life and Work Transformed Our Own*. Pp. 1–16. Analouise Keating and Gloria Gonzalez-Lopez, eds. Austin: University of Texas Press, 2011.

Keating, Sandra Toenis. 'Habib Ibn Khida Abu Ra'ita al-Takriti's "The Refutation of the Melkites concerning the Union of the Divinity and Humanity in Christ, III"'. *Christians at the Heart of Islamic Rule: Church Life and Scholarship in Abbasid Iraq*. Pp. 39–53. David Thomas, ed. Leiden: E. J. Brill, 2003.

Khach'er, Khach'ik. *Ashk-i Sheshum (The Sixth Tear)*. Tehran: Nashr-i Chishmih, 2000.

Khach'er, Khach'ik. 'Hayots' Yerge' (The Armenian Song). *Im Chakatagri Sove: Patmevatskner Zhoghovats'u (The Sea of My Destiny: A Collection of Short Stories)*.

Pp. 137–38. Antilias: Printing House of the Armenian Catholicosate of Cilicia, 2011.

Khach'er, Khach'ik. 'Hakasutyun' (Contradiction). *Im Chakatagri Sove: Patmevatskner Zhoghovats'u* (*The Sea of My Destiny: A Collection of Short Stories*). Pp. 135. Antilias: Printing House of the Armenian Catholicosate of Cilicia, 2011.

Khorenatsi, Movses. *History of the Armenians*. Robert W. Thomson, ed. and trans. Venice: [n. p.], 1881.

Khosronejad, Pedram, ed. *Iranian Sacred Defence Cinema: Religion, Martyrdom and National Identity*. Canon Pyon: Sean Kingston Publishing, 2012.

Khosronejad, Pedram, ed. *Unburied Memories: The Politics of Bodies of Sacred Defense Martyrs in Iran*. London and New York: Rutledge, 2012.

Kim, Lucian. '"The Wound Is Very Deep": Azerbaijanis and Armenians in Russia Long for Peace'. *NPR*, 6 November 2020, www.npr.org/2020/11/05/931702222/the-wound-is-very-deep-azerbaijanis-and-armenians-in-russia-long-for-peace

Kimball, Charles A. *Angle of Vision: Christians and the Middle East*. New York: Friendship Press, 1992.

Kishi, Roudabeh, and Sam Jones. 'Demonstrations and Political Violence in America: New Data for Summer 2020'. *ACLED*, 21 January 2021, acleddata.com/2020/09/03/demonstrations-political-violence-in-america-new-data-for-summer-2020/

Koorkchian, Soukias Hacob (Varand). *An-veradardz* (*Irreversible*). Tehran: Alik Publishers, 1999.

Koorkchian, Soukias Hacob (Varand). *Sharach'ogh Shght'aner* (*Thundering Chains*). Tehran: Alik Publishers, 2011.

Koven, Michele. 'Two Languages in the Self/the Self in Two Languages: French Portuguese Bilinguals' Verbal Enactments and Experiences of Self in Narrative Discourse'. *Ethnos* 26.4 (1998): 410–55.

Kristeva, Julia. 'Word, Dialogue, and Novel'. *Desire in Language: A Semiotic Approach to Literature and Art*. Pp. 64–91. Leon S. Roudiez, ed. New York: Columbia University Press, 1980.

Kuortti, Joel. *Writing Imagined Diaporas: South Asian Women Reshaping North American Identity*. Newcastle-upon-Tyne: Cambridge Scholars Publishing, 2007.

Kymlicka, Will. 'Misunderstanding Nationalism'. *Theorizing Nationalism*. Pp. 131–40. Ronald Beiner, ed. Albany, NY: State University of New York Press, 1999.

LaFromboise, Teresa, and Wayne Rowe. 'Skills Training for Bicultural Competence: Rationale and Application'. *Journal of Counseling Psychology* 30 (1983): 589–95.

LaFromboise, Teresa, Hardin L. K. Coleman and Jennifer Gerton. 'Psychological Impact of Biculturalism: Evidence and Theory'. *Psychological Bulletin* 114 (1993): 395–412.

Lahiri, Shompa. *Indians in Britain: Anglo-Indian Encounters 1880–1930*. London: Frank Cass, 2000.

Lapierre, Jean-William. *Le pouvoir politique et les langues*. Paris: Presses Universitaires de France, 1988.

LaPierre, Richard. 'The Armenian Colony in Fresno County, California: A Study in Social Psychology'. Ph.D. diss., Stanford University, 1930.

Larin, Stephen J. 'Is It Really About Values? Civic Nationalism and Migrant Integration'. *Journal of Ethnic and Migration Studies* 46.1 (2020): 127–41.

Lazarian, Zhanet D. *Danishnamih-yi Iranihay-i Armani (The Encyclopedia of Armenian Iranians)*. Tehran: Hirmand Publications, 2003.

Lee, Jennifer, and Frank D. Bean. 'America's Changing Color Lines: Race/Ethnicity, Immigration, and Multiracial Identification'. *Annual Review of Sociology* 30 (2004): 221–42.

Lenormant, François. *Histoire ancienne de L'Orient jusqu'aux Guerres Mediques*, vol. 1. Paris: A. Lévy, Libraire-Editeur, 1881.

'Lilith Terian Was One of the Pillars of the University, But They Expelled Her'. *ISNA*, 16 March 2019, https://www.isna.ir/news/97122513455/

'Loris Tjeknavorian: Don't Call Us Minorities So Much'. *Fararu*, December 2014. fararu.com/fa/news/214937

'Loris Tjeknavorian: Imam Abbas Has Helped Me Several Times'. *Jahan News*, 25 August 2020, https://www.jahannews.com/news/737934/

Maalouf, Amin. *On Identity*. New York and London: Random House, 2000.

Madadian, Andy. 'Gnank Hayastan' (Let's Go to Armenia). *YouTube*, December 2014, https://www.youtube.com/watch?v=cMJ2NCVh5S0

Malcom, Vartan. *The Armenians in America*. Boston: The Pilgrim Press, 1919.

Malešević, Siniša. *Grounded Nationalisms: A Sociological Analysis*. Cambridge: Cambridge University Press, 2019.

Malhi, Rebecca, Susan Boon and Timothy Rodgers. '"Being Canadian" and "Being Indian": Subject Positions and Discourses Used in South Asian-Canadian Women's Talk about Ethnic Identity'. *Culture and Psychology* 15.2 (2009): 255–83.

Matian, Azad. 'Mi Yerazanki Masin' (About a Dream). *Grakan Ashkharh* (Literary World), *Nayiri Newspaper* (2008): 160–65.

McCabe, Ian B. 'Global Trading Ambitions in Diaspora: The Armenians and their Eurasian Silk Trade'. *Diaspora Entrepreneurial Networks*. Pp. 27–50. Ian Baghdiantz McCabe, Gelina Harlaftis and Ioanna P. Minoglou, eds. New York: Berg, 2005.

Meillet, Antoine. *Esquisse d'une grammaire comparee de l'Armenienne classique.* Vienna: [n. p.], 1936.

Mercer, Kobena. *Welcome to the Jungle: New Positions in Black Cultural Studies.* London: Routledge, 1994.

Mesrobian, Nerses D. *Karot-e Hayi (Armenian Longing).* Glendale, CA: Yerevan Printing, 2014.

Migliorino, Nicola. *(Re)Constructing Armenia in Lebanon and Syria.* New York: Berghahn Books, 2008.

Miller Donald E., and Lorna Touryan Miller. *Survivors: An Oral History of the Armenian Genocide.* Berkeley, Los Angeles and London: University of California Press, 1993.

Mills, Jean. 'Connecting Communities: Identity, Language and Diaspora'. *International Journal of Bilingual Education and Bilingualism* 8.4 (2005): 253–74.

Minassian, Hovik, and Mojtaba Qanbari. *Gurihzar: A Relic from Ancient Iran.* Tehran: Navayih Danish, 2005.

Minassian, Hovik, Mojtaba Qanbari and Leyla Mohtasham. *History and Culture of the Armenians of Arak and the Kazaz Region.* Tehran: Nayiri Publishers, 2019.

Minh-ha, Trinh T. *Elsewhere, Within Here: Immigration, Refugeeism and the Boundary Event.* New York and London: Routledge, 2010.

Mirak, Robert. *Torn Between Two Lands: Armenians in America, 1890 to World War I.* Cambridge, MA: Harvard University Press, 1983.

Mitchell, William John Thomas. *Picture Theory: Essays on Verbal and Visual Representation.* Chicago: University of Chicago Press, 1994.

Mitchell, William John Thomas. 'What Do Pictures Really Want?' *October* 77 (1996): 71–82.

Mitchell, William John Thomas. *What Do Pictures Want? The Lives and Loves of Images.* Chicago: University of Chicago Press, 2005.

Montoya, Margaret E. 'Silence and Silencing: Their Centripetal and Centrifugal Forces in Legal Communication, Pedagogy and Discourse'. *University of Michigan Journal of Law Reform* 33 (2000): 263–327.

Morawska, Ewa. 'Immigrant Transnationalism and Assimilation: A Variety of Combinations and the Analytic Strategy It Suggests'. *Toward Assimilation and Citizenship: Immigrants in Liberal Nation-States.* Pp. 133–76. Christian Joppke and Ewa Morawska, eds. Basingstoke: Palgrave Macmillan, 2014.

N., B. 'Chishmih-yi hamishih jushan' (The Ever-Boiling Spring), *Theater and Cinema of Arby Ovanessian.* Pp. 740–47. Majid Lashkari, ed. Tehran: Ruzanih Publications, 2014.

Naderi, Afshin. 'A Report on the Status of Armenians in Iran'. *Akhbar-i Adian* 1.1 (2004): 46–55.

Nercissians, Emilia. 'Life and Culture of Armenians in Iran'. *International Sociology Association (ISA): Language and Society* 2 (2012): 31–54.

Norris-Holt, Jacqueline. 'Motivation as a Contributing Factor in Second Language Acquisition'. *The Internet TESL Journal* 8.6 (2001), http://iteslj.org/Articles/Norris-Motivation.html

Oakes, Leigh. *Language and National Identity: Comparing France and Sweden.* Amsterdam and Philadelphia: John Benjamins, 2001.

O'Connor, Thomas. 'The Armenian Experience: Roots of the Past, Realities of the Present'. *The Armenians of New England.* Pp. 5–8. Marc C. Mamigonian, ed. Belmont, MA: Armenian Heritage Press, 2004.

Ojakians, Anahid. 'Chiragh-ha ra man khamush mikonam'. *Namih Farhangistan* 21 (2003): 166–74.

Okoomian, Janice. 'Becoming White: Contested History, Armenian American Women, and Racialized Bodies'. *Contested Boundaries* 27.1 (2002): 213–37.

Ordjanian, Anahid Victoria. 'Children of Ararat: Political Economy and Ideology at an Armenian Ethnic School in the United States'. Ph.D. diss., Temple University, 1991.

Oskanian, Kevork. 'Perspectives: Stereotypes and Hatred Drive the Nagorno-Karabakh Conflict'. *Eurasianet*, 5 October 2020, eurasianet.org/perspectives-stereotypes-and-hatred-drive-the-nagorno-karabakh-conflict

Ouyang, Win-chen. 'Semiology of Madness'. *Politics of Nostalgia in the Arabic Novel: Nation-State, Modernity and Tradition.* E-book. Pp. 77–103. Edinburgh: Edinburgh University Press, 2013.

Ovanessian, Arby. *Ghara Kelisa* (*Lebbaeus Whose Surname Was Thaddaeus*). Tehran: Studio Chaplin, 1967, http://iranahaytv.com/2020/04/23/ghara-kelisa-a-documentary-film-by-arbi-ovanisian/

Ovanessian, Arby. *Cheshmeh* (*The Spring*). Teheran: National Iranian Radio and Television, 1972.

Pahlavanian, Hovannes L. *Iranahay Hamaynk: 1941–1979.* Erevan: Khach Ga Publishers, 1989.

Pahlavan-nijad, Muhammad Reza, and Faizih Varzi-nijad. 'Barresi-yi sabk-i roman-i *Chiragh-ha ra man khamush mikunam* ba ruykard-i fara-naqsh mian fardi nazari-i naqsh-girayi' (The Study of the Style of *Things Left Unsaid* with Interpersonal Theory of Metafunction). *Adab Pazhuhi* 7–8 (1388/2010): 51–78.

Panossian, Razmik. *The Armenians: From Kings and Priests to Merchants and Commissars.* New York: Columbia University Press, 2006.

Parati, Graziella, and Marie Orton. *Multicultural Literature in Contemporary Italy*. Madison: Farleigh Dickinson University Press, 2007.

Parmar, Maya. 'Reading the Double Diaspora: Representing Gujarati East African Cultural Identity in Britain'. *Journal of the Spanish Association of Anglo-American Studies* 35.1 (2013): 137–55.

Pasdermajian, Hrand. *Tarikh-i Armanistan (The History of Armenia)*. Muhammad Ghazi, trans. Tehran: Nur-i Jahan Publishers, 1993.

Pavlenko, Aneta. 'Bilingualism, Gender, and Ideology'. *International Journal of Bilingualism* 5.2 (2001): 117–51.

Penninx, Rinus, Kraal Karen, and Maria Berger, eds. 'Identity, Representation, Inter-ethnic Relations and Discrimination'. *The Dynamics of International Migration and Settlement in Europe: A State of the Art*. Pp. 201–32. Amsterdam: Amsterdam University Press, 2006.

Phillips, Jenny. *Symbol, Myth and Rhetoric: The Politics of Culture in an Armenian American Population*. New York: AMS Press, 1989.

Pirzad, Zoya. *Chiragh-ha ra man khamush mikonam*. Tehran: Nashr-i Markaz, 2002.

Pirzad, Zoya. 'I Look for Simplicity and Accuracy'. *Courrier International*, 11 March 2009, https://www.courrierinternational.com/article/2009/10/30/je-recherche-la-simplicite-et-la-justesse

Pirzad, Zoya. *The Space Between Us*. Amy Motlagh, trans. London: OneWorld Publications, 2014.

Pirzad, Zoya. *Things We Left Unsaid: A Novel*. Franklin Lewis, trans. London: OneWorld Publications, 2013.

Pirzad, Zoya. 'Yik Ruz Qabl az 'iyd-i Pak'. *Sih Kitab*. Pp. 225–319. Tehran: Nashr-i Markaz, 2011.

Plumly, Vanessa D. 'Linked Security and 'Rhetorical Ethics': Breaking Frames and Opening Cracks of Identification through the Narrative Fissures of Olumide Popoola and Annie Holmes's *Breach* (2016)'. *The Many Voices of Europe: Mobility and Migration in Contemporary Europe*. Pp. 13–29. Gisela Brinker-Gabler and Nicole Shea, eds. Berlin: De Gruyter, 2020.

Portes, Alejandro, and Min Zhou, 'The New Second Generation: Segmented Assimilation and Its Variants'. *The Annals of the American Academy of Political and Social Science* 530 (1993): 74–96.

Rajaee, Farhang. *The Iran-Iraq War: The Politics of Aggression*. Gainesville, FL: The University Press of Florida, 1993.

Rastegar, Kamran. 'Treacherous Memory: Bashu the Little Stranger and the Sacred Defense'. *Moments of Silence: Authenticity in The Cultural Expressions of The Iran-Iraq*

War, 1980–1988. Pp. 61–87. Arta Khakpour, Mohammad Mehdi Khorrami and Shouleh Vatanabadi, eds. New York: New York University Press, 2016.

Roberts, Murat H. 'The Problem of the Hybrid Language'. *The Journal of English and Germanic Philology* 38.1 (1939): 23–41.

Roosens, Eugene. *Creating Ethnicity: The Process of Ethnogenesis.* Newbury Park: Sage, 1989.

Rushdie, Salman. *Imaginary Homelands: Essays and Criticism, 1981–1991.* New York: Penguin Books, 1992.

Russell, James R. *Zoroastrianism in Armenia.* Cambridge, MA: Harvard University Press, 1987.

Safarian, Robert. 'Dar Fasili-yi du Kuch' (Between Two Migrations), 2010–13, https://vimeo.com/user35586486

Safarian, Robert. 'Is Multiculturalism the Right Word for a Description of the Armenian Community in Iran?' *Writings and Photos of Robert Safarian,* 19 December 2014, https://robertsafarian.com/?p=2165

Safarian, Robert. 'Qisi-yi far'i-i khanum-i Nurulahi va Shutayt' (The Secondary Story of Mrs. Nurollahi and Shutait). *Haft* 1 (2004): 24–26.

Safarian, Robert. *Sakin-i du farhang: Diaspora-yi Armani dar Iran* (*Living in Two Cultures: Armenian Diaspora in Iran*). Tehran: Nashr-i Markaz, 2020.

Safran, William. 'Language, Ethnicity and Religion: A Complex and Persistent Linkage'. *Nations and Nationalism* 14.1 (2008): 171–90.

Sahafi, Mohamad Javad. 'Musighi, 'eshq, va azadi-khahi: barresi-yi zindigi-yi pur faraz va nashib-i Loris Tjeknavorian' (Music, Love, and Freedom-Seeking: A Study of the Ups and Downs of Loris Tjeknavorian's Life). *Honar-i Musighi* 23 (2020): 16–21.

Sahami, Navid. 'Naqdi bar kitab-i *Chiragh-ha ra man khamush mikunam*' (A Study of *Things Left Unsaid*). *Chista* 200 (2004): 819–25.

Said, Edward. 'Reflections on Exile'. *Reflections on Exile and Other Essays.* Pp. 173–86. Cambridge, MA: Harvard University Press, 2001.

'San Francisco FBI Offering $50,000 Reward in Armenian Church Arson'. *CBS San Francisco,* 17 December 2020, sanfrancisco.cbslocal.com/2020/12/17/san-francisco-fbi-offering-50000-reward-in-armenian-church-arson/

Sanasarian, Eliz. *Religious Minorities in Iran.* Cambridge: Cambridge University Press, 2000.

Sarkissian, Henry A. *Tales of 1001 Iranian Days.* New York and Los Angeles: Vantage Press, 1981.

Saroyan, William. 'The Armenian and the Armenian'. *Ararat* 25.2 (1984): 7. [First published as *Inhale and Exhale.* New York: Random House, 1936.]

Sarvarian, Leonid. 'Tkhrutyun' (Sorrow). *Sirt-e Gravor* (*Written from the Heart*). Pp. 18–19. Tehran: [n. p.], 1997.

Shahrizai, Zahra. 'Rivayat-i khandani az iyd didani dar khani-yi avalin shahid-i Armani' (An Interesting Narrative about New Year's Visit to the House of the First Armenian Martyr). *Mehr News Agency*, 10 January 2016. mehrnews.com/xxH3V

Sharkey, Heather. 'Coming Together, Moving Apart: Ottoman Muslims, Christians, and Jews at the Turn of the Century'. *A History of Muslims, Christians and Jews in the Middle East*. pp. 243–300. Cambridge: Cambridge University Press, 2017.

Shirinian, Lorne. *The Landscape of Memory: Perspectives on the Armenian Diaspora*. Toronto: Bule Heron Press, 2004.

Sidaghat-kish, Arvin. 'Rival-hayi mushabih va manabi' si-ganih dar ahang-sazi-yi Loris Tjeknavorian' (Similar Trends and Three Sources of Loris Tjeknavorian's Compositions). *Honar-i Musighi* 23 (2020): 8–14.

Silva, Kumarini. 'Brown: From Identity to Identification'. *Cultural Studies* 24.2 (2010): 167–82.

Silva, Kumarini. 'What is Brown? Theorizing Race in Everyday Life'. *Brown Threat: Identification in the Security State*. Pp. 25–51. Minneapolis: University of Minnesota Press, 2016.

Simon, Bernd, and David L. Hamilton, 'Self-Stereotyping and Social Context: The Effects of Relative In-Group Size and Out-Group Status'. *Journal of Personality and Social Psychology* 66 (1994): 699–711.

Simpson, George Eaton, and J. Milton Yinger. *Racial and Cultural Minorities: An Analysis of Prejudice and Discrimination*. 5th ed. New York: Plenum Press, 1985.

Smith, Anthony. *The Ethnic Origins of Nations*. Hoboken, NJ: Blackwell, 1986.

Smith, Anthony D. 'Nations and History'. *Understanding Nationalism*. Pp. 9–31. Montserrat Guibernau and John Hutchinson, eds. Oxford: Polity Press, 2005.

Smith, Michael Peter. 'Translocality: A Critical Reflection'. *Translocal Geographies: Spaces, Places, Connections*. Pp. 181–98. Katherine Brickell and Ayona Datta, eds. Farnham: Ashgate, 2011.

Smolicz, Jerzy J. 'Language Core Values in a Multicultural Setting: An Australian Perspective'. *International Review of Education* 37.1 (1991): 33–52.

Smolicz, Jerzy J. 'Minority Languages as Core Values of Ethnic Cultures: A Study of Maintenance and Erosion of Polish, Welsh, and Chinese Languages in Australia'. *Maintenance and Loss of Minority Languages*. Pp. 277–305. Willem Fase, Konen Jaspaert and Sjaak Kroon, eds. Amsterdam: Benjamins, 1992.

Sökefeld, Martin. 'Religion or Culture? Concepts of Identity in the Alevi Diaspora'. *Diaspora, Identity and Religion: New Directions in Theory and Research*. Pp. 133–55.

Caroline Alfonso, Waltraud Kokot and Khachig Tölölyan, eds. London: Routledge, 2004.

Stewart, Alan. *Persian Expedition: The Australians in Dunsterforce 1918*. Sydney: Australian Military History Publications, 2006.

Suny, Ronald Grigor. *Looking toward Ararat: Armenia in Modern History*. Bloomington: Indiana University Press, 1993.

Suny, Ronald Grigor. *They Can Live in the Desert But Nowhere Else: A History of the Armenian Genocide*. Princeton, NJ: Princeton University Press, 2015.

Suny, Ronald Grigor. 'Writing Genocide: The Fate of the Ottoman Armenians'. *A Question of Genocide: Armenians and Turks at the End of the Ottoman Empire*. Pp. 15–41. Ronald Grigor Suny, Fatma Muge Gogek and Norman M. Naimark, eds. Oxford: Oxford University Press, 2011.

Suny, Ronald Grigor, and Geoff Eley, eds. *Becoming National: A Reader*. Oxford: Oxford University Press, 1996.

Suny, Ronald Grigor, and Michael D. Kennedy, eds. *Intellectuals and the Articulation of the Nation*. Ann Arbor, MI: Michigan University Press, 1999.

Tabouret-Keller, A. 'Language and Identity'. *The Handbook of Sociolinguistics*. Pp. 315–26. Florian Coulmas, ed. Oxford: Blackwell, 1998.

Taheri, Amir. 'Deep Roots in the Land'. *Armenian Review* 22.2 (1969): 45–48.

Tajfel, Henri. *Human Groups and Social Categories: Studies in Social Psychology*. Cambridge: Cambridge University Press, 1981.

Tajpour, Muhammad Ali. *Tarikh-i du aqaliat-i mazhabi-i yahud va masihiyat dar Iran (The History of Two Religious Minorities in Iran: Jews and Christians)*. Tehran: Farahani Publishers, 1965.

Takooshian, Harold. 'Armenian Immigration to the United States from the Middle East'. *Journal of Armenian Studies* 3.1–2 (1986–7): 133–55.

Talai, Vered. 'Mobilization and Diffuse Ethnic Organization: The London Armenian Community'. *Urban Anthropology* 13 (1984): 197–218.

Tamir, Yael. 'Not So Civic: Is There a Difference Between Ethnic and Civic Nationalism?' *American Review of Political Science* 22 (2019): 419–34.

Taylor, Stephanie. 'The Meanings of Place for Identity'. *Narratives of Identity and Place*. Pp. 1–20. Abingdon: Routledge, 2009.

'The Number of Iranian Minority Martyrs Speaks to the Unity of Iranian People'. *Alikonline*, 26 December 2019, alikonline.ir/fa/news/social/item/10483

Tölölyan, Khachig. 'Elites and Institutions in the Armenian Transnation'. *Diaspora: A Journal of Transnational Studies* 9.1 (2000): 107–36.

Tölölyan, Khachig. *Redefining Diaspora, Old Approaches, New Identities: The Armenian Diaspora in International Context*. London: Armenian Institute, 2002.

Tölölyan, Khachig. 'The Role of the Armenian Apostolic Church in the Diaspora'. *Armenian Review* 41.1 (1988): 55–68.

Tölölyan, Khachig, and Taline Papazian. 'Armenian Diasporas and Armenia: Issues of Identity and Mobilization: An Interview with Khachig Tölölyan'. *Contemporary Armenian Studies* [special issue on 'Jews, Armenians: A Century of Sainthood'] 3 (2014): 83–101.

Tsadik, Daniel. *Between Foreigners and Shi'is: Nineteenth-Century Iran and Its Jewish Minority*. Palo Alto: Stanford University Press, 2007.

Turkamani Bar-anduzi, Vajihih, and Sanaz Chamani Gulzar. 'Persona az didgah-i Zoya Pirzad' (Persona in Zoya Pirzad's View). *Baharistan-i Sukhan: Adabiyat-i Farsi* 26 (2015): 145–62.

Turner, John C. 'Social Comparison and Social Identity: Some Prospects for Intergroup Behaviour'. *European Journal of Social Psychology* 5 (1975): 5–34.

Turner, John C., and Rupert Brown, 'Social Status, Cognitive Alternatives and Intergroup Relations'. *Differentiation Between Social Groups*. Pp. 201–34. Henri Tajfel, ed. London: Academic Press, 1978.

Turner, John C., Michael A. Hogg, Penelope J. Oakes, Stephen D. Reicher and Margaret S. Wetherell. *Rediscovering the Social Group: A Self-Categorization Theory*. Oxford: Blackwell, 1987.

Turner, Victor. *The Ritual Process: Structure and Anti-Structure*. Ithaca: Cornell University Press, 1969.

Uras, Esat. *The Armenians in History and the Armenian Question*. Ankara: Documentary Publications, 1988.

Van Gennep, Arnold. *The Rites of Passage*. Chicago: University of Chicago, 1960.

Van Gorder, A. Christian. *Christianity in Persia and the Status of Non-Muslims in Modern Iran*. Washington, DC: Lexington Books, 2010.

Van Londen, Selma, and Arie De Ruijter. 'Ethnicity and Identity'. *Culture, Ethnicity and Migration*. Pp. 69–79. Marie Claire Foblets and Ching Lin Pang, eds. Leuven/Leusden: Acco, 1999.

Vardanyan, Emmanuel P. *The Well of Ararat*. Belmont, MA: The National Association for Armenian Studies and Research Inc., 2005.

Vaux, Bert. 'The Fate of the Armenian Language in New England'. *The Armenians of New England*. Pp. 207–16. Marc C. Mamigonian, ed. Belmont, MA: Armenian Heritage Press, 2004.

Verkuyten, Maykel, and Angela de Wolf. 'Being, Feeling and Doing: Discourses and Ethnic Self-Definitions among Minority Group Members'. *Culture and Psychology* 8.4 (2002): 371–99.

Voskani Avakian, Arlene. 'Are We What We Eat? Armenian-American Women's Ethnic Identity and Food'. *The Armenians of New England*. Pp. 219–23. Marc C. Mamigonian, ed. Belmont, MA: Armenian Heritage Press, 2004.

Wacks, David. *Double Diaspora in Sephardic Literature: Jewish Cultural Production Before and After 1492*. Bloomington: Indiana University Press, 2015.

Waterfield, Robin E. *Christians in Persia: Assyrians, Armenians, Roman Catholics and Protestants*. London and New York: Routledge, 1973.

Waters, Mary. *Ethnic Options: Choosing Identities in America*. Berkeley: University of California Press, 1990.

Wennerstrom, Ann. 'Immigrant Voices in the Courts'. *International Journal of Speech, Language and the Law* 15.1 (2008): 23–49.

Winter, Joanne, and Anne Pauwels. 'Language Maintenance and the Second Generation: Policies and Practices'. *Maintaining Minority Languages in Transnational Contexts*. Pp. 180–200. Anne Pauwels, Joanne Winter and Joseph Lo Bianco, eds. New York: Palgrave Macmillan, 2007.

Woodward, Kath. *Understanding Identity*. London: Arnold, 2002.

Woollett, Anne, Harriette Marshall, Paula Nicholson, and Neelam Dosanjh. 'Asian Women's Ethnic Identity: The Impact of Gender and Context in Accounts of Women Bringing up Children in East London'. *Feminism and Psychology* 4.1 (1994): 119–32.

Wortham, Stanton. 'Linguistic Anthropology of Education'. *Annual Review of Anthropology* 37 (2008): 37–51.

Yack, Bernard. 'The Myth of the Civic Nation'. *Theorizing Nationalism*. Pp. 103–18. Ronald Beiner, ed. Albany, NY: State University of New York Press, 1999.

Yaghoobi, Claudia. 'Multiple Consciousness and Transnationalism in Iranian Armenian Cultural Productions'. *Middle East Critique* 31.1 (2022): 81–97.

Yaghoobi, Claudia. 'Racial Profiling of Armenian Iranians in the US: Omid Fallahazad's "Citizen Vartgez"'. *Iran-Namag: A Bilingual Quarterly of Iranian Studies* 6.2 (2021): 154–72.

Yaghoobi, Claudia. 'The Significance of Armenian Language in Iranian Armenian Diasporic Literature'. *The Doha Institute Arab Center for Research and Policy Studies*, September 2021, https://www.dohainstitute.org/en/PoliticalStudies/Pages/The-Significance-of-the-Armenian-Language-in-Iranian-Armenian-Diasporic-Literature.aspx?fbclid=IwAR0O8HbZWoDN3bv2k6AEo8qCtTW_SThcCpukCw8lkwy8xVImb0fMhnN8hSA

Yaghoobi, Claudia. 'Pirzad's Diasporic Transnational Subjects in "A Day Before Easter"'. *International Journal of Persian Literature* 3.1 (2018): 110–32.

Yaghoobi, Claudia. 'The Fluidity of Iranian-Armenian Identity in Zoya Pirzad's *Things We Left Unsaid*. *International Journal of Persian Literature* [special issue on 'Iranian Minority Women'] 4.1 (2019): 103–20.

Yaghoobi, Claudia. 'Iranian Armenians in Zoya Pirzad's Works: Diasporic Transnational Identity'. *Persian Media Productions*, 2020: 1–4, https://persianmediaproduction.org/article/%d8%a7%d8%b1%d8%a7%d9%85%d9%86%d9%87-%d8%a7%db%8c%d8%b1%d8%a7%d9%86-%d8%af%d8%b1-%d8%a2%d8%ab%d8%a7%d8%b1-%d8%b2%d9%88%db%8c%d8%a7-%d9%be%db%8c%d8%b1%d8%b2%d8%a7%d8%af-%d9%87%d9%88%db%8c%d8%aa-%d8%af/

Yaghoubian, David N. *Ethnicity, Identity, and the Development of Nationalism in Iran*. Syracuse, NY: Syracuse University Press, 2014.

Young, Robert. *Colonial Desire: Hybridity in Theory, Culture and Race*. London: Routledge, 1995.

Yuki, Masaki. 'Intergroup Comparison versus Intragroup Relationships: A Cross-Cultural Examination of Social Identity Theory in North American and East Asian Cultural Contexts'. *Social Psychology Quarterly* 66.2 (2003): 166–83.

'Zindigi-namih: Marcos Grigorian (1925–2007)'. *Hamshahrionline*, 17 June 2011, hamshahrionline.ir/x3bnR

Zentella, Ana Celia. 'Latin@ Languages and Identities'. *Latinos: Remaking America*. Pp. 321–38. Marcelo Suárez-Orozco and Mariela Páez, eds. Berkeley: University of California Press, 2009.

Zopf, Bradley J. 'A Different Kind of Brown: Arabs and Middle Easterners as Anti-American Muslims'. *Sociology of Race and Ethnicity* 4.2 (2018): 178–91.

INDEX

Note: *italic* signifies illustrations, n signifies notes

EU representative:
Easy Access System Europe
Mustamäe tee 50, 10621 Tallinn, Estonia
Gpsr.requests@easproject.com

www.ingramcontent.com/pod-product-compliance
Lightning Source LLC
Chambersburg PA
CBHW050645270326
41927CB00012B/2884